John Dryden and the Poetry of Statement

John Dryden

and the
Poetry of Statement

by
K. G. HAMILTON

MICHIGAN STATE UNIVERSITY PRESS
1969

Copyright 1967 University of Queensland Press

First American edition 1969

Library of Congress Catalog Card Number: 68-56157

Preface

The subject of this study is indicated by its title: *John Dryden and the Poetry of Statement*. Its immediate reference is to the poetry of Dryden, but its field of interest is a form of poetic expression rather than the work of any particular poet. In scope it is both narrower and wider than a study of Dryden: narrower because its concern is limited to an analysis of his work as "poetry of statement"; and wider because ultimately its interest goes beyond the work of this one poet to what can be learned from it about the nature and limits of poetry as a form of discourse. The choice of Dryden is more than incidental, because no other poet has made such consistent and successful use of the kind of poetry I am concerned with; but an understanding of the poetry of statement is not something that begins and ends with an appreciation of Dryden.

In an earlier work, *The Two Harmonies*,[1] my endeavour was to define seventeenth century concepts of the nature and function of poetry by looking at the kind of distinctions made by that period between poetry and prose as different forms of discourse. Some of the definitions reached in that work are here applied to the poetry of Dryden, particularly with a view to resolving an apparent contradiction between

[1] K. G. Hamilton, *The Two Harmonies; Poetry and Prose in the Seventeenth Century* (Oxford: Clarendon Press, 1963).

what is now commonly regarded as the nature of poetry and the acceptance of much of Dryden's best work as poetry of statement. To this extent the present study is an extension of the analysis of Renaissance poetic theory begun in *The Two Harmonies.*

Primarily, however, this book is intended for the general student of seventeenth century poetry, and my purpose has been to contribute towards a greater understanding and appreciation of a kind of poetry that is often unfamiliar to the present-day student and to which he is not readily sympathetic. Dryden has received at least his fair share of attention from critics and literary historians in recent years, and the man and his work are now the subject of a very considerable literature: including the first volumes of the much needed new edition which are now beginning to appear from the University of California Press, with a promise of great things to come for all students of Dryden. Many of these studies, however, have been peripheral to Dryden's actual poetic art: studies concerned with questions of interpretation, biography, thought, historical background, influences. With the exception perhaps of Arthur Hoffman's *John Dryden's Imagery*, Dryden has thus far mainly escaped the attention of the "new criticism", and there have been no really sustained attempts to analyze the qualities that go to make up his poetry. His art of translation has been treated generally by Frost, and, with special reference to the *Aeneid*, by Proudfoot; and Ian Jack has dealt with his contribution to Augustan satire. Allan Roper's *Dryden's Poetic Kingdoms*, and Bernard Schilling's *John Dryden and the Conservative Myth*, both seem to draw their inspiration ultimately from an interest in the ideas and the thought rather than from the poetry itself. There is, of course, the still very valuable study of his poetry by Mark Van Doren, first published in 1920; and also, among other things, Bonamy Dobrée's quite delightful pamphlet. But these are descriptive rather than analytical in approach: while studies such as Sister Mary Hoefling's of the sentence structure of the satiric *characters* are rather too specialized.

The present study is concerned immediately with the structure of Dryden's verse, with his technique, his craftsmanship. But it is a commonplace of literary history that both the strengths and the weaknesses of Dryden's poetry are in part a reflection of the spirit of his time; and, too, his poetry of statement is so closely related to his concept of the nature of poetry, and to his view of life as it is expressed in words, that a study of it will inevitably go deeper and wider

than an analysis of technique. None the less, an exhaustive
study, for its own sake, of Dryden's achievement as a poet
is not intended. The treatment of individual poems is taken
only as far as is necessary to meet the needs of the problem
immediately under discussion, and as a result is often more
or less piecemeal and incomplete. Attention is also largely
concentrated on poems that are most revealing of the particular qualities I have been concerned to examine: which
means, in effect, a relatively short list of poems on which
most of Dryden's current reputation depends—poems that
appeared between the publication of *Absalom and Achitophel* in 1682 and *The Hind and the Panther* in 1687,
dealing particularly with *Absalom and Achitophel* itself,
with the other two great satires, *The Medall* and *Mac-
Flecknoe*, and with *Religio Laici*, the lines *To the Memory
of Mr. Oldham*, and also the Pindaric ode, *To the Memory
of Mrs. Anne Killigrew*. (It is in fact to this group of poems
of the 1682-1687 period that I wish to be understood as
referring when I speak of Dryden's mature, or most successful
work: the poems in which his poetry of statement achieves
its highest and most sustained expression.) But while there
are many things that this study does not attempt to do, the
more important of these are, I think, matters that have been
most adequately dealt with elsewhere. What it does attempt
is to get to the essence of Dryden's whole achievement as a
poet, and this, I believe, is what most needs to be done, at
least from the point of view of the general student of Dryden,
and it is something that has not hitherto been undertaken
in any systematic or sustained way.

After an introductory chapter in which some of the problems posed by the nature of Dryden's poetry are defined and
illustrated, I have endeavoured in Chapter 1 to lay the basis
for an analysis of the poetry of statement by reconciling this
concept with the pervasive Renaissance idea of poetry as an
"art of imitation". For this purpose I have referred mainly
to the verse essay *Religio Laici*, chosen because its acknowledged nearness to prose seems to place it at the crux of the
problem of defining those qualities which, by separating
Dryden's poetry of statement from prose, allow it the title of
poetry. The next chapter seeks to analyze the structure of
meaning in Dryden's poetry, particularly the relationship
between meaning at the level of discursive statement and the
total poetic meaning. This theme is extended in Chapter 3
to a study of the role of sound and rhythm as a means of
enriching and enlarging the significance of the statement,
while the following chapter is concerned to investigate the

kinds of imagery Dryden habitually uses and its function in his poetry. In Chapter 5 attention is turned from these more universally accepted elements of poetry to something that belongs more closely to the particular tradition in which Dryden wrote: the art of rhetorical "amplification" that perhaps more than anything else stands in the way of an adequate appreciation of his work by the twentieth century reader. And finally the study concludes with some suggestions regarding the implications for poetic theory generally of an acceptance of Dryden's poetry of statement as genuine poetry.

Although it is concerned with the nature of poetry as a form of expression, this study does not seek to put forward any new theory of poetry as a means of justifying Dryden's work. On the contrary it suggests the need for a renewal of interest in the now generally outmoded concept of poetry as "imitation", as the soundest basis for an appreciation of the kind of poetry that Dryden excelled in writing. The method I have used depends mainly on a close analysis of the poetry itself. However I do not believe that this kind of analysis, particularly when it is applied to poetry of an age other than our own, can be as autonomous as some exponents of the new criticism would like to make it. Rather it must be accompanied by what might be called an "historical consciousness"; a sense of period, an awareness of the environment in which the poetry was written, and particularly of the concepts of the nature and function of poetry that may have influenced its composition.

Thus I have begun from the position that "poetry" may not have meant quite the same thing, nor have been intended to serve the same purposes in all ages: and in analyzing the qualities of Dryden's verse I have endeavoured always to rely on what could be learned from an examination of the poems themselves, but subject to the check of its relevance to the poetic tradition in which they were written. In other words, I have sought to reach an appreciation of his poetry in terms that Dryden himself might have been expected to understand and accept, rather than in terms of twentieth century preconceptions of what poetry should be. If in the process I have, for some readers, done for Dryden what Empson, I think it was, claimed Miss Tuve had achieved for Donne, by making them more aware of the very things they dislike in his poetry, this may be aesthetically unfortunate, but from the point of view of the literary historian unavoidable, and even desirable.

I have endeavoured to make this study as self-contained as

possible, without getting too far away from the immediate subject of the poetry of statement: however those matters of Renaissance theory with which it is frequently concerned are the main subject of *The Two Harmonies*, to which I would refer the reader for some further or more exact treatment of points that may seem to be inadequately dealt with here. I have also tried to keep in mind the primary purpose of the book, the re-orientation of the present-day student to a type of poetry that may be unfamiliar and often uncongenial to him; and I have pursued matters only so far as seemed necessary or desirable for this purpose. I would hope that what I have written will supplement, and in places correct, the material already available for the study of Dryden, but I certainly have not intended to replace it.

The Bibliography that is appended lists most of the works that have directly or indirectly influenced the writing of this book. It covers most aspects of Dryden study, but is not intended to be definitive: its main emphasis is on works related to Dryden's achievement as a poetic artist and to the ideas about the nature and function of poetry that belong to the tradition in which he worked.

Any study of Dryden's poetic art must inevitably pay attention to the sound and movement of his verse. Despite the strength and naturalness of his rhythms, which virtually cause his verse to "read itself", I am aware that everyone may not agree with my particular reading of any one line; and also that, in any case, it is not possible to know how Dryden himself would have expected his lines to be read. But to avoid the endless repetition of such phrases as "by my reading" I would ask that this sort of qualification be accepted as implied throughout the study: although I do not believe that Dryden sought or achieved the kind of niceties of enunciation that would make an important issue of variant readings of this type.

By far my most considerable indebtedness in making this study is to Miss Jill Patten, for allowing me to incorporate in it material from a dissertation that she wrote under my guidance. Without many of the insights deriving from her work, insights that spring from a rare combination of a keenly analytical mind and a delicate sensitivity to the working of words, this study would have been much poorer than it is.

To those who, at various stages, read and commented on the manuscript, and particularly to A. D. Hope, I also offer my sincere thanks.

Much of the earlier work for this book was done while on sabbatical leave from the University of Queensland, as a Fellow of the Folger Shakespeare Library in Washington, D.C. To the Trustees of the Folger, and to its Director (Dr. Louis Wright) and his staff, I would express my gratitude for their unfailing assistance and courtesy.

K. G. H.
University of Queensland,
1966

Contents

Introduction   1

Chapter one   Imitation   21

Chapter two   Meaning   38

Chapter three   Sound   63

Chapter four   Imagery   91

Chapter five   Amplification   124

Chapter six   The Poetry of Statement and Literary Theory   157

Bibliography   179

Index of Names   191

Introduction

There can be few men of letters of equal eminence who in their lifetime suffered more criticism, more downright abuse, even physical violence, than did John Dryden. Yet in his own time Dryden's position and reputation as a poet were secure enough, and for the most part of the last thirty years of the seventeenth century he maintained from his favourite chair in Will's Coffee House a virtually unchallenged dictatorship over the English literary scene. After his death his reputation, if anything, grew in strength: the testy old critic, John Dennis, who had not always been uncritical of Dryden in his lifetime, paid this tribute in a letter of 1715:

If Mr. *Dryden* has Faults (as where is the Mortal who has none?) I by searching for them perhaps would find them. But whatever the mistaken world may think, I am always willing to be pleas'd. ... Wherever Genius runs through a Work, I forgive its Faults; and wherever that is wanting, no Beauties can touch me. Being struck by Mr. *Dryden's* Genius, I have no eyes for his Errors. ...[1]

And in the reliable opinion of Edmond Malone, Dryden's first critical biographer, this reputation survived undiminished

---

1 John Dennis, "Letter to Jacob Tonson, (dated 4 June 1715)", *The Critical Works of John Dennis*, ed. E. N. Hooker (2 vols.; Baltimore: Johns Hopkins Press, 1939), II, 400-401.

throughout the eighteenth century. In concluding his life of the poet published in 1800, Malone wrote:

Since the death of Dryden nearly a century has elapsed; during the latter part of which his reputation has greatly increased, in common with that of our other most famous poets ... the reputation of Dryden ... is now elevated beyond the reach of envy, ridicule, or satire; and posterity, to whose judgement with great calmness and magnanimity he appealed from his contemporary adversaries has done him ample justice, by allotting to him that distinguished place in the Temple of Fame, to which no one now presumes to controvert his title.[2]

Dr. Johnson, too, in his *Life of Pope*, had earlier compared the achievements of the two great poets of the Augustan age, and finally, "with some hesitation", had attributed to Dryden the superiority of "genius"—"that power which constitutes a poet; that quality without which judgement is cold and knowledge is inert; that energy which collects, combines, amplifies and animates".[3]

But herein lay the rub: already before Johnson had made this comparison, Joseph Warton, in an *Essay on the Genius and Writings of Pope* (1756) that was to be one of the early indicators of the way the wind was blowing towards the nineteenth century, had relegated Pope to the second rank of poets. Despite his ostensible purpose in the *Essay* of praising Pope, Warton divided poetry into four kinds, and would allow him only a superiority over all other poets in the second of these kinds—that is, in moral, ethical, and panegyrical poetry, in which there is seen "true poetical genius, in a more moderate degree", as compared with the first kind, which is distinguished by the sublime and the pathetic, "the two chief nerves of all genuine poetry".[4] This latter kind of poetry Warton refers to as "pure poetry", perhaps the first use of the term in this sense, reflecting the growing desire to purify poetry by separating it from other, non-poetic influences, and to exalt the lyric as the expression of personal passion.

2 Edmond Malone, *The Critical and Miscellaneous Prose Works of John Dryden* (3 vols., in 4; London: 1800), I, 547-48.
3 Samuel Johnson, "Life of Pope", in *Lives of the English Poets* (London, 1779), ed. G. Birkbeck Hill (3 vols.; Oxford: Clarendon Press, 1905), III, 222.
4 Joseph Warton, "An Essay on the Genius and Writings of Pope" (London, 1756), *Eighteenth Century Critical Essays*, ed. Scott Elledge (2 vols.; New York: Cornell University Press, 1961), pp. iii-x.

In the face of this rising tide of Romanticism, to be ranked ahead of Pope might be only a hollow triumph. At the end of the eighteenth century Malone could still write of Dryden: "The great author of the following works has long had the honour of being ranked in the first class of English Poets; for to the names of Shakespeare, Spenser, and Milton, we have now for near a century been in the habit of annexing those of Dryden, and his scholar Pope."[5] But the habit of ranking poets had also caught on, and in the nineteenth century Dryden was to go with Pope inexorably into the second division. Reviewing Scott's 1826 edition of Dryden, the *Edinburgh Review* has no doubts in declaring, apparently as a compliment, that the "public voice has assigned to Dryden the first place in the second rank of our poets";[6] or in summing up its judgment of his work as that of a man "possessed of splendid talents, which he often abused, and of a sound judgement, the admonitions of which he often neglected; a man who succeeded only in an inferior department of his art, but who in that department succeeded pre-eminently".[7]

The same cry, sometimes with more, sometimes with less favourable intonations, is to be heard throughout the nineteenth century: "Johnson ascribes to Dryden more genius than to Pope; but he has less than Spenser or Milton. Nay he was not of the same order of minds. . . . Nor can we liken Dryden to the great poets of his own day [*sic*]—to Coleridge, Wordsworth, Shelley or Keats."[8] And again, from a lecture of 1867 by H. T. Reid on *The Age of the Restoration: Dryden*:

I am anxious to render justice to Dryden's powers, and shall strive to do so. Neither do I wish to limit literary research or taste to the productions of the *great masters*; for English poetry abounds with poems of unnumbered degrees of merit. . . . But when I hear people talk of the poets carelessly or ignorantly, or, it may be, intentionally coupling in an indiscriminate series Spenser, Milton, Dryden and Pope, every principle of judgement and feeling and taste revolts.

5 Malone, *op. cit.*, I, i.
6 *Edinburgh Review*, XLVII, No. 93 (January 1828), 1.
7 *Ibid.*, p. 36.
8 John A. Heraud, one-time editor of *Monthly Magazine*, speaking in 1862.

Or from an 1864 series of lectures on *Our Great Writers*, by
G. E. Turner, this one dealing with "The Life, Dramas, and
Poetry of Dryden":

We have now arrived at a period in the history of our literature
to which we can only look back with feelings of shame and
contempt. . . . Dryden . . . completely represents the spirit of his
times, his genius was formed by the age in which he wrote. . . .
He cannot be regarded as a successor of the great writers who
adorned the reigns of Elizabeth and the first two Stuarts. . . . He
must be compared with Waller, Donne, or Cowley, but never
with Shakespeare, Milton, or Fletcher.

For Matthew Arnold the habit of ranking the poets that
was so popular during the century took the form of his
famous "touchstones" of poetry, and here there was no
place for Dryden. With Pope he was distinguished as a classic
"not of our poetry but our prose".[9] And for Walter Pater,
too, Dryden's poetry was found to be "prosaic"; while Rossetti
makes a comparison between the Elizabethans who "created
a style in poetry and by misapplying some of its qualities
formed their prose", and the Augustans (or "Annians") who
"created a style in prose and wrenched its characteristics to
form their poetry".[10]

Dryden is no longer universally relegated, as he tended to
be by the nineteenth century, to the "second rank of poets":
at least not so explicitly, if only for the reason that critics
today are generally wise enough to avoid the placing of
poets in ranks. Yet, apart from the interest of a relatively
small band of Dryden scholars, and despite the very considerable volume of significant work done on his poetry in recent
years, I am not sure that for the general reader or student of
poetry the situation now is so very different from what it was
in 1913, when Sir Walter Raleigh prefaced his lecture on
Dryden with the observation that "whoever speaks today in
praise of John Dryden speaks to a world that is far from
being disposed in his favour. The poetry of today has many

9 Matthew Arnold, "The Study of Poetry", in *Essays in Criticism; Second
Series*, ed. S. R. Littlewood (London: Macmillan Co., 1938), p. 25.
10 D. G. Rossetti, *Works* (London: Ellis & Elvy, 1901-2), Preface.

kinds of excellence, but they are all remote from the excellence of Dryden."[11] Certainly the most influential attitudes to poetry in this century have provided no real basis for a defence of Dryden's work any more convincing than the earlier adverse criticism of it. The Victorian critics who disliked Augustan poetry regarded its subjects as not properly belonging to poetry, or, like Arnold and Pater, saw it as being not really poetry at all. Twentieth century criticism, on the other hand, has generally not denied Dryden's work the title of poetry. But though nineteenth century attitudes no longer dominate poetic taste, a profound change in ideas about the nature of poetry in relation to other forms of discourse formed an essential part of the development of Romantic and post-Romantic theories of poetry; and this change remains to stand between the present-day reader and a ready appreciation of Dryden.

Neither Dryden's aims as a poet nor the special qualities of his work conform to the common basic assumptions of modern poetic and aesthetic theory. In particular, its insistence on an absolute dichotomy between poetry and other forms of discourse makes this theory difficult to reconcile with either the theory or practice of Dryden, whose own judgments and those of his age recognized no final distinction between the literary and non-literary, or between the poetic and non-poetic uses of language. In writing poetry Dryden sought to give it qualities, in addition to those thought of as specifically poetic, which it would share with other forms of discourse. Ultimately for him poetry must succeed not only as poetry but as discourse: it cannot be judged by wholly poetic criteria, because it is never envisaged as having a sufficiently autonomous existence as poetry for this to be done.[12] And because these modern theories too seldom leave room for kinds of poetry other than those they have been specifically designed to describe; and because they are almost without exception put forward as theories of poetry,

---

11 Sir Walter Raleigh, "John Dryden and Political Satire" (The Henry Sidgwick Memorial Lecture delivered at Cambridge, November 1913) in *Some Authors* (Oxford: Clarendon Press, 1923), p. 156.
12 The seventeenth century relationship between poetry and prose as forms of discourse is the subject of K. G. Hamilton, *The Two Harmonies* (Oxford: Clarendon Press, 1963) to which I would refer the reader for a further discussion in support of the conclusions stated here.

and not simply as one kind of poetic expression (of "Imagism", "Symbolism", "Expressionism", or the like), they have contributed to a climate of ideas about poetry that has little real sympathy for Dryden.

T. S. Eliot, who claims for Dryden that he is "one of the tests of a catholic appreciation of poetry",[13] has provided some inspired appreciations of the poet's more memorable lines; but when he attempts to generalize on the nature of their poetic qualities he is less satisfactory. "Dryden's words," he says, ". . . are precise, they state immensely, but their suggestiveness is often nothing";[14] and again, with reference to the elegy *To the Memory of Mr. Oldham*: "the lack of suggestiveness is compensated by the satisfying completeness of the statement."[15] To the question that he admits "may justly be asked", "Whether without this which Dryden lacks verse can be poetry?" he can only answer, "What man is to decide what poetry is?"[16] But there are many men, including Eliot himself, I think, on other occasions where the context is less difficult, who are ready to decide what poetry is; and it is then that Dryden's work is likely to cause problems.

Eliot's emphasis is on Dryden's power of precise statement in verse; and the term "poetry of statement" is one that has become widely attached to Dryden's work. "Dryden was most at home when he was making statements," says Mark Van Doren. "His poetry was the poetry of statement."[17] But this term "poetry of statement" is one that has led critics into difficulties; and indeed it would have led them into greater difficulties if there had been more tendency to attempt a reconciliation between what is said and inferred about the poetry of statement and what is said and inferred about poetry in general. R. L. Sharp is one critic who at least notices the difficulty: he begins his account of the progress of

13 T. S. Eliot, "John Dryden" (1922), in *Selected Essays* (London: L. & V. Woolf, 1932), p. 305.
14 *Ibid.*, p. 315.
15 *Ibid.*, p. 316.
16 *Ibid.*, p. 315.
17 Mark Van Doren, *John Dryden: A Study of his Poetry* (Bloomington, Indiana: Indiana University Press, 1946), p. 67. Originally published as *The Poetry of John Dryden* (New York: Harcourt, Brace & Howe, 1920).

seventeenth century poetry from Donne to Dryden by commenting on the movement during the century towards a
greater simplicity in the style of both prose and verse. The
greater simplicity in the style of poetry he finds "more
surprising" than the corresponding change in prose, because,
he says, "prose as distinguished from poetry is primarily the
language of statement". Poetry, he believes, "we normally
expect to be something else".[18]

The word "statement" normally has two main areas of
connotation. Sharp (and also Eliot, I think, when he speaks
of "the satisfying completeness of the statement") is referring
to qualities of simplicity, directness, precision, accuracy, and
the like as they are found in "plain" or "scientific" prose;[19]
prose that seeks to draw as little attention to itself as possible,
aiming to serve only as a transparent medium for the communication of its subject: that is, the "close, naked, natural"
way of writing advocated by Dryden's contemporaries of the
Royal Society of London. "Statement" is also associated with
the spoken word, particularly with public speech, in the
sense of "making a statement", and this is what Van Doren
seems to have meant when applying the term to Dryden's
poetry: in the original edition of his study of Dryden the
sentence quoted earlier read: "Dryden was most at home
when he was making statements. His poetry was the poetry
of declaration." In this meaning, too, "statement" implies
qualities of simplicity and directness.

Each of these meanings of "statement" has significance for
the term "poetry of statement". Dryden's own particular
poetic genius was formed in the theatre. Here the rhymed
heroic play demanded a continuously elevated tone and a
declamatory style of speech which Dryden nevertheless contrived to make sound surprisingly natural, and this is a
quality that is retained in almost all his mature poetry. At
the same time this poetry belongs to the rhetorical tradition
that had dominated medieval and Renaissance attitudes to
poetry, and Dryden writes very much as the public orator,

---

18 R. L. Sharp, *From Donne to Dryden* (Chapel Hill: University of North
Carolina Press, 1940), p. ix.
19 The term "prose" is itself an awkward one to use, because of the wide
variety of expression that can be included in it. In the present study, unless
the context clearly indicates otherwise, I have used it to refer to this strictly
"plain", denotative use of language, while still being aware of the difficulty
of avoiding purely verbal effects in any prose, no matter how plain.

"armed with the power of verse".[20] Closely associated, too, with this rhetorical tradition is the acceptance of a moral and didactic function for poetry, derived ultimately from the *Ars Poetica* of Horace. Poetry for Dryden must give delight, but the purpose of its delight is that it may also instruct; and for this a "plain and natural" style is required.[21] The element of statement in Dryden's poetry, in the sense both of public utterance and of a directness and clarity of meaning, is thus closely associated with the tradition of poetry in which he wrote, and it is as a combination of these meanings that the word should be understood as part of the term "poetry of statement".

It is a good deal more difficult to define the other half of this term: that is, "poetry". But if statement is synonymous with direct utterance or plain prose, then in saying that we expect poetry to be something other than statement, Sharp, of course, is right. It must be taken as axiomatic that poetry is something more than statement, and that, if Dryden's lines achieve the quality of poetry through "the satisfying completeness of the statement", this phrase must have a special meaning. Prose does not become poetry simply by being very good prose, and this is particularly true of plain prose. An imaginative richness or complexity that goes beyond direct statement is essential to poetry, and where Dryden's work does not achieve a multidimensional structure through the usual kinds of poetic suggestiveness, it must do it in some other way if it is to deserve the title of poetry. "Poetry" and "statement" as modes of expression are in some degree opposites, each tending to depend on qualities that the other seeks to avoid or repel. If the concept of a poetry of statement is to have any meaning, and is not to be a contradiction in terms, it must refer to poetry in which there is a fusion of these normally contrary qualities; poetry in which the direct, discursive statement remains the central core, but is so organized and controlled that it evokes an effective response on more than one level of mental experience, *without however losing its essential character and importance as*

---

20 Dryden, "A Discourse concerning the Original and Progress of Satire" (1693), *Essays of John Dryden*, ed. W. P. Ker (2 vols.; Oxford: Clarendon Press, 1900), II, 22.
21 Dryden, "Preface to 'Religio Laici: or, a Layman's Faith. A Poem'" (1682), *The Poems of John Dryden*, ed. J. Kinsley (4 vols.; Oxford: Clarendon Press, 1958), I, 311.

statement: poetry, that is, which is successful both as poetry and as statement, and not as either statement or poetry alone.

In practice this means that the "poetic" elements of such verse, more than in some other forms of poetry, will remain closely subordinated to the statement and less inclined to generate an independent life of their own that would tend to weaken the effectiveness of the statement by drawing attention away from it. It does *not* mean that for poetry to become poetry of statement it must eschew the usual devices of poetry altogether. There may be times when, as Eliot says, the "suggestiveness" of Dryden's lines is "nothing": but these are the exceptions rather than the rule, even when suggestiveness is taken to include only the usual means to poetic suggestiveness. Dryden does not avoid imagery; his language is frequently figurative and rich in allusion and associative value; he can be a master of irony. But when his poetry can properly be described as poetry of statement these things are controlled, subordinated, so that they fulfil their allotted purpose without blurring the precision, the clarity, of the direct statement. The reader can give the same undivided attention to the direct meaning that he gives to the meaning of plain prose, but unlike such prose the poetry of statement has a richness to which the imagination can also respond.

The poetry of statement seeks to have the best of both of the worlds of poetry and statement: something that John Dennis may have been thinking of when he said of the blank verse of Dryden's *Spanish Fryar* that "though at the same time it has the purity and easiness of Prose, it has the dignity and strength of Verse".[22] It is the aim of this study to demonstrate that Dryden is consistently at his best when he maintains this balance between the demands of poetry and statement; and that, despite the frequent charge that he is "prosaic", when he fails it is more likely to be because of the undue dominance of distinctly *poetic* rather than of prosaic[23] elements in his work. Yet it must be remembered

22 John Dennis, "The Impartial Critic: Or, Some Observations upon a Late Book, entitled, 'A Short View of Tragedy', written by Mr. Rymer" (London, 1693), ed. E. N. Hooker, *op. cit.*, I, 14.
23 The word "prosaic", unless the context indicates otherwise, is used throughout this study to mean simply "having the qualities of plain prose", and without any of the derogatory connotations often attaching to the word in modern usage.

that this is a balance, and one that is easily disturbed. There is no absolute or clear cut difference between what is poetry of statement and what is not. The term "poetry of statement" is simply a convenient, but essentially theoretical classification that can be used to differentiate poetry which tends towards the kind of dependence on direct statement that has been described from poetry that conveys its meaning primarily in other ways.

Because it does seek this balance between statement and imaginative richness, there can be no such thing as "pure" poetry of statement, in the way that some poetry might be described as "pure" lyric. It is not a "kind" of poetry, in the sense of a poetic genre. Dryden, both as a critic and as a poet, was keenly aware of the different kinds of poetry and the varying demands they made on the poet. He would think of himself as creating a poem in accord with an established form (Juvenalian satire, the heroic poem, the Pindaric Ode, the Horatian Epistle, or whatever his particular chosen form might be), and not as writing poetry of statement. What has come to be called his poetry of statement was partly the result of a general attitude towards poetry that he shared with his age and partly the result of his own poetic genius. It affects not only satire, the verse essay, and occasional poetry—forms to which it was especially well suited—but his more purely lyric poetry as well. The role it plays is different in these different kinds of poetry, but the effects are similar; and if in this study the differences between kinds of poetry become blurred, this is because attention is being directed less to the differences than to this common influence of the poetry of statement.

The opening passage of *Absalom and Achitophel* will serve as a preliminary illustration of some of the things that must be covered by the term "poetry of statement" if it is to play a useful part in the description of Dryden's poetic achievement. The choice of this passage is fair to Dryden because, true to his training in rhetoric under Dr. Busby at Westminster School, he habitually composed his opening lines —his exordium, as it were—with great care. And by the same token it is convenient as an extreme example with which to test the concept of the poetry of statement, in that here all Dryden's resources as a poet are thrown into the endeavour to gain and hold the attention of the reader, to give richness and vitality to his subject. Certainly this is not simply plain or direct statement.

In pious times, e'er Priest-craft did begin,
Before *Polygamy* was made a sin;
When man, on many, multiply'd his kind,
E'r one to one was, cursedly, confin'd:
When Nature prompted, and no law deny'd
Promiscuous use of Concubine and Bride;
Then, *Israel's* Monarch, after Heaven's own heart,
His vigorous warmth did, variously, impart
To *Wives* and Slaves: And, wide as his Command,
Scatter'd his Maker's Image through the Land.[24]

An extraordinary amount of alliterative binding and emphasis, and a fine rhetorical climax, serve to mould these lines into a formal verse paragraph with a very complex purpose. It launches the narrative on which the allegorical structure of the poem is based; the diction and the conventional manner in which the time and setting of the narrative are established give it a proper heroic tone; the King's immoral behaviour, because it cannot be ignored or glossed over, is offset by the gently ironic humour of its treatment (which apart from its immediate purpose has a wider significance in the whole poem, deriving from the contrast it provides with the implacable figure of absolute justice who speaks to end the narrative); the vitally important identification with God of the divinely appointed King is suggested; and the opportunity is not lost to make one or two oblique thrusts at the King's enemies. The passage is narrative statement to be sure, but the effects it achieves, which even this list does not exhaust, go far beyond the limits of direct statement; and they derive from a variety of poetic devices, as well as from the subtle control of the statement itself.

The lines are heroic (they serve to set the heroic tone of the poem as a whole), but they are also humorous. Their humour, however, comes not from any sudden deflation of the heroic elevation, as in the mock heroic style of *Mac-*

---

24 *Absalom and Achitophel; A Poem* (1681), lines 1-10. All passages, unless otherwise specified, are repeated from Kinsley, *op. cit.*

Flecknoe: although the mock heroic element is certainly present in the incongruity between the epic style and the promiscuity of the King, the elevation is too much tempered by a tone of easy familiarity for this element to be exploited. The more effective humour comes from the manner in which Dryden has handled the delicate situation posed by the King's questionable moral behaviour (a situation that is not only morally and poetically delicate but also, for a poet-laureate charged with the duty of furthering his employer's cause, personally delicate). This humour is deeply embedded in the whole complex structure of the passage, but it is firstly a matter of syntax.

The heroic couplet, as the Augustan poets used it, characteristically encouraged a loosely co-ordinate sentence structure, in which the devices of balance and antithesis predominated. But here there is only one brief flash of this sort of precision, in the line:

When Nature prompted, and no law deny'd.

The long sentence is not alien to Dryden's use of the heroic couplet: *Religio Laici* has many of them. But the more complex type of subordinate sentence structure, in which the core of meaning is held in abeyance until it is reached climactically (as in the so-called "Ciceronian" period), is relatively rare, and its use here is basic to the whole tone of the passage. These lines still proceed by means of discursive statement, but because of the delicacy of the subject, demanding indirectness, even evasiveness, the statement itself tends to be devious.

The unusual syntax of the passage contributes to the general heroic elevation, but its tentativeness also enables it to capture an effect of hesitancy, when combined with the hovering, checked quality of the rhythm. When Dryden had strengthened and toughened his style, as he certainly had done by the time he came to write *Absalom and Achitophel*, he had learned to avoid the weak form of verbs that abound in the smooth but weak verse of Waller, and also in his own early poems like *Annus Mirabilis*. The repeated use of the auxiliary "did" in these carefully structured opening lines can safely be accepted as a conscious mannerism. It deliberately weakens the force of the opening line:

In pious times, e'er Priest-craft did begin,

which in turn prepares for the deviousness of line 8, where the verb is not only weak in form but also carefully separated in its parts:

His vigorous warmth did, variously, impart.

The progression of thought is rendered hesitant, but yet remains orderly and controlled. Syntax, though with a mimetic evasiveness, articulates the passage, adding a nicely delicate flavour, but without in any way concealing or distorting the meaning. The statement still means what it says, but because of its manner it operates on an affective as well as a cognitive level.

Rhythm, too, follows closely on the sense and serves to control, to guide, rather than to overwhelm, the literal meaning. The opening sentence culminates in its final four lines:

Then *Israel's* Monarch, after Heaven's own heart,
His vigorous warmth did, variously, impart
To *Wives* and Slaves: And, wide as his Command,
Scatter'd his Maker's Image through the Land.

Even here the first couplet continues to hold the thought in abeyance and the rhythmic flow is uneven. Only the final line and a half are uninterrupted or undislocated in syntax and rhythm, and there evasiveness is suddenly cast aside with the sudden directness of statement in:

Scatter'd his Maker's Image through the Land,

where the rhythmic plunge deriving from the inversion of the first metrical foot combines with the straightforward syntax and the forceful diction—Dryden is a master of the forceful verb—to give strength and significance to the whole paragraph. The abruptness of "scatter'd" and its metrical force in the line receive added power from their climactic position in a context of tentative progression, and in their turn serve to highlight the evasiveness of what has gone before. The alliterative binding throughout the passage, too, helps to enhance the impression of a delicately hesitant statement, by setting it off against a pattern of formal orderliness.

And within this overall mimetic structure of syntax and rhythm the paragraph achieves other more incidental and indirect effects by minor adjustments of diction and movement. Ostensibly the diction is elevated, as suits an heroic poem. Polysyllabic abstractions, such as "polygamy" (Greek

in origin), impart an air of self-conscious dignity; "promiscuous" was in the seventeenth century one of those consciously "poetic" words inherited by Dryden from Sylvester
and Sandys, which afforded a measure of ostentatious elevation; as it does in this triplet from the *Aeneid* (without, of
course, any humorous or ironic intent):

Still pressing onward, to the Walls he drew,
Where Shafts, and Spears, and Darts promiscuous flew;
And sanguine Streams the slipp'ry Ground embrew.[25]

The only word with any directly ironical flavour is the
"priest-craft" of the first line, and this is interesting because
of the manner in which a word that in the seventeenth
century apparently meant simply the "craft" or "business"
of a priest gains this added significance.[26] The word occurs
too early in the passage for it to reflect any tinge of irony
from its literal context: as yet the diction has been relatively
neutral. But it draws attention to itself by its length relative
to the other words in the line, and the slowness of the
spondaic metre, which in the seventeenth century was aptly
considered "grave and majestic", combines with the texture[27]
and the indirect syntax to produce the need for a careful,
even hesitant articulation:

In pious times, e'er Priest-craft did begin.

Against this background, the alliteration of plosive consonants (an element that Dryden uses frequently to contribute
to the development of satire)[28] and the connotations of

25 *Aeneid*, Bk. 12, lines 1001-3.
26 According to the OED "priestcraft" originally meant "the *craft* or business
of a priest" or "the exercise of priestly functions". In Dryden's line, again as
defined by the OED, the word means "priestly craft or policy; the arts used
by ambitious priests to impose upon the multitude or further their interests".
If the OED is to be accepted in this matter, Dryden was the first to use
the word "priestcraft" with this particular meaning.
27 The term "texture" in this study is used to refer to the patterning of vowels
and consonants in the line, and may include such effects as alliteration,
consonance, and assonance.
28 Josephine Miles, from editing the *Concordance to the Poetical Works of John
Dryden* (California: University of California Press, 1957), believes that his
"major vocabulary is clearly an heroic one", and that his own "characteristic
words are terms of deliberation". These things are no doubt true, but they
seem to be more an accident of the type of poems that Dryden wrote, and
of the age in which he wrote them, than something that is essential to his
own particular poetic genius. I suspect that the fact that approximately 7
per cent of Dryden's words in his poetry begin with the highly effective
plosive consonant p, by comparison with a figure of less than 3 per cent in a
wide selection of his prose, is at least as significant as any usage of words in
terms of meaning or reference.

"pious" and "craft" lend an intangible sense, a new piquancy of tone, to the word, unsupported as yet by anything in the direct meaning.

The same deft control of sound and sense is apparent throughout the passage: the word "polygamy" dominates the second line, not solely because of its intrinsic meaning but also because it echoes the alliteration placed on the key words of the previous line, and because, like "priest-craft", it has syllabic dominance in a line composed mainly of monosyllables. The use of words with auditory dominance, without an accompanying rhetorical inflation, to give a strongly ironic effect, is a trick that Dryden uses with considerable success in mock heroic passages: in *MacFlecknoe* for example:

Then thus, continu'd he, my Son advance
Still in new Impudence, new Ignorance.[29]

The same control, too, helps give these lines from *Absalom and Achitophel* dignity and elevation, but with an urbanity, a conversational ease of expression, essential to their tone of delicate humour. The amplification of lines 3–6, strictly unnecessary except as a means of raising the tone:

When man, on many, multiply'd his kind
E'r one to one was, cursedly, confin'd:
When Nature prompted, and no law deny'd
Promiscuous use of Concubine and Bride;

is blended with a smooth, almost suave use of alliteration and consonance. The sound of the verse is assured though the treatment is delicate, and perfect ease is combined with the formal patterning of precisely balanced syllables.

One final reference to the passage will serve to demonstrate Dryden's habit of inserting into his verse a rather unobtrusive word or phrase that is yet charged with structural significance. Close reading may be necessary to realize the full implications of:

Scatter'd his Maker's Image through the Land.

The apparently casual use of the phrase "his Maker's Image" here, made more inconspicuous by the prominence of "scatter'd", serves none the less to begin the establishment of

---

29 *MacFlecknoe; or, A Satire upon a True-Blue Protestant Poet*, T. S. (1682), lines 145-46.

a primary structural link within the poem: the identification of King *David* with God, a link with important ramifications for the whole allegory, for the tone of the poem, and for its ultimate meaning. And there are other indirect meanings and shades of meaning that point to the difficulty of describing the passage as poetry of statement, if by that is meant poetry which follows wholly the methods of plain prose or direct utterance: the ironic treatment of *David* and his complaisant concubines, the ambivalence of the phrase "after Heaven's own heart", the ironical glance at the Whig claim that Monmouth's mother was married to the King, in the words "*Wives* and Slaves". Yet it is characteristic of Dryden at his best that these oblique meanings can, and should, remain unobtrusive, in order that they do not destroy or even lessen the narrative quality of the statement.

For though the richness of the lines goes beyond their direct statement, it is not—and this is particularly important because it introduces a basic aspect of the problem of reconciling Dryden's work with the demands of a great deal of present-day poetic theory and taste—it is not a richness that gains by acting contrary to the statement. To put the main emphasis on possible ambiguities in Dryden's poetry, on tensions between what is said and the way of saying it, is more often than not to go in the wrong direction, except of course for the obvious irony of the mock heroic. Dryden usually means first and foremost what he says directly: even in mock heroic poems he sometimes gains his purpose by saying, somewhat unexpectedly, just exactly what he means. The first lines of *MacFlecknoe*, for instance, could not state their meaning any more specifically than they do:

All humane things are subject to decay,
And, when Fate summons, Monarchs must obey:
This *Fleckno* found, who, like *Augustus*, young
Was call'd to Empire, and had govern'd long:
In Prose and Verse was own'd, without dispute
Through all the Realms of *Non-sense*, absolute.[30]

In its way this last couplet might be regarded as the essence, the "touchstone" perhaps, of the poetry of statement.

But the astonishing thing about the opening of *Absalom and Achitophel* is that, despite all that it contrives to do, it

---

30 *Ibid.*, lines 1-6.

still sounds natural. Despite the formality of its carefully managed deviousness, its heroic elevation, its constant alliterative pattern that controls the movement of almost every line: despite all this artifice, and more, it still sounds like someone beginning to speak with a straightforward, easy familiarity, a half-humorous seriousness. It is, indeed, only this successful welding of artifice, of formality, with a conversational ease that enables Dryden to get away with an outrageous proposition that neither familiarity nor formality alone could have made acceptable: that promiscuity may be justified by Heaven. And it is this, more consistently than anything else, that saves Dryden's poetry of statement from the danger of being dull or prosaic: where nothing else in his verse seems to raise it above the level of prose, it still has the vitality, the verisimilitude, to be derived from a controlled and imaginative use of the rhythms of the speaking voice.

To read Dryden too closely, to be constantly on the lookout for fine and subtle shades of ambiguous meaning and implication, will almost certainly result in a degree of misplaced ingenuity. Dryden belongs essentially to the tradition of a relatively simple, straightforward oral poetry, and most of his richness is available to whoever will listen to him with the same sensitive ear that he himself possessed. But he is still a highly conscious artist, and too complete a concentration on his "divine energy", too ready a surrender to his "long majestic march", runs the risk of missing much along the way. In saying that "when Dryden became fired he only wrote more plainly" Van Doren was not altogether right: he would have been more accurate if he had said "he only *appears* to write more plainly". And in this respect the lines we have been looking at from *Absalom and Achitophel* are characteristic of Dryden at his best. They have the appearance and the strength of meaning, of simple, clear, decisive narrative statement, but with a richness and complexity so perfectly contrived that it remains unobtrusive though wholly effective.

And yet, of course, these lines cannot really be declared typical of Dryden. There is no other passage in his work quite like them, just as there is nothing quite like the *character* of *Zimri* in *Absalom and Achitophel* that Dryden himself thought "worth the whole poem"; nothing quite like the magnificence of the opening stanza of the ode *To the Memory of Mrs. Anne Killigrew* or the beautifully modulated lines in memory of his fellow poet Oldham; nothing quite like the voice of the "honest *Layman*" as it is heard speaking throughout *Religio Laici*. Each of these has its own special qualities; but the beginning of *Absalom and Achitophel* is still sufficiently typical to give some guidance in what to look for. It is typical in its use of a structure of discursive statement, in the essential directness of its meaning, and in the complex pattern of sound, movement, and texture that has been woven into that meaning to give it richness and vitality. It is not simple statement, and yet it still deserves the title "poetry of statement" because the statement remains important in the poetry: it does not become transformed into something else or serve merely as a framework for other, non-discursive effects.

And it is typical, too, in the toughness of its art. This is not the intangible, evanescent kind of poetry that threatens to vanish under the least analytical or intellectual pressure. It is no kindness to any poet, perhaps, to take to pieces his carefully wrought artifice in order to see how it is made. But because of their central core of direct statement Dryden's creations have a resilience that usually enables them to stand up to analysis, even when it is taken to the lengths it has been here. The most heavyhanded of critics could not go far towards destroying, except of course by sheer obtuseness, the quality of lines like these, which follow shortly after the passage we have been discussing and refer to the people of London:

The Jews, a Headstrong, Moody, Murmuring race,
As ever try'd th'extent and stretch of grace;
God's pamper'd people whom, debauch'd with ease,
No King could govern, nor no God could please;
(Gods they had tri'd of every shape and size
That God-smiths could produce, or Priests devise:).[31]

For this reason one may embark on a close analysis of Dryden's poetic art with less misgiving than otherwise might

31 *Absalom and Achitophel*, lines 45-50.

be the case. Where one does no good, at least one is unlikely to do very much harm; after doing one's worst the poetry will remain to be enjoyed at least as much as before. And an analysis such as has been attempted of the opening verse paragraph of *Absalom and Achitophel* suggests that a careful examination of some of the best or most characteristic of Dryden's work would serve to make us more receptive to his way of working, to what his poetry of statement has to offer. This will be the purpose of the chapters that follow.

and again: " 'Tis true, that to imitate well is a poet's work."[5]
As late as 1725, John Dennis, though in some ways his ideas
look forward to the Romanticism that was finally to reject
imitation as the basis of poetry, can still thump the table
and declare, in refutation of Leonard Welsted's attack on
imitation, that "if to imitate is purely mechanical, why then
all poetry is mechanical because all poetry is an Imitation of
nature. Whoever writes poetically imitates, and every work
of nature that is poeticall, is a Downright imitation".[6]

Because this concept of poetry as imitation, as "fiction" or
"fable", is so widely accepted in Dryden's own time as to be
almost taken for granted, it is important, I think, to begin
with an attempt to place his work against this background:
to understand in what way his poems are "imitations", and
what are the consequences for a view of his work as poetry
of statement if it is also seen as imitation.

Because of its acknowledged nearness to prose argument,
Dryden's verse essay *Religio Laici; or, a Layman's Faith*, the
poem in which he argues the Anglican theological position
that he was himself soon to abandon, has special significance
for this attempt to define those qualities which, by separating
his poetry of statement from prose, allow it the title of
poetry. *Religio Laici* is without doubt poetry of statement
in the purest form it can achieve, in the sense that no other
poem achieves poetic quality while retaining its character as
statement so completely: in no other poem does the "poetry"
interfere with or inhibit less the reader's response to the
statement purely as statement. In such poems as *Absalom
and Achitophel* or even *The Hind and the Panther*, though
our response must be primarily to the discursive meaning,
we are more immediately conscious of the imaginative force
of the lines.

Religio Laici may, indeed, be the closest that this kind of
poetry can come to prose and yet continue to be recognized
and accepted as poetry. Dryden himself spoke in the poem of:

5 *Ibid.*, I, 113.
6 John Dennis, "The Causes of the Decay and Defects of Dramatick Poetry,
and of the Degeneracy of the Publick Tast", ed. E. N. Hooker, *The Critical
Works of John Dennis* (2 vols.; Baltimore: Johns Hopkins Press, 1939), II, 285.

chapter one

Imitation

Poetry, declared Sir Philip Sidney in his *Apologie*, is "... an arte of imitation ... that is to say, a representing, counterfetting, or figuring foorth: to speak metaphorically, a speaking picture: with this end, to teach and delight".[1] And if there is anything certain about the seventeenth century it is that the majority of its poetry was written against the background of a tacit acceptance of this concept of poetry as an art of imitation. For Francis Bacon poetry is "nothing else but an imitation of history at pleasure";[2] and Ben Jonson describes the poet as

a Maker, or a fainer: his Art, an Art of imitation or faining, expressing the life of man in fit measure, numbers and harmony. ... Hence he is called a *Poet*, not he which writeth in measure only, but that fayneth and formeth a fable, and writes things like the truth. For the Fable and Fiction is, as it were, the form and Soul of any Poeticall worke or Poeme.[3]

As for Dryden, "I never heard," he says, "of any other foundations of Dramatic Poesy than the imitation of Nature";[4]

1 Sir Philip Sidney, "Apologie for Poetrie" (*ca.* 1583), ed. G. G. Smith, *Elizabethan Critical Essays* (2 vols.; Oxford: Clarendon Press, 1904), I, 158.
2 Francis Bacon, "De dignitate et augmentis scientiarum libros IX" (London, 1623), ed. J. Spedding and R. H. Ellis, *The Philosophical Works of Francis Bacon* (5 vols.; London: 1861), IV, 315.
3 Ben Jonson, "Timber; or, Discoveries" (London, 1641), Section 128, ed. C. H. Herford and E. Simpson, *Ben Jonson* (12 vols.; Oxford: Clarendon Press, 1947), VIII, 635.
4 Dryden, "Defence of an 'Essay of Dramatic Poesy'", prefixed to the second edition of *The Indian Emperour* (London, 1668), ed. W. P. Ker, *Essays of John Dryden* (2 vols.; Oxford: Clarendon Press, 1900), I, 123.

... this unpolish'd rugged Verse, I chose;
As fittest for Discourse, and nearest Prose.[7]

And in his Preface to the poem he described his style as
being "legislative":

The Expressions of a Poem, design'd purely for Instruction, ought
to be Plain and Natural, and yet Majestick: for here the Poet is
presum'd to be a kind of Law-giver, and those three qualities
which I have named are proper to the Legislative style. The
Florid, Elevated and Figurative way is for the Passions; for Love
and Hatred, Fear and Anger, are begotten in the Soul by shewing
their Objects out of their true proportion; either greater than the
Life, or less; but Instruction is to be given by shewing them
what they naturally are. A Man is to be cheated into Passion,
but to be reason'd into Truth.[8]

Thus in some respects, even to Dryden himself, the poem is
deliberately "unpoetic": there is to be no painting of the
subjects larger than life, no playing on the passions of the
reader. He is concerned with fact, and fact does not require
any elaborate devices of poetry to sustain it:

For, while from *Sacred Truth* I do not swerve
Tom Sternhold's or *Tom Shadwell's Rhimes* will serve.[9]

But as well as being "plain and natural", the style of
Religio Laici is required to be "majestick", and against the
other assertions of the poet the poem itself opens with an
exordium as splendid as anything that Dryden did, and
"poetry" in any sense of the word. And it must also be
remembered that in *Religio Laici* Dryden is seeking to teach:
the situation is different from what it ostensibly was when,
in his *Defence of an "Essay of Dramatic Poesy"*, he defended
himself against the charge of being "magesterial" by maintaining that

my whole discourse was sceptical, according to that way of reasoning which was used by Socrates, Plato, and all the Academies of
old, which Tully and the best of the Ancients followed, and which
is imitated by the modest inquisitions of the Royal Society. That
this is so, not only the name will show, which is an Essay, but

7 *Religio Laici*, lines 453-54.
8 "Preface to 'Religio Laici' " (1682), *The Poems of John Dryden*, ed. J. Kinsley
   (4 vols.; Oxford: Clarendon Press, 1958), I, 311.
9 *Religio Laici*, lines 455-56.

the frame and composition of the work. You see it is a dialogue sustained by persons of several opinions, all of them left doubtful, to be determined by the readers in general. . . .[10]

Here Dryden is claiming for the *Essay of Dramatic Poesy* a use of words as that kind of "transparent medium" demanded by the new experimental science, which required that words should intrude as little as possible between the subject and the reader. *Religio Laici*, by contrast, has an admittedly didactic purpose. Men are to be "reason'd into truth", instead of the matter being left "to be determined by the readers in general", and, "plain and natural" as its expression may be, it still must have the delightfulness that enables poetry to teach. Though it is a poem "design'd purely for Instruction", nevertheless "delight is the chief, if not the only end of poesy; instruction can be admitted but in second place, for poesy only instructs as it delights".[11]

But irrespective of Dryden's own attitude or purpose, already by the middle of the eighteenth century, and by such a staunch neoclassicist as Dr. Johnson, the subject of *Religio Laici* was found to be "argumentative rather than poetical", and the poem itself thought to be intended only as "a specimen of metrical disputation". The poem has achieved a considerable reputation, but frequently one that betrays some uneasiness about its poetic qualities: its excellence is seen as being of a unique kind, rather than as something to be accounted for by the usual poetic criteria. Thus Dr. Johnson, "nor will it be easy to find another example equally happy of this middle kind of writing which, though prosaick in some parts, rises to high poetry in others, and neither towers to the skies nor creeps along the ground".[12] Percival Stockdale, on the other hand, in his *Lectures on the English Poets* (1807) is one who had no doubts: he thought that "to give poetry to controversial and scholastick theology . . . was reserved by the God of Nature, for the genius of Milton and of Dryden".[13] And Van Doren: ". . . Dryden has achieved an effect of his own which has been achieved by no other writer

10 "Defence of an 'Essay of Dramatic Poesy'", Ker, *op. cit.*, I, 124.
11 *Ibid.*, p. 113.
12 Samuel Johnson, "Life of Dryden", in *Lives of the English Poets* (London, 1779), ed. G. Birkbeck Hill (3 vols.; Oxford: Clarendon Press, 1905), III, 222.
13 Percival Stockdale, *Lectures on the Truly Eminent English Poets* (2 vols.; London: 1807), I, 286.

in prose or verse."[14] Van Doren judges *Religio Laici* to be "a truly engaging poem . . . for which Grays's 'thoughts that breathe and words that burn' is not an impossible phrase"; but at the same time he believes it "hardly worth while to become exercised over the question whether Dryden's ratiocinative poems are really poems". And he is echoed by Christopher Hollis:

It is not necessary to delay over the somewhat fruitless enquiry whether the debate in verse is, or is not of its very nature a bastard business, whether it is not the function of poetry to express emotion and of prose to argue . . . if Dryden's use of verse form makes it easier for us to read what he has to say, then the use of verse form is justified;[15]

which is good common sense of a kind (and something Dryden himself may well have agreed with), but not much use as poetic theory. Fruitless or not, the question as to what does, and does not constitute poetry will continue to be asked.

It is a question that might be asked regarding these lines from *Religio Laici*:

Shall I speak plain, and in a Nation free
Assume an honest *Layman's Liberty?*
I think (according to my little Skill,
To my own Mother-Church submitting still:)
That many have been sav'd, and many may,
Who never heard this Question brought in play.[16]

These are not particularly striking or distinguished lines, but they are the stuff of which the poem is made. They illustrate what A. D. Hope, who accepts Samuel Johnson's description of such verse as "the middle kind of writing", but who, unlike Johnson, has no hesitation in accepting it as poetry (as in fact the real backbone of poetry, what he describes as its "discursive mode") means when he speaks of how "metre and the unaffected skill of the poet draw the

14 Mark Van Doren, *John Dryden: A Study of his Poetry* (Bloomington, Indiana: Indiana University Press, 1946), p. 170.
15 Christopher Hollis, *Dryden* (London: Duckworth, 1933), pp. 104-5.
16 *Religio Laici*, lines 316-21.

natural words and syntax into a movement that constitutes the dance of language we call poetry".[17] The rhythmic movement based on the metric of the heroic couplet transforms the statement, giving it a vitality, an energy, a life that it would not otherwise have.

"Poetry," Robert Frost tells us, "is what gets lost in the translation", and if we could "translate" these lines from *Religio Laici* into statement—if we could think of them only in terms of the kind of meaning conveyed by strictly plain prose, what we would lose in the process is primarily the effect of its characteristic movement, its "dance of language". There would be other things as well: the slightly unusual word order, for instance, is likely to have psychological overtones quite apart from those deriving from sound or movement. But it is to the rhythmic movement of the verse that we mainly respond, apart from the literal meaning of the words.

Professor Morris Croll, although concerned immediately with the theory of the cadence in seventeenth century oratorical prose, attempts an explanation of the origins of verse that may add something of interest here:

the psychological explanation of verse in to be found in the dance in which it originated. In the dance the regularity of beat is the means by which energy is artificially maintained at uniform level higher than that of ordinary human occupations and movements. In poetry the regularity of accent stimulates the energy of utterance which always tends to flag and die away, and keeps it at an artificial height throughout the line or stanza. And of course this energy of utterance accompanies, interprets, stimulates, energy of emotion. Prose on the other hand, even oratorical prose, cannot, does not aim to move uniformly on a high level. Its foundation is laid on the basis of common and matter-of-fact speech.[18]

There is much more to Dryden's rhythm than regularity of beat, but the rhythmic strength of the heroic couplet makes the general idea expressed here by Croll relevant to it. Dryden's lines carry a series of stresses, induced partly by the formal structure of the heroic verse and partly by their

17 A. D. Hope, "The Discursive Mode; Reflections on the Ecology of Poetry", *Quadrant*, I (1956-57), 31.
18 M. W. Croll, "The Cadence of English Oratorical Prose", *SP*, XVI (1919), 50-51.

exploitation of its rhetorical potentialities:[19] the parallel of "plain" and "free" in the first line of the passage quoted earlier, for instance, gives the words added emphasis, and points to the attitude of the "honest *Layman*" of the second line; which in its turn is given slightly more prominence than it would otherwise receive, from the position of these words across a change of texture between the two half lines:

Shall I speak *plain*, and in a Nation *free*
Assume an *honest Layman's* Liberty?[20]

Similarly with the line:

To my own Mother-Church submitting still:

where a slight rearrangement of the usual word order, preceded by a smoothing of the stress pattern, gives full emphasis to "Mother-Church", reinforced by the alliteration of the following "submitting still". These stresses, which belong to the verse and not to the statement as such, yet help to sustain the statement, to give it energy of utterance apart from that deriving from the intrinsic interest of what is said.

This energy of utterance resulting from the rhythm Croll sees not only as stimulating but also as "interpreting" energy of emotion. In other words rhythm can give meaning or direction to the emotion it arouses, and consequently, if organized and controlled, can be used to develop an emotional dimension with significance in the poem's pattern of meaning. In *Religio Laici* this emotional dimension deriving from the rhythm remains subordinate to the direct, ratiocinative element in the pattern, but its contribution to the total poetic structure of the poem is nevertheless a very real one. In the passage we have been discussing the metrical stresses on "plain" and "free" lead to a slightly greater energy of utterance; and the result is to arouse not simply a general vitality but one that gives a significant emotional colouring to the "honest *Layman*" of the following line.

19 These rhetorical potentialities have been discussed in a number of works, e.g.:
Ruth Wallerstein, "The Development of the Rhetoric and Metre of the Heroic Couplet, especially 1625-1645", *PMLA*, I (1935), 166-210.
G. E. Williamson, "The Rhetorical Pattern of Neo-classical Wit", *MP*, XXXIII (1935), 55-81.
W. C. Brown, *The Triumph of Form: A Study of the Later Masters of the Heroic Couplet* (Chapel Hill: University of North Carolina Press, 1948).
20 My italics here.

But the poetic quality of *Religio Laici* is not to be gauged primarily from a close analysis of individual lines. It is to be found, or rather it is to be heard, by listening to the tone of the poem as a whole, although this tone is itself derived from individual auditory, rhythmic qualities of the kind that have been discussed. An answering "antiphonal" rhythm is natural to the neoclassic use of the couplet form, and Dryden's lines allow this rhythm to correspond with the movement of the reasoning mind as it grapples with the points of the argument. The clearly defined periods of the couplets fit the propositions as they are put forward, and the points of stress in rhythm and argument are similarly matched:

But stay: the *Deist* here will urge anew,
No *Supernatural Worship* can be *True*:
Because a *general Law* is that alone
Which must to *all*, and every *where* be known:
A Style so large as not *this* Book can claim
Nor aught that bears *reveal'd* Religions *Name*.
'Tis said the sound of a *Messiah's Birth*
Is gone through all the habitable Earth:
But still that Text must be confin'd alone
To what was *Then* inhabited, and known:
And what Provision cou'd from *thence* accrue
To *Indian* Souls, and Worlds discover'd *New*?
In other parts it helps, that Ages past,
The Scriptures there were *known*, and were *imbrac'd*,
Till Sin spread once again the Shades of Night:
What's that to these who never *saw* the Light?[21]

The emphases gained by sound and movement in this passage are continuous and varied: the syllabic prominence of "*Supernatural Worship*"; the careful enunciation required by "*general Law*"; the two pauses in the following line; the deliberation of the string of more or less evenly stressed monosyllables followed by the alliterated "*reveal'd* Religions"; and so on through the passage. All these add to the strength of the formal stress pattern of the lines. But they are not emphases that the poem invites us to dwell upon or analyze. They are cumulative in their effect rather than to be savoured individually. They give added energy and an emotional

21 *Religio Laici*, lines 168-83.

colouring to a passage whose tone comes from a mastery of
rhythm that allows sufficient stress to the final rhyme word
to finish each line and each couplet neatly and definitely,
and makes each second line seem to "answer" or complete
the first, but yet with sufficient variety and interest within
the lines and couplets to prevent monotony and to reinforce
their meaning. "The favourite exercise of his mind was
ratiocination", Dr. Johnson once said of Dryden, and here
the rhythmic pattern of the poem is an "imitation" of that
exercise, with all the neat but varied movement of an alert,
reasonable, enlightened mind, fully in control of itself.

Yet the poem does not have a single tone or rhythmic
pattern throughout. Its argument is divided into clearly
defined sections, each of which tends to have its own characteristic movement, its own distinct rhythmic pattern, appropriate to the direction being taken by the argument at the
time, which separates it off from those on either side of it.
This gives *Religio Laici* a larger unity, approximating to
the blank verse paragraph of Milton, and helping overcome
the excessive fragmentation likely to result from the use of
the couplet form. The lines quoted below allow for the
development of an easier, more meditative movement, by
comparison with the more formal control of those just
discussed: this being achieved mainly by a more frequent
use of enjambment within the couplets, thereby allowing a
greater degree of prose fluidity, while at the same time
retaining the decisive definition of points by the regular end-
stopping of the couplets themselves:

For granting we have Sin'd, and that th'offence
Of *Man*, is made against *Omnipotence*,
Some Price, that bears *proportion*, must be paid;
And *Infinite* with *Infinite* be weigh'd.
See then the *Deist lost*: *Remorse* for *Vice*,
Not paid, or *paid, inadequate* in price:
What farther means can *Reason* now direct,
Or what Relief from *humane Wit* expect?
That shews us *sick*; and sadly are we sure
Still to be *Sick*, till Heav'n reveal the *Cure*:[22]

This matching of rhythmic and auditory qualities to the
movement of the argument in *Religio Laici*, by which means

22 *Ibid.*, lines 111-20.

interest and vitality are sustained at a level beyond that deriving intrinsically from the subject of the argument itself, is something that pervades the whole poem. The discussion of this particular quality has not been intended to imply that there are not other and more immediately noticeable or more striking poetic qualities to be found in selected lines and passages of the poem: in the splendidly lyrical opening lines, for instance. The poem does have its moments of "high poetry", noticed by Dr. Johnson, that would lift it for the time being above the level of prose (or verse), and this is not likely to be disputed by anyone who is familiar with it. But the immediate problem has been to define the basic qualities that characterize the work as a whole, and that enable it to be seen as poetry, again as a whole: that is, as a *poem* and not as prose argument with occasional flashes of poetry.

Donald Davie, in his *Articulate Energy*, a study of the role of syntax in poetry, makes a suggestion that has some relevance to the poetic structure of *Religio Laici*. "If all poems are born as rhythms," he says, "then some it seems may be born as rhythms of ideas, that is, as patterns of syntax rather than patterns of sound." This rhythm of ideas based on syntax is claimed by Davie to be something quite apart from the usual poetic concept of the sound as an echo of the sense: "when we speak of music in relation to poetic syntax we mean something that can be appreciated in silent reading without the reader having to imagine how the poem would sound if it were uttered aloud."[23] The separation of ideas from sound makes Davie's theory inadequate for Dryden's poetry, in which sound can never be neglected. Dryden's rhythms are almost always those of the speaking voice, and his ideas are habitually expressed in the manner of spoken rather than silent language. Nevertheless, the presence in his poetry of a strong pattern of ideas, regulated in the normal manner by syntax, is quite apparent; and the total rhythmic pattern of *Religio Laici*, shown in the previous discussion as working parallel to the pattern of ideas or argument, is one that is determined by an interaction of prose, or speech rhythms, in which syntax plays its usual role, and rhythms deriving from the formal structure of the couplets. In some passages it is apparent that the prose syntax is

23 Donald Davie, *Articulate Energy* (London: Routledge & Kegan Paul, 1955), p. 32.

allowed to become a dominant element in determining the movement at least within the couplets, giving the easier, meditative movement to the thought that has been commented on. This results in what Davie would call the "subjective" use of syntax. "Poetic syntax is subjective," he says, "when its function is to please us by the fidelity with which it follows the 'form of thought' in the poet's mind."[24]

Davie himself believes that the heroic couplet, "at least as used by Dryden and Pope, is capable of rendering only one sort of movement through the mind; it is committed by its very nature to a syntax of antithesis and razor sharp distinctions".[25] There is some truth in this judgment (and more in relation to Pope than to Dryden), in so far as it points to the most common type of neoclassical wit. But its inadequacy as a general description of the movement of ideas in *Religio Laici* will already have been made apparent. And although the restrictive nature of the couplet form does not normally encourage or allow some of the more complex patterns of metre and syntax discussed by Davie, something of the variety that can be achieved is indicated by this passage:

Proof needs not here, for whether we compare
That Impious, Idle Superstitious Ware
Of *Rites, Lustrations Offerings*, (which before,
In various Ages, various Countries bore)
With *Christian Faith* and *Vertues*, we shall find
None answ'ring the great ends of humane kind
But *This one Rule of Life*: That shows us best
How God may be appeas'd, and Mortals blest.[26]

The long sentence here takes almost no account of the couplet form, and achieves a sinuous, meandering movement that approaches the flexibility, the ease and continuity of spoken prose. The enjambments, though the rhymes are not weak, give an effect of fluidity, which results in the sentence rather than the line or couplet being the unit of rhythm. The metre is not pronounced, and the movement through the passage depends more on length of syllables than on metrical stress. Emphatic monosyllables effectively bracket one section of the argument:

24 *Ibid.*, p. 68.
25 *Ibid.*, p. 79.
26 *Religio Laici*, lines 126-33.

Proof needs not here . . .

. . . .

But *This one Rule of Life* . . .

and polysyllabic words in the second and third lines destroy
any tendency towards a metrical flow. Yet the rhythm is
carefully controlled, and it is typical of Dryden that in this
longer, more complicated type of sentence the sense is not
obscured but continues to be closely followed. At the same
time the modulated rhythm of the passage has a mimetic
rather than a strictly semantic role in the total pattern: the
meditative, slowly reasoned movement of the lines makes
the verse reflective in tone as well as argumentatively precise
in meaning. The movement follows the "form of thought",
and some further words of Dr. Johnson are applicable: "The
measure of time in pronouncing may be varied so as strongly
to represent, not only the measure of external motion, but
the quick or slow succession of ideas, and consequently the
passions of the mind."

Everywhere in *Religio Laici* the rhythm of the verse has
this quality of imitating, or imaging, the "passions of the
mind". The variations of sound and movement and texture
are subordinated to the rhetorical expression of the meaning; but they are, too, indicative of a thinking mind:

Must *all Tradition* then be set aside?
This to affirm were Ignorance, or Pride.
Are there not many points, some needfull sure
To saving Faith, that Scripture leaves obscure?
Which every Sect will wrest a several way
(For what *one* Sect Interprets, *all* Sects *may*:)
We hold, and say we prove from Scripture plain,
That *Christ* is GOD; the bold *Socinian*
From the *same* Scripture urges he's but MAN.
Now what Appeal can end th'important Suit;
Both parts *talk* loudly, but the Rule is mute?[27]

From this abrupt but varied pattern of propositions reflecting in its rhythms the state of intellectual confusion it outlines, there arises the easy, reasoned statement of the "honest
Layman", speaking plainly and freely, from which this discussion of the poem began:

27 *Ibid.*, lines 305-15.

Shall I speak plain, and in a Nation free
Assume an honest *Layman's Liberty*?

In the context of the poem this statement is heard as the
authentic and unmistakable voice of the narrator, whose
"faith" the poem expresses, to be recognized whenever it is
heard, as unmistakable as the voices of Milton's *Paradise
Lost*, a voice expressive of what has been described as the
"commonsense of the layman weary of the warring theologians";[28] or of the scepticism that Louis Bredvold has
shown to be the prevailing tenor of much of Dryden's
thought.[29] Dryden in his Preface to the poem confesses himself as "naturally inclin'd to scepticism in philosophy", and
this is an attitude that is everywhere reflected in the poem,
though it is seldom to be found in the discursive argument
as such.

Yet in spite of this *Religio Laici* cannot be said to exist as
a poem simply for what it may reveal of the workings of
Dryden's mind, or of his philosophical attitude to religion
or to the world. The essence of the poem, its *raison d'être*, is
the intellectual statement of the argument: it means what it
states directly and exists in order to state it. It is written in
poetry because Dryden saw this as the most effective form of
expression for his purpose, a form whose special delightfulness would lead men to moral action. Its ability to reflect,
by the means discussed in the foregoing pages, the mental
experience that lies behind the argument serves only as
something that Dryden himself would have described as
poetic ornament; as the equivalent in a verse essay of what
he calls "the proper wit" of an heroic poem, which he says,
"sets before your eyes the absent object as perfectly, and
more delightfully than nature";[30] or as the poetic version
of the *energia* of the rhetoricians, defined by Thomas Wilson
in his *Arte of Rhetorique* (1553) as "an evident declaration
of the thing as though we see it even now done". The poem
gives us not a report or summary of the argument, but the
argument itself in an especially vital form.

28 George Sampson, *Concise Cambridge History of English Literature* (Cambridge: Cambridge University Press, 1941), p. 407.
29 See Louis Bredvold, *The Milieu of John Dryden* (Ann Arbor: University of
Michigan Press, 1934).
30 Dryden, "Preface to 'Annus Mirabilis: The Year of Wonders MDCLXVI'"
(1667), Ker, *op. cit.*, I, 15.

The changing patterns of argument in *Religio Laici* constitute the imitation, the fiction, without which poetry, in the tradition to which Dryden belonged, could not exist. It is this imitation that makes the poem a thing of the imagination, that gives it a seeming reality over a wider and more complex field of experience and response than is offered by the actual reality of the subject that is the limit of its discursive statement. The reader is better induced to believe in the interest and importance of the argument because it comes to him, not as a dead or static thing, but as a living, dynamic pattern of ideas and attitudes: not as a flat, intellectually abstract statement, but as an image, an imitation of that statement in the minds of men to whom it is a vital issue. He is thus enabled and encouraged to live for himself the problems posed by the poem. Or, to put it more simply, he will be delighted by the appearance of reality in what he reads, and will therefore be more likely to be affected by it.

The fiction, the imaginative setting, of *Religio Laici* may be more clearly illuminated, by contrast, if the poem is placed alongside what in some ways is a companion work, *The Hind and the Panther*, an allegorical treatment of the religio-political situation written from the Roman Catholic viewpoint to which in 1687 Dryden had been newly converted. The didactic purpose of this poem is made quite clear by Dryden in his Preface. If the *Declaration for Liberty of Conscience* had been made before he finished, he tells us,

... I might have spar'd my self the labour of writing many things which are contain'd in the third part of it. But I was alwayes in some hope, that the Church of England might have been perswaded to have taken off the Penal Lawes and the Test, which was one Design of the Poem when I propos'd to my self the writing of it;[31]

and a good part of the poem is taken up with arguments similar in kind to those of *Religio Laici*, though often of even greater dialectical brilliance. But here Dryden's poetic

31 Dryden, "Preface to 'The Hind and the Panther. A poem, in Three Parts'" (1687), Kinsley, *op. cit.*, II, 468.

invention works in quite another direction, to create an entirely different kind of fiction. Rather than being given an imaginative awareness of the variety of mental experience behind the actual argument, the poem is dominated imaginatively by the allegorical figure of the *Hind*, representing the Catholic Church:

A milk white *Hind*, immortal and unchang'd,
Fed on the lawns, and in the forest rang'd;
Without unspotted, innocent within,
She fear'd no danger, for she knew no sin.
Yet had she oft been chas'd with horns and hounds
And Scythian shafts, and many winged wounds
Aimed at Her heart, was often forc'd to fly,
And doom'd to death, though fated not to dy.[32]

Every reference to the *Hind* contributes to a picture of innocence, of purity, of patience, of tragic aloneness; and this gives an imaginative colouring that washes over both the intellectual brilliance of the argument and the savagery of the satire in passages like those attacking the sects, adding greatly to the richness, to the emotional intensity, of the experience they offer.

In its sheer imaginative power, indeed, *The Hind and the Panther* reaches heights not achieved by *Religio Laici*; yet as a complete poem it is less successful. The nature of the imitation makes an integration of the imaginative setting with the direct statement difficult to sustain, and though there are many passages where the fusion is complete, where the allegory exists only as an emotional undertone to the argument, there are others where it either becomes too obtrusive or ceases for the time being to be effective at all. As statement the two poems are basically similar, and it may be that in *The Hind and the Panther* Dryden has chosen a fiction that is ultimately incompatible with this kind of ratiocinative statement. But neither poem is simply prose statement made "easier to read" by being cast into verse form. In their different ways each has a dimension beyond the discursive statement to which the imagination of the reader may respond, and hence each is worthy of the title of poetry. And, too, each may be described as poetry of statement, because this poetic dimension serves, not to carry the

[32] *The Hind and the Panther*, lines 1-8.

statement or to replace it as a vehicle for meaning, but to evoke a wider response, to give the subject an appearance of reality over a wider field of experience than is covered by its direct statement.

In this chapter I have been concerned to reconcile *Religio Laici*, as an extreme example of the poetry of statement, with the Renaissance concept of poetry as an art of imitation, and to show the basic consequences of such a reconciliation for an understanding of the poetry of statement. I have tried to demonstrate how in *Religio Laici* Dryden creates a fiction within which his subject achieves poetic life and reality, without in any way lessening the precision or definitiveness of the direct statement. And I believe that it is the creation of the fiction, the invention of the imaginative setting of the poem, that reveals Dryden's poetic genius—that shows him as a poet and not merely a highly competent technician or "a classic of our prose". Any other of his major poems might have been chosen, and though the nature of the imitation may have been found to differ, its role in bringing life and vitality to the poem would have been found the same. In *Absalom and Achitophel*, for example, the imaginative development of the allegory gives the poem a verisimilitude over a range of human experience and response beyond that of the political squabble that was Dryden's immediate concern in devising the poem.

By comparison with Pope, Dryden has relatively few single lines or phrases that are really memorable. He does not consistently have the exquisiteness of touch that is found so often in Pope and that has led T. S. Eliot to describe him as a "master of miniature". It is as wholes, as complete things, that we can best savour Dryden's poems. His work has a largeness of conception: the transformation of his subject into poetry has a grandness of scale that enables it to embrace the whole poem. Whether it was the spirit of the age or his own limitations that stood in the way of the epic that he would dearly have loved to write, the epic is his imaginative sphere; and in the invention of the imitation he can lend epic magnificence, not only to satire, but to occasional verse, to the verse essay, to narrative, indeed to anything he touches.

It is, therefore, fitting that this matter of the imitation should have been dealt with first. *MacFlecknoe* delights by the brilliance of its humour, the fineness of its ironic thrusts. But it succeeds as a poem because its effective satire of Shadwell is embodied in a fiction of grandiose proportions, made of scraps of the London scene, of the world of writers, actors, publishers, of literary allusion, of Christian and classical culture; a fiction that presents the reader with a caricature that is no longer Shadwell but a figure infinitely more arresting, more impressive in its grotesqueness than any merely dull poet could ever hope or fear to be. And no amount of emphasis on the poem's power of statement should be allowed to blind us to this.

"Poetry is an art of imitation ... with this end, to teach and delight." And it is the imitation that links together the delight and the instruction and thereby enables statement to become poetry. It is the imitation that provides a unified structure for the imaginative enrichment of the statement, for the elaboration of detail, which when clothed with the beauty and magic of words gives the poem its special delightfulness. But the imitation is not simply something added to the statement for the purpose of giving pleasure. From the imitation the statement gains the verisimilitude that is not only part of the poem's delightfulness, but also the means whereby the instruction—the statement itself—is given its ultimate meaning as something belonging to life, is enabled to become an expression of "the life of man in fit measure, numbers, and harmony. . . ."

chapter two

Meaning

In *The Second Part of Absalom and Achitophel*, when Dryden has the midwife advise *Og* to:

Drink, Swear and Roar, forbear no lew'd delight
Fit for thy Bulk, doe any thing but write,[1]

he is making a statement that for directness, for precision, for "satisfying completeness", could hardly be bettered. And at the same time he is making an effective contribution to the caricature of Shadwell that is a main part of the fiction, of the imaginative setting in which the subject of the poem is presented. At this point in the poem, poetry and statement are almost identical in the demands they make on expression; as they are, too, in this very different line from the speech of King *David* in *Absalom and Achitophel*:

Beware the Fury of a Patient Man.[2]

But a reconciliation of the demands of poetry and statement are not always to be met in an equally straightforward fashion. This line, which concludes a description of *Sh—* at his "coronation" in *MacFlecknoe* reveals a wider gap between direct statement and imaginative significance:

And lambent dullness plaid arround his face.[3]

---

1 *The Second Part of Absalom and Achitophel: A Poem* (1682), lines 478-79.
2 *Absalom and Achitophel*, line 1005.
3 *MacFlecknoe*, line 111.

Because the subject and its imaginative presentation, when they come together in the poetry of statement, must be given effective expression simultaneously through the same words, their relationship is one that works its way down into the very warp and woof of the verse, into the meanings and associations of words, into sound and rhythm and imagery. In the chapters that follow attention will be directed to various aspects of this relationship, looking first at the relationship between meaning at the level of direct statement and the total poetic meaning. Rhythm and imagery are always likely to be more or less important factors in determining this relationship and they will be given detailed treatment in later chapters. For the time being, though they can seldom be ignored, they will not be the centre of interest.

The *character* of George Villiers, Duke of Buckingham, the *Zimri* of *Absalom and Achitophel*, will provide a further convenient test of the nature of Dryden's poetry of statement, though a test of a different kind from that furnished by *Religio Laici*. This is a good passage to use, because in some respects it is the exception that proves the rule of the poetry of statement. By his own account in his *Essay on the Original and Progress of Satire*, Dryden's intention ideally in these satiric *characters* was an indirect one: "to make a man appear a fool, a blockhead or a knave, without using any of those opprobrious terms! ... This is the mystery of that noble trade. . . ."[4] And, too, he himself thought this one of *Zimri* well done—"worth the whole poem", as he said. Thus we would expect to find all his resources as a poet brought into play to transform the "statement" of the passage towards this indirect end:

In the first Rank of these did *Zimri* stand:
A man so various, that he seem'd to be
Not one, but all Mankinds Epitome.
Stiff in Opinions, always in the wrong;
Was every thing by starts, and nothing long:
But, in the course of one revolving Moon,

4 Dryden, "A Discourse concerning the Original and Progress of Satire" (1693), *Essays of John Dryden*, ed. W. P. Ker (2 vols.; Oxford: Clarendon Press, 1900), II, 93.

Was Chymist, Fidler, States-Man, and Buffoon:
Then all for Women, Painting, Rhiming, Drinking;
Besides ten thousand freaks that dy'd in thinking.
Blest Madman, who coud every hour employ,
With something New to wish, or to enjoy!
Rayling and praising were his usual Theams;
And both (to shew his Judgement) in Extreams:
So over Violent, or over Civil,
That every man, with him, was God or Devil.
In squand'ring Wealth was his peculiar Art:
Nothing went unrewarded, but Desert.
Begger'd by Fools, whom still he found too late:
He had his Jest, and they had his Estate.
He laught himself from Court, then sought Relief
By forming Parties, but coud ne're be Chief:
For, spight of him, the weight of Business fell
On *Absalom* and wise *Achitophel*:
Thus, wicked but in will, of means bereft,
He left not Faction, but of that was left.[5]

> Dryden's diction here shows a lack of any great subtlety or
> richness of ambiguous meaning. The passage opens in a
> tone of apparent approval of *Zimri*, a virtuoso in an age of
> virtuosos, but switches too soon to open ridicule to make
> much capital from this particular irony: the word "various"
> quickly gives a clue to the particular character to be pre-
> sented. In these twenty-four lines there is only one genuinely
> equivocal word (one used extensively by the ironist Gibbon)
> viz. "peculiar", which in Dryden's line captures the full force
> of its imprecise implication because it balances metrically
> the directly abusive "squand'ring", and because its syllabic
> prominence in the second half of the line and its position
> before the rhyme word demand sensitive enunciation:

In squand'ring Wealth was his peculiar Art:

> There are other more doubtful examples as well. When
> Dryden uses a favourable adjective in the line:

On *Absalom* and wise *Achitophel*:

> he might be suspected of ironical intent. But it is not charac-
> teristic of him to use words with this kind of veiled impli-
> cation only, no matter how denigratory the context, and the

5 *Absalom and Achitophel*, lines 544-68.

use of "wise" here reflects an important element in the earlier *character* of *Achitophel* himself—the insistence on the greatness of the man, which, because it is misguided, makes his threat to the State all the more terrible:

In Israel's Courts ne'r sat an *Abbethdin*
With more discerning Eyes, or Hands more clean:
Unbrib'd, unsought, the Wretched to redress;
Swift of Dispatch, and easie of Access.
Oh, had he been content to serve the Crown,
With vertues only proper to the Gown;

. . . . . .

David, for him his tunefull Harp had strung,
And Heaven had wanted one Immortal song.[6]

> *Zimri*, by contrast, is simply bad; or rather, mad: there is no element of greatness or wisdom in *his* rebellion against the King. Far from being ironical or equivocal, the word "wise" in this context has direct structural significance that would suffer rather than gain from any richness of ironical meaning. And in the penultimate line of the passage:

Thus, wicked but in will, of means bereft,

> the word "means", as well as amplifying the first part of the line, may refer to the second half of the earlier line:

He had his Jest, and they had his Estate.

> But it is doubtful whether Dryden intended such a double meaning, and even if he did its effectiveness would very likely be lost in the rush and snap of the lines.

So then, even when Dryden deliberately sought indirectness of expression he did not achieve a delicate ambiguity of meaning through the choice of suggestive words. Indeed, even the avoidance of "opprobrious terms" that he claims for the portrait can be overstressed. Such words as "buffoon", "freaks", "madman", and "squand'ring" leave one wondering whether Buckingham was after all amused or sufficiently "witty" not "to resent it as an injury".[7] Such words could hardly be more directly abusive, or more appropriate to poetry that "says what it means"; and these are the words that tend to set the tone of the passage. There is, too, a

---

6 *Ibid*., lines 188-93 and 196-97.
7 Dryden, "A Discourse concerning the Original and Progress of Satire", *op. cit.*

crude vigour, a colloquial vitality in much of the phrasing: "Stiff in Opinions", "Beside ten thousand freaks that dy'd in thinking", "begger'd by Fools"; and this vitality goes a long way towards nullifying any ironical effect of "pity" that Dryden may have sought to infuse into the passage as part of his technique of "fine raillery". If indirectness enters the portrait of *Zimri* at all it certainly does not do so through a fineness of implication in the individual words or phrases.

A feature of the passage is its apparently close mode of expression. The Augustan ideal of energy or strength in verse meant among other things an ability to crowd much meaning into limited space; and because words were generally shorn of any loose implication or depth and because they were used with the full weight of their primary meanings, compression or closeness of expression at times tended to be more structural than semantic. Often, as happens in this passage on *Zimri*, compactness of syntax concealed either a diffuseness or an emptiness of meaning: the structure itself became tightened in form while the content lost in density.[8] The pattern of expression is what might be called a sleight of hand, dependent on syntactical trickery. In the first couplet, the phrases:

. . . . that he seem'd to be
Not one, but all Mankinds Epitome.

are a loose and hyperbolic extension of the one word "various". And the antithesis in the line:

Was every thing by starts, and nothing long:

while syntactically close and even truncated in expression (the omission of the subject pronoun "he" intensifies the sense of condensed urgency), is empty of meaning. Even the use of a phrase to fill out a line inertly, as in:

With something New to wish, or to enjoy!

8 George Williamson, *Senecan Amble: A Study of Prose Form from Bacon to Collier* (London: Faber & Faber, 1951), p. 38n., has pointed to the impossibility of logical advance in sentences adopting the strictly paratactic structure that is characteristically exploited by the neoclassic couplet: "Members when united in paratactic structure and unified in thought do not advance logically; they repeat or vary the main idea or present different facets of it. When thrown into parallel form they acquire a formal unity." The portrait of *Zimri* would seem an excellent example of this linguistic phenomenon.

tends to be overlooked in this effect of compression. Some lines rely for their force on the element of surprise coming from a nice twist of syntax:

He had his Jest, and they had his Estate,

or:

He left not Faction, but of that was left.

This is the kind of surprise that is found most often in Dryden's verse, but it is not founded on any deep paradox of thought, where the clash of diction expresses something that is too rich in its implications to be stated directly.

The whole of Dryden's portrait of *Zimri* gives this impression of a hasty vitality and compression that evaporates when it is subjected to any close semantic scrutiny. The syntactical tightness does not co-ordinate with any real depth of meaning. The portrait has compactness of expression but not compression of thought: a basic weakness of content recognized by Van Doren when he declared that Dryden often seemed to be saying the last word about a man "when actually he said almost nothing; he seemed to weave a close garment about his subject when in truth he only latticed him over with antitheses".[9] The portrait confines itself to the general (*Zimri* is the type of the "various" or "inconstant" man), and it is almost completely lacking in any precise detail. The first ten lines, in spite of their structural condensation, are used loosely to elaborate the one aspect of *Zimri's* "variousness", and the whole portrait is not to be relished for the quality of its thought, in the manner of Goldsmith's portraits of the preacher or of the schoolmaster in *The Deserted Village*, or of any of the portraits from Chaucer's *Tales*. Dryden's attack is not based on any fine perceptiveness of character or acuteness of psychological insight.

Yet the portrait of *Zimri* "lives", by the sheer audacity and verve of its language. It is composed of a cumulative series of quick phrases, rather than a closely articulated group of sentences. Significantly it is lacking in Dryden's usual array of strongly expressive verbs, which might have given more character to the sentences, as sentences. The form of syntactical expression communicates itself to the rhythm; and, to use Donald Davie's words, because of the weakness in

9 Mark Van Doren, *John Dryden: A Study of his Poetry* (Bloomington, Indiana: Indiana University Press, 1946), p. 158.

the sense, "the articulation is by rhythm, and syntax only seems to be doing the articulation—it is a play of empty forms".[10] This is to be seen very clearly in the tumbling, breathless lines:

But, in the course of one revolving Moon,
Was Chymist, Fidler, States-Man, and Buffoon:
Then all for Women, Painting, Rhiming, Drinking;
Besides ten thousand freaks that dy'd in thinking.

In the opening lines of *Absalom and Achitophel* that were discussed in the introductory chapter, metre and syntax were found to be complementary, both working to define and enrich the meaning of the passage. But in these lines the rhythmical urgency follows only the broad meaning, tending to overwhelm, rather than to articulate closely, any subtle implication in the individual words. In the first line the metrical stress falls strongly on the polysyllabic "revolving", because of its syllabic dominance in the line, instead of on the insinuating rhyme word "Moon": Dryden misses the opportunity to emphasize metrically the potential associations of lunacy inherent in the word "Moon", mentioned earlier in the poem when he speaks of the "giddy Jews . . . govern'd by the Moon". The stress is less on any specific idea such as lunacy than on the loosely general notion of breathless haste. And in the next two lines the strongest potentiality for satire lies in the incongruity of the word "States-Man", in its juxtaposition with other words denoting the trivial activities of the courtier, and especially in its placement alongside the directly abusive "buffoon". But because of the resistless metrical urgency of the line the implications of the word itself cannot be fully realized. The rhythm achieves a hectic rush in which the reader is virtually denied the opportunity to dwell on individual words, which become metrical counters in the rhythm, rather than meaningful points in the syntax.

It is the rhythm that dominates the *character* of *Zimri* as a whole: a rhythm energetically turbulent, with no single line lacking at least one sharp medial pause, and with only three lines not separated by strong intervening commas. It is a mimetic rhythm that mirrors the restlessness of *Zimri*'s own mind: a rhythm that often seems to jump from one

10 Donald Davie, *Articulate Energy* (London: Routledge & Kegan Paul, 1955), p. 106.

point to the next—points that are often loosely repetitive
and empty of syntactic progress—just as *Zimri*'s "variousness", his tendency to be "everything by starts and nothing
long", leads to a life that is all violent movement, but without progress or meaning. The statement carrying this rhythm
has a strength that is more apparent than real, and the same
might be said of the passage as poetry of statement. It still
means what it does say directly, and the poetic elements in
it still co-operate with, still imitate this meaning. But if, as
Van Doren says, Dryden has said "almost nothing" about
Zimri, this is because there is almost nothing to say about
him: nothing coherent or connected, that is. From a wider
point of view he has said everything there is to say about his
victim, which in the end amounts to the empty form full of
energy but without end or purpose imaged in the rhythms
and in the meaninglessness of the statement. Here the poetry
of statement, in meeting the demands imposed by its subject,
assumes a special character that is to some extent a negation
of its nature. But its method remains essentially the same.

Both the *Zimri* portrait and the arguments of *Religio
Laici* depend for their poetic quality on a particular combination of discursive and metrical elements. A direct meaning is expressed by the discursive statement, and it is given
life and vitality—an imaginative dimension—by being cast
into a form where metre, texture, alliteration, rhyme, set up
a pattern in sound and movement that gives a richer significance to the statement. The potentialities of this interplay
of effect resulting from a juxtaposition of syntactical and
metrical patterns, in the absence of a more immediately or
obviously "poetic" use of words, have led some critics with
an interest in Augustan poetry to approach it in a manner
that has some relevance to the present study. These critics
(W. K. Wimsatt, Jr. and Maynard Mack in particular) find
in the work of poets who, like Dryden, use language in an
apparently discursive manner, words and phrases having the
richness and suggestiveness of metaphor without necessarily
the actual use of metaphor in the strict sense of the word:
not, that is, in the usual way of poetry, by virtue of the
meanings or associations attaching to the words themselves,

but from the way the words are put together—the effect again being one that derives primarily from the metrical and syntactical arrangement of the words, and not from the mere bringing of them together in the poem.

The prime aim of these critics is to show what are usually regarded as no more than aids to poetic expression (what William Empson calls "the incidental conveniences of language") as having in Augustan poetry direct poetic force; and this aim might be seen as leading to some sort of concept of "pure" poetry, of poetry as "pattern" or "music", were it not applied to verse in which the discursive elements are so obviously strong. These discursive elements, which provide the basic syntactic structure, are seen as redirected, dislocated, or otherwise changed by effects and counter-effects arising from the metrical pattern. The closed heroic couplet, particularly, demands a fine organization of words, a nicety of syntax, which in the hands of Pope became an almost geometric manipulation. Words used in such close conjunction can tend to interact counter-logically, and by means of the resulting "reflection" of meaning the language assumes a metaphorical quality.

Maynard Mack provides a convenient illustration of the strength of this interplay of metrical and syntactical structure, which he aptly terms "couplet rhetoric", and which he demonstrates as capable of being even more dominant in its effect than imagery. He shows[11] how both Pope and Dryden, starting from the same image found in Donne's *Second Anni-*

---

11 Maynard Mack, "Wit and Poetry and Pope: some observations on his Imagery", in *Pope and His Contemporaries: Essays Presented to George Sherburn*, ed. J. L. Clifford and L. A. Lander (Oxford: Clarendon Press, 1949), pp. 26-27. The image as Donne uses it occurs in the lines:

> She whose faire body no such prison was
> But that a Soule might well be pleas'd to passe
> An age in her. (*Second Anniversarie*, lines 221-23.)

With Dryden these lines become:

> ....imprison'd in so sweet a cage
> A soul might well be pleas'd to pass an age.
> (*To the Duchess of Ormond*, lines 118-19.)

And finally in Pope's *Elegy on the Memory of an Unfortunate Lady* (lines 17-22):

> Most souls, 'tis true, but peep out once an age,
> Dull sullen pris'ners in the body's cage:
> Dim lights of life that burn a length of years,
> Useless, unseen, as lamps in sepulchres;
> Like Eastern kings a lazy state they keep,
> And close confin'd to their own palace sleep.

versarie of the soul as the prisoner of the body, have used it in such a way as to "subdue" the image by putting it "in competition with other forms of complication". All the effects gained, he says, "grow out of the potentialities of couplet rhetoric, not out of the image; and though they may co-operate with the imagery, as here, they have a life of their own which tends to mute it". Instead of being itself the end towards which poetic expression strives, the image becomes only a starting point, the foundation on which expression is built. The true figurative meaning of the lines arises from "other forms of complication" in the syntactical/metrical pattern.

The concept of poetic structure developed by these critics would serve to confirm the applicability, even to Augustan poetry, of a view of poetry that sees its resources as "working to repel the logical and progressive tendencies" represented by the prose syntax. This would be particularly true of the ideas of W. K. Wimsatt, Jr., regarding the effects of rhyme in Augustan poetry. Poetry, for Wimsatt, is "never altogether, or even mainly, poetry of statement", and he writes:

I wish to develop the idea that verse gives to poetry a quality of the concrete and particular not merely in virtue of being a simultaneous and partly irrelevant performance, but in virtue of *a studiously and accurately alogical character*[12] by which it imposes upon the meaning a counterpattern and acts as a fixative or preservative of the sensory quality of words.[13]

But despite its emphasis on the essentially alogical quality of poetry, Wimsatt's whole thesis regarding the function of rhyme, namely that rhyme achieves its effects mainly by running counter to expectations raised by the syntax, depends on the strength of the syntactical structure against which it acts. As he says, "words have no character as rhymes until they become points in a syntactical succession";[14] and again: "the principle on which I am intent is one that concerns rhyme as a fusion of sound and sense".[15] In fact, his thesis is unlike much twentieth century poetic theory in requiring

12 My italics.
13 W. K. Wimsatt, Jr., "One Relation of Rhyme to Reason", *MLQ*, V (1944), 323-24.
14 *Ibid.*, 327.
15 *Ibid.*, 335.

the recognition of a constant and effective presence of discursive, logical prose statement underlying the poetic structure. It would thus seem particularly applicable to the theory of a poetry of statement, combining as it does what it regards as the essential alogicality of poetry with that basic structure of logical statement that has been found dominant in Dryden's poetry.

Dryden's method of giving an imaginative dimension to statement does have some affinity with the patterning of syntactical and metrical structures discussed by Wimsatt and Mack. But ultimately, because of their emphasis on the essential alogicality of poetry, their theories are largely inapplicable to Dryden. The structural complexity of Dryden's verse characteristically works alongside the statement, serving to give it a greater vitality and richness, but without concealing or distorting its meaning. It is something deriving from the manner of the statement, but in order to enrich it, not to replace it or work against it. The statement remains important in its own right: its strength remains its own and does not serve simply to add strength to alogical effects which overwhelm it. Words are made to interact in a way that is not strictly flat or prosaic, but the interaction is not counter-logical, or contrary to the stated meaning of the poem. For this reason attempts to read into Dryden's diction a metaphorical quality arising from the interplay of meaning in the manner, for instance, of the metaphysical poets, will more often than not result in an ingenuity belonging more to the subtlety of the reader than to the skill of the poet.

This is not always true. There is something of alogical subtlety in these lines from *MacFlecknoe*, where compression of syntax within the structure of the couplet (combined perhaps with a complex pattern of classical reference)[16] gives ironic richness, counter to the logical meaning, to the conjunction of "Poppies", "nodding", "consecrate", and "head". The nodding becomes associated in an alogical manner with "head", instead of the "Poppies" to which it belongs:

His Temples last with Poppies were o'erspread,
That nodding seem'd to consecrate his head.[17]

16 The OET edition of Dryden cites references from classical literature for three associations of "poppies". Whether or not these allusions were intended by Dryden, they do not, I think, contribute materially to the effect of the lines.
17 *MacFlecknoe,* lines 126-27.

Here the form of expression exploits the connotations of "Poppies" in a way that is contrary to the discursive meaning. And similarly, in these lines from *Alexander's Feast*:

Revolveing in his alter'd Soul
  The various Turns of Chance below,[18]

there is an alogicality arising from the implicit verbal parallelism between "revolveing" (meaning "meditating") and the noun "turns" (which suggests the turning or "revolving" wheel of fortune).[19] There are certainly other examples, too, but especially in Dryden's more successful poems these are the exceptions rather than the rule: exceptions which indicate that his poetry does not always consistently maintain its character as poetry of statement. But he could not be said to exploit this kind of pattern, and it is significant that critics like Mack and Wimsatt have devoted more attention to Pope than to Dryden. Pope's metrical practice was more rigidly "correct" than was Dryden's: by comparison with Dryden he almost always allows the strict metrical form of the couplet to shape the outline of the rhythmic pattern, relying for variety on diction rather than metre, and on unexpected or otherwise striking combinations of metrical and syntactical stresses, or on unusual dislocations of the expected syntactical pattern by the dominant metrical form. The rhythms of Dryden's poetry, by contrast, are closer to the rhythms of prose, and there is consequently less opportunity for the development of these alogical effects.

The inadequacy of theories such as Wimsatt's in providing an explanation for the poetic quality of Dryden's work arises from an insistence on the necessarily alogical, non-discursive nature of poetry, even when it seems to be logical and discursive. Any such restriction of poetry is likely to become difficult to sustain when faced with the use made of discursive structure by Dryden. Poetry to Dryden was "heightened" prose: prose enriched and adorned, made majestic or delightful by all the resources of language available to the poet, but none the less obeying fundamentally the same rules of dis-

---

18 *Alexander's Feast: or, The Power of Music* (1697), lines 85-86.
19 This is more or less parallel to Wimsatt's example from Pope (*The Verbal Icon*, Lexington, Kentucky: University of Kentucky Press, 1954, p. 178):
  With earnest eyes and round unthinking face,
  He first the snuff-box open'd, and then the case.
Here the word "case" becomes a pun because of its position near "snuff-box".

course as prose. He could not be expected to have understood or accepted poetry as something that achieves its ends by defeating or even working against the kind of meaning to be reached by the logical and progressive structure of discursive statement.

On the contrary, Dryden believed that the poet should make it his general rule "that the words be placed as they are in the negligence of prose",[20] and not be inverted for the sake of rhyme:

This is what makes them say, rhyme is not natural, it being only so when the poet either makes a vicious choice of words, or places them, for rhyme sake, so unnaturally as no man would in ordinary speaking; but when 'tis so judiciously ordered, that the first word in the verse seems to beget the second, and that the next, till that becomes the last word in the line, which in the negligence of prose would be so. . . .[21]

Wit, for Dryden, is "best conveyed to us in most easy language; and is most to be admired when a great thought comes in words so commonly received that it is understood by the meanest apprehensions. . . ."[22]

But though Dryden's pattern of expression has not the complexity that would give it independent levels of metaphorical meaning or significance counter to the discursive statement, some degree of multidimensional richness is not incompatible with its character as poetry of statement; and, indeed, is essential to it, if it is to be poetry as well as statement. His words are not simply prosaic—not prosaic, for instance, in the sense of the word as defined by Northrop Frye when he writes: "prose by itself is a transparent medium: it is at its purest—that is, farthest from the *epos* and other metrical influences—when it is least obtrusive and presents its subject matter like plate glass in a shop window."[23] In prose, that is, according to Frye, words exist only to denote "things", and are in themselves toneless and inexpressive. This is the quality of the bare, scientific type of diction advocated in Dryden's own time by the Royal Society of London, and despite Dryden's association with the Society's

20 Dryden, "An Essay of Dramatic Poesy" (1668), Ker, *op. cit.*, I, 98.
21 Dryden, "Epistle Dedicatory to 'The Rival Ladies' " (1664), Ker, *op. cit.*, I, 98.
22 Dryden, "An Essay of Dramatic Poesy" (1668), Ker, *op. cit.*, I, 52.
23 Northrop Frye, *The Anatomy of Criticism* (Princeton: Princeton University Press, 1957), p. 265.

achieved a varied richness of expression without going
beyond the bounds of a poetry of statement.

There are occasions when the statement is in danger of
becoming no more than a framework for highly suggestive
words, as it is in much of the *Og* portrait in *The Second Part
of Absalom and Achitophel*, or in these lines from *Mac-
Flecknoe*:

Nor let thy mountain belly make pretence
Of likeness; thine's a tympany of sense.
A Tun of Man in thy Large bulk is writ,
But sure thou'rt but a Kilderkin of wit.[34]

These lines, beginning with their allusion to Ben Jonson's
"mountain belly", have a quite appropriate discursive meaning; but words like "tympany", "Tun", and "Kilderkin" in
this context can achieve a strong effect without reference to
their exact significance: many modern readers might give
the wrong meaning to "tympany", and even to "Tun", and
not worry at all about "Kilderkin", and still thoroughly
enjoy the lines. But this is not typical of Dryden. It is not
likely to happen except when, as here, he is striving for an
effect of grotesqueness. His connotative richness is mostly
less obtrusive: a common word with an unusual meaning,
an unexpected intrusion of colloquialism, a quick change of
tone, a word with Latin connotations that give richness to
the expression. This passage from *The Hind and the Panther*,
for instance, where the formal flow of statement is brought
to an unexpectedly direct end:

Could He his god-head veil with flesh and bloud
And not veil these again to be our food?
His grace in both is equal in extent,
The first affords us life, the second nourishment.
And if he can, why all this frantick pain
To construe what his clearest words contain,
And make a riddle what He made so plain?
To take up half on trust, and half to try,
Name it not faith, but bungling biggottry.[35]

The most obvious examples of the enrichment of statement
come from satire—particularly from what, following Pope's
Peri Bathous, has become known as the "art of sinking in

34 *MacFlecknoe*, lines 193-96.
35 *The Hind and the Panther*, Part 1, lines 134-42.

committee for purifying the language, his use of words, at
least in poetry, does not conform to their standard. His
words are neither toneless nor inexpressive, nor do they
exist only as a "transparent medium" to convey thoughts: as
a poet Dryden was interested in the expressiveness of words
as well as in the communication of thoughts.

On the other hand the poetry of statement cannot, by its
nature, use words in the manner defined as poetic by William
Empson: "a poetical word is a thing conceived in itself and
includes all its meanings, and may have been used differently."[24] Because he aims at precision and clarity of statement, Dryden would not normally use a word in a manner
that "includes all its meanings". His diction is lacking in
those "mental reverberations" whereby words have an indefinable and inexhaustible richness of meaning or depth of
implication.[25] His words have not the intensity we are accus-
tomed to, for instance, in the verse of Gerard Manley
Hopkins, who composes a mosaic in which individual words
often have the depth of a compressed image. "Dryden is not
interested in the echoes and recesses of words", Empson
declares with some justification. But when he goes on to say:
"he uses them flatly; he is interested in the echoes and
recesses of human judgement",[26] he is unduly limiting the
alternatives, and (especially in his use of the word "flat",
which he later employs to describe the prosaic function of
words) failing to see what in Dryden's poetry takes the place
of the delicate shades of meaning, the richness of ambiguity
or irony within individual words, that he himself tends to
look for in the language of poetry. Though Dryden's words
seldom have this depth of implication or richness of suggestion within themselves, they none the less can and do interact
imaginatively within the meaningful progress of the statement.

Dryden's diction, while it is denotative in that it exists to
convey relatively specific things, is seldom if ever neutral to
the point of colourlessness. It is chosen partly for what Dr.

24 William Empson, *Seven Types of Ambiguity* (London: Chatto & Windus,
1947), p. 252.
25 Cf. Herbert Read, *Collected Essays in Literary Criticism* (London: Faber &
Faber, 1938), p. 45: "Poetry depends not only on the sound of words, but
even more on their mental reverberations."
26 Empson, *op. cit.*, p. 199.

Johnson has called its "strong impressions" and its "delightful images". In writing of Dryden he declared:

Words too familiar, or too remote . . . defeat the purpose of a poet. From those sounds which we hear on small or on coarse occasions we do not easily receive strong impressions or delightful images; and words to which we are nearly strangers, wherever they occur, draw attention on themselves which they should transmit to things.[27]

Words in poetry should be expressive, but should not be so interesting in themselves as to absorb attention at the expense of the communication of ideas. Dryden helped inaugurate an age which fostered verbal precision and clarity rather than a vaguely connotative use of language. He reflected a reaction away from the idiosyncrasy and ambiguity of the decaying metaphysical tradition, and he preceded the quest of the Romantic poets for an imaginative selection of words. He conformed generally to the neoclassical ideal of "chastity" in diction, which among other things demanded that the language of the poet be sanctioned by common usage and literary precedent—an ideal expressed later by Pope in his *Essay on Criticism*:

In Words as Fashions the same Rule will hold,
Alike fantastick if too new or old,
Be not the first by whom the new are try'd,
Nor yet the last to lay the old aside.[28]

Originality in the choice of unusual words was not the criterion for poetic diction, as might be inferred from the apologetic note with which Dryden draws attention to his use of new words in his *Annus Mirabilis*: "you have taken notice of some new words which I have innovated (if it be too bold for me to say refined) upon his Latin; which as I offer not to introduce into English prose, so I hope they are neither improper nor altogether inelegant in verse";[29] or from his criticism of Shakespeare, the fury of whose fancy, he said, "often transported him beyond the bounds of judgement, either in coining new words and phrases, or racking

27 Samuel Johnson, "Life of Dryden", in *Lives of the English Poets* (London, 1779), ed. G. Birkbeck Hill (3 vols.; Oxford: Clarendon Press, 1905), I, 450.
28 Pope, *Essay on Criticism*, lines 333-36.
29 Dryden, "Preface to 'Annus Mirabilis: The Year of Wonders MDCLXVI'" (1667), Ker, *op. cit.*, I, 17.

words which were in use, into the violence of a catachresis".[30] Rather the emphasis was on propriety, on judgment and good taste. Solecisms, archaisms, obscurity, and ambiguity were generally to be avoided because they detracted from the lucidity and precision of the statement. For instance, archaisms were permissible, but only when "sound and significancy is wanting in the present language"; and even then it is necessary that their sense be made clear by the context: "in my opinion, obsolete words may then be laudably revived, when either they are more sounding, or more significant, than those in practice; and when their obscurity is taken away, by joining other words with them, which clear the sense. . . ."[31] Dryden's last word, in fact, would probably be that "unnecessary change . . . runs into affectation",[32] and this would certainly include words either revived or newly coined purely for purposes of originality. In an age that fostered syntactical nicety, and (despite the protestations of John Wilkins, of the Royal Society, and at times of Dryden himself) such rhetorical devices as balance, antithesis, and amplification, the emphasis was likely to be on verbal arrangement and structure, rather than on verbal selection.[33] Words tended not to be imaginative, or striking, or original in themselves, but rather to interact within an interesting and significant pattern of meaning, directed or reinforced by the interwoven pattern of sound, movement, and texture.

Within this middle field of writing, neither conforming to the requirements of a flat, neutral type of expression in which words exist only to denote specific things and have no life of their own, nor allowing words to develop an imaginative existence independent of a discursive meaning, Dryden

30 Dryden, "Preface to 'Troilus and Cressida'" (1679), Ker, *op. cit.*, I, 224. John Dennis, on the other hand, said of Dryden that ". . . never any one was a greater coiner than he" in "Reflections on an 'Essay upon Criticism'", (1711), *The Critical Works of John Dennis*, ed. E. N. Hooker (2 vols.; Baltimore: Johns Hopkins Press, 1939), I, 407.
31 Dryden, "A Discourse concerning the Original and Progress of Satire", Ker, *op. cit.*, II, 241.
32 *Ibid.*, p. 29.
33 These brief comments do not, of course, do justice to the complexities of Restoration ideals of language. The subject is discussed more fully in K. G. Hamilton, *The Two Harmonies* (Oxford: Clarendon Press, 1963), particularly chap. 3.

poetry". This couplet from *The Medall*, for example, where the word "Ideots" with one stroke alters the direction of the poem:

Of all our Antick Sights, and Pageantry
Which *English* Ideots run in crowds to see.[36]

The word "Ideots" is effective enough in itself, both for its precisely apposite meaning and for its sound, but both its semantic and its auditory value is enhanced by the context. The satire may be seen as beginning in the first line, with the equivocal "Antick", which in the seventeenth century could equally well mean either "antic" (grotesque) or "antique" (ancient).[37] But the real nicety of effect lies in the incongruous juxtaposition of the words *"English* Ideots", pointed by their similarity of initial sound and by the quality of their texture, both of which, in a line consisting otherwise of monosyllables, demand a slightly deliberate enunciation.[38] To appreciate this effect we might compare the use of "Ideots" in this couplet with that of the same word as it occurs in Dryden's version of the *Tale of the Cock and the Fox*:

An honest Man may take a Knave's Advice,
But Ideots only will be couzen'd twice.[39]

The way in which the word "Ideots" becomes relatively innocuous when left to stand alone is apparent here. And another example of this adjustment of tone by a word this time quite lacking in intrinsic tonal significance is provided by this line from *MacFlecknoe*:

When thou on silver Thames did'st cut thy way,[40]

36 *The Medall; A Satyre against Sedition* (1682), lines 1-2.
37 Dryden's use of the word "Antick" in other contexts—e.g. "An ample Goblet stood of antick mold" (Ovid's *Metamorphoses*, Bk. 12, line 330)—usually has rather the meaning "grotesque", but with little or no denigratory flavour. Even in the lines from *The Medall* the word may be confined to this meaning and the first line yet remain heroic: it only becomes mock heroic retrospectively, as a result of the intrusion of the *"English* Ideots".
38 By comparison with Dryden's couplet, Pope characteristically depends much more strongly on individual words for a similar deflating effect. For instance, from *The Dunciad*:
   High on a throne of royal state,
   That far outshone Henley's gilt tub.
This is rich in mock heroic allusion, but the effect is finally driven home by the sheer incongruity of sound and association in the word "tub".
39 *The Cock and the Fox; or, The Tale of the Nun's Priest* (1700), lines 797-98.
40 *MacFlecknoe*, line 38.

where the effect built up by the beautiful liquid movement of the line is shattered by the abruptness, the brittle quality of "cut".

Dryden relies heavily on the irony arising from these straightforward but nicely surprising juxtapositions. Words that are discordant in sound or sense (or both) are frequently brought together with an implicit but nevertheless obvious ironical intent. The simplest examples are those witty adjective-noun combinations, one of which, "*English* Ideots", has already been discussed: there are many others: "blest madman", "monumental brass", "Solymean rout", "suburban muse", "pleasing rape", "pious hate", "anointed dulness", "sav'ry deities", and that one which T. S. Eliot picked out from the dullness of *The State of Innocence and Fall of Man*, the "sad variety" of Hell. The nature of these juxtapositions is by no means uniform, and the exact role of each is determined by the context in which it occurs. But they all have an element of surprise that adds liveliness and vigour to the verse by continually upsetting any tendency towards evenness of tone: though the words still "mean what they say", creating no metaphorical meaning distinct from their literal one.

And the same quality, on a slightly more extended scale, is to be found in lines like these from *The Medall*:

The Wretch turn'd loyal in his own defence;
And Malice reconcil'd him to his Prince,[41]

where the discrepancy is between subject and verb, or between the motive and the deed. Or it may come from such an overt clash of diction, both in sound and meaning, as in:

Whether, inspir'd by some diviner Lust,
His Father got him with a greater Gust;[42]

or from the use of contrasting epithets in a form that suggests that one would compensate for the other:

Never was a Patriot yet, but was a Fool;[43]

or from the juxtaposition of contrasting infinitives as if they were logically parallel:

41 *The Medall*, lines 51-52.
42 *Absalom and Achitophel*, lines 19-20.
43 *Ibid.*, line 968.

Thus, heaping Wealth, by the most ready way
Among the Jews, which was to Cheat and Pray.[44]

> And when the emphasis is on "propriety", the "improper"
> use of a word can have a witty effect without the need for
> ambiguity or irony, as it has when the unfortunate Shadwell
> is seen as never deviating, not from, but into sense:

The rest to some faint meaning make pretence,
But *Sh*— never deviates into sense.[45]

> Similarly the parenthesis, or aside, can be juxtaposed in a
> manner that may appear deceptively innocuous, as in:

Athens, no doubt, did righteously decide,
When *Phocion* and when *Socrates* were try'd:[46]

> or in *Absalom*'s address to the crowd, when Dryden's mastery
> of the ironic aside is turned to brilliant account:

Take then my tears (with that he wip'd his Eyes)
'Tis all the Aid my present power supplies.[47]

> Or he can give interest to a line by an unexpected twist of
> meaning that gains by being more apparent than real:

At first without, at last against their Prince.[48]

> And a similar nicety of inversion is used to indicate the
> speciousness of *Achitophel*'s arguments:

. . . . The People have a Right Supreme
To make their Kings; for Kings are made for them.[49]

> Yet for all their effectiveness, each of these verses depends
> on nice adjustments of the statement, and not on something
> independent of or counter to its meaning. And this kind of
> surprise, too, though an important instrument in Dryden's
> satire, is not sufficiently organic to it to be regarded as an
> essential element of his poetry. His juxtapositions give the
> reader a pleasant jolt, but they do not indicate a tissue of
> tantalizing implications. They enrich the total meaning, but
> do not determine it. There is nothing in them to correspond
> to the paradoxes of the metaphysical poets: it is not surpris-

44 *Ibid.*, lines 591-92.
45 *MacFlecknoe*, lines 19-20.
46 *The Medall*, lines 95-96.
47 *Absalom and Achitophel*, lines 717-18.
48 *The Medall*, line 212.
49 *Absalom and Achitophel*, lines 409-10.

ing that despite the prevalence of this kind of incongruity
Dr. Johnson did not find in Dryden the "heterogeneous ideas
yoked with violence together" that he objected to in the
poetry of the earlier part of the seventeenth century. And
without making too much of his distinction between "fancy"
and "imagination", it is perhaps significant that Thomas
Hobbes differentiated between those who, like Dryden, are
able to observe nicely incongruous differences and who are
"sayd to have a good Judgement", and those who like the
metaphysical poets can perceive neat and ingenious correspondences and who " are sayd to have a *Good Wit*; by which
in this occasion is meant a *Good Fancy*".[50]

Enrichment of the discursive statement can also derive
from the use of words that have significance within an
already established tonal context; as the word "Reason" has
significance beyond its immediate meaning in these lines
from the second verse paragraph of *Religio Laici*:

Our Reason prompts us to a future State,
The *last Appeal* from *Fortune*, and from *Fate*:
Where God's all-righteous ways will be declar'd;
The *Bad* meet *Punishment*, the *Good, Reward*.[51]

These lines are presented as an argument which the following paragraph proceeds to deflate:

Vain, wretched Creature, how art thou misled
. . . .
. . *Reason* saw not, till *Faith* sprung the Light.

But if the poem has been read sensitively the speciousness
of the argument will already have been made apparent. The
word *"Reason"* is not used here in a flatly denotative way,
but has acquired a weight of ironical implication from the
first eleven lines of the poem, where the inadequacy of reason
in matters of faith is illustrated:

Dim, as the borrow'd beams of Moon and Stars
. . . .
Is *Reason* to the *Soul*: . . . . .

50 Hobbes, *Leviathan*, I, VIII. For a discussion of Hobbes's distinction between
"fancy" and "judgement" see Hamilton, *op. cit.*, pp. 166-69.
51 *Religio Laici*, lines 58-61.

"Reason" has thus accumulated a certain colouring that adjusts its meaning in the new context; and this meaning is subtly reinforced by the tone of the context itself—for example, by the expression of facile optimism in the final line:

The *Bad* meet *Punishment,* the *Good, Reward.*

But this richness of verbal implication is one that results from the use of the word within the poem's synthetic structure, and not from an imaginative selection of individual words. And it is a richness that continues to build up as the tone of each successive use of the word contributes to the same effect:

Canst *Thou,* by *Reason,* more of *God-head* know;[52]

and:

What farther means can *Reason* now direct;[53]

or:

To what can *Reason* such effects assign;[54]

and so on through the poem.

It is important to realize just what Dryden is achieving here. Strictly—or logically—speaking, he is committing the fallacy of using reason to prove that reason is inadequate. But reason is the only means open to the poet to lead men to truth: "The florid, elevated and figurative way is for the passions. . . . A man is to be cheated into passion, but reason'd into truth." And it is part of the *poetic* effectiveness of *Religio Laici* that though it must depend on reason for its argument it can still invest "reason" with an aura of inadequacy in matters of faith. What might be a fallacy in prose can be avoided in poetry, but without resorting in this case to a deliberately alogical structure: while retaining, that is, the character of statement that expresses its meaning directly, but giving it a further tonal dimension.

The easily familiar aside in these four lines from the portrait of *Shimei* in *Absalom and Achitophel* reveals a similar complexity of structural meaning:

52 *Religio Laici,* line 78.
53 *Ibid.,* line 117.
54 *Ibid.,* line 164.

If any leisure time he had from Power,
(Because 'tis Sin to misemploy an hour;)
His business was, by Writing, to Persuade,
That Kings were Useless, and a Clog to Trade.[55]

Shimei is treated ironically as the type of the "godly" man, and the reference to sin here is part of this conventional *character*. The last line also develops an unobtrusive identification between mercenary and political motives that is sustained throughout the poem, though never explicitly condemned. Within this framework the inconspicuous word "Sin" becomes associated with *Shimei*'s rebellion against the King, thereby continuing another identification in the poem, that of religious and political values: a connexion basic both to Dryden's own intellectual position, which made rebellion against the King who rules by Divine Right a violation of the will of God, and to his development of the allegory, in which King *David* speaks unmistakably with the voice of the omnipotent God the Father of the Third Book of *Paradise Lost*, and in which *Achitophel*, "hell's dire agent", begins to tempt *Absalom* to rebellion against the King by playing on the same weakness that Satan had used to bring Eve to rebellion against God: "Desire of Greatness," he tells *Absalom*, "is a Godlike Sin."[56] The apparently bland aside in the portrait of *Shimei* draws attention to itself superficially as a means of softening the bitter irony of the lines—as a means of reducing "all to pleasant ridicule" by its wit, in accord with Dryden's professed ideal of satire. The more serious charge against *Shimei*, which paradoxically this seemingly softening aside introduces, lies hidden beneath the wit.

The subtlety behind these lines from *Religio Laici* is something of the same kind:

---

55 *Absalom and Achitophel*, lines 612-15.
56 *Ibid.*, line 372. Almost the same ironic juxtaposition had already been exploited earlier in the same portrait of *Shimei*—a not unusual example of repetitiveness on Dryden's part. *Shimei*, he writes:

Did wisely from expensive sins refrain
And never broke the Sabbath but for gain.

Within the context of the poem's Biblical allegory, and that of the *character* of the "godly" man, these juxtapositions can, of course, be made quite naturally.

This *general Worship* is to PRAISE, and PRAY:
One part to *borrow* Blessings, one to *pay*.
And when frail Nature slides into *Offence*,
The *Sacrifice* for *Crimes* is *Penitence*.[57]

> In this last line the legal term *"Crimes"* is used in unobtru-
> sive juxtaposition with the religious terms *"Sacrifice"* and
> *"Penitence"*, where in this case "sins" might rather have
> been expected. Once again the transference seems to be
> more than accidental or conventional, with a special signifi-
> cance in the larger unity of the poem. *Religio Laici* is a
> rationalistic, legal, or social document, rather than a spiritual
> expression of religious faith; and the word *"Crimes"* takes
> its place in a consistent but unobtrusive pattern of legal
> terminology: such words as "partial", "justice", "appeal",
> "suit", "effects", "forfeit", "fine", and "mulct" are consis-
> tently used for the expression of religious notions. For
> example:

Look humbly upward, see his Will disclose:
The *Forfeit* first, and then the *Fine* impose:
A Mulct thy Poverty cou'd never pay.[58]

> Here again the result is structural rather than belonging to
> the individual words themselves. Dryden summons, through
> the continued use of these words, an additional plane of
> reference by employing its terminology; and in doing so gives
> to the poem a new and distinctive flavour. He is not seeking
> the startling or original type of incongruity employed, for
> instance, by Donne: rather it is a familiar, "decorous" incon-
> gruity for which there was ample precedent—in Milton's
> line, for example: "with reiterated crimes . . . Heap on him-
> self Damnation".[59] His aim is an adjustment of meaning,
> not its transformation.
>
> Words used in these ways tend to have repercussions *beyond*
> themselves, but not *within* themselves, and this power of
> association is both extended and controlled by the pattern of
> which the words are part. Through this means Dryden
> escapes the woolliness of connotation of some Romantic

57 *Religio Laici*, lines 50-51.
58 *Ibid.*, lines 101-3.
59 *Paradise Lost*, I, 214. The OED also cites *Othello*, V, ii, 26, and Addison
  to illustrate the equation of "crime" and "sin".

poetry, where this kind of precise structural control is missing, while avoiding, too, the potential monotony of a strictly
denotative use of words.

Speaking of Augustan poetry, which, he says, was "mainly
the creation of Dryden", F. W. Bateson claims that its
achievement "was by shearing words of their secondary and
irrelevant associations to release the full emphasis of their
primary meanings".[60] The relationships between the meaning of Dryden's words as direct statement and their full
meaning in terms of the poem as a whole discussed in this
chapter will show the inadequacy of this kind of judgment
when applied to Dryden. In its desire for clarity and precision, the poetry of statement does strive to avoid "irrelevant
associations" and to retain the "full emphasis of primary
meanings". But this is not all it does. And when Bateson
gives a more general definition of poetry, whose "devices"
(listed as "the metre, the rhymes, the alliterations and the
associative value of words") he sees as serving to "repel the
logical and progressive tendencies that are always active in
speech",[61] he is going to an opposite extreme that is equally
difficult to reconcile with Dryden's work. Because he seeks
to give his material an added richness, an added piquancy,
that at its best serves both to vitalize the immediate context
and to help build up an imaginative dimension for the poem
as a whole, Dryden's words do not always have the simplicity
of meaning, the singleness of purpose suggested by Bateson's
definition of Augustan poetry: on the other hand the nature
of the poetry of statement demands that the devices of
poetry should not be used to weaken the opportunities for
adequate statement inherent in a logical, progressive mode
of expression.

Again it is a question of writing that seeks to achieve the
richness of poetry, but without sacrificing the qualities of
good prose. Dryden's meanings achieve strength and subtlety,
not from an opposition, or even a balance, or tension, of
prose and poetry, but from an harmonious blending of their
qualities.

60 F. W. Bateson, *English Poetry and English Language: An Experiment in
  Literary History* (Oxford: Clarendon Press, 1934), p. 58.
61 *Ibid.*, pp. 19-21.

chapter three

Sound

Prose is the art of manifest statement: the periods and diction may vary with the emotional mood, but the latent meanings of the words that compose it are largely disregarded. In poetry a supplementary statement is framed by a precise marshalling of these latent meanings; yet the reader would not be aware of more than the manifest statement were it not for the heightened sensibility induced in him by the rhythmic intoxication of verse.[1]

In the previous chapter we have seen how, even in the poetry of statement, there can be this "precise marshalling ... of latent meanings"; and we turn now to a closer examination of the role of sound and rhythm in transforming "manifest statement" into poetry.

Dryden's poetry is one of powerful rhythms. These lines from the *Og* portrait in *The Second Part of Absalom and Achitophel* make the utmost use of almost every one of the five stresses in each line, consistently reinforcing the metrical stress with some emphasis of sound, or meaning, or association:

Now stop your noses Readers, all and some,
For here's a tun of Midnight-work to come,
Og from Treason Tavern rowling home.
Round as a Globe, and Liquor'd ev'ry chink,
Goodly and Great he Sayls behind his Link;

1 Robert Graves.

With all this Bulk there's nothing lost in *Og*,
For ev'ry inch that is not Fool is Rogue:
A Monstrous mass of foul corrupted matter,
As all the Devils had spew'd to make the batter.
When wine has given him courage to Blaspheme,
He Curses God, but God before Curst him;
And if man cou'd have reason none has more,
That made his Paunch so rich and him so poor.[2]

> Or this passage from *Religio Laici*, where the argument is developed through an elaborate patterning of sound, until it reaches its climax in the emphatic repetition of the last line:

For granting we have Sin'd, and that th'offence
Of *Man*, is made against *Omnipotence*,
Some Price, that bears *proportion*, must be paid;
And *Infinite* with *Infinite* be weigh'd.[3]

> There are two main sources of rhythm available to the poet: the "formal" or artificial rhythm—that is the rhythm imposed by or deriving from the form of the poem, from its metrical structure as it is reinforced and/or varied by the meaning of the words and by the devices of sound and movement; and the "natural" rhythms of the speaking voice that tend to assert themselves whenever they are given the opportunity. The rhythm of any individual poem is the result of a combination of these formal and natural rhythms, and the poet has a number of alternatives to choose from in determining the rhythmic nature of his verse. He can make the formal rhythm imposed by the verse sufficiently strong and insistent virtually to block out any tendency towards a natural rhythm; he can mute the verse rhythms to the point where the formal quality is all but lost and the rhythm becomes that of the normal speaking voice; he can so manage the movement of the verse that a state of near balance, or tension, is set up between the formal and natural rhythm, seeking sometimes to gain energy from the attempt of the two rhythms to assert themselves; or he can control or vary the formal rhythm in such a way that it maintains its own quality, but yet adheres closely to the natural rhythm of the speaking voice.

2 *The Second Part of Absalom and Achitophel*, lines 457-69.
3 *Religio Laici*, lines 111-14.

This last course is the one followed characteristically by Dryden. Hear, for instance, the painful change as Nahum Tate takes over from Dryden after the first eight lines of this passage from *The Second Part of Absalom and Achitophel*:

These Gloomy, Thoughtfull and on Mischief bent,
While those for mere good Fellowship frequent
Th'Appointed Clubb, can let Sedition pass,
Sense, Non-sence, anything t'employ the Glass;
And who believe in their dull honest Hearts,
The Rest talk Treason but to shew their Parts;
Who n'er had Wit or Will for Mischief yet,
But pleas'd to be reputed of a Set.
    But in the Sacred Annals of our Plot,
Industrious AROD never be forgot:
The Labours of this Midnight-Magistrate,
May Vie with Corah's to preserve the State;
In search of Arms, He fail'd not to lay hold
On War's most powerful dang'rous Weapon, GOLD.[4]

Dryden's lines, unlike Tate's, sound perfectly natural, but nevertheless they still derive a good deal of advantage from the formal shape and movement of the heroic couplet.

This is something that Dryden learned as part of his technique of dramatic writing. His years of apprenticeship in the theatre, and the many thousands of couplets that make up his heroic plays, lie behind the "speaking voice" of *Absalom and Achitophel* and the other great poems of the 1680's. It is in the heroic plays, and in the constant thinking and theorizing about poetry expressed in his essays and dedications, that the smoothness of Waller's verse, and the strength of Denham's were forged into a natural and powerful instrument of statement. Here is *Almanzor* as he faces his mother's ghost in *The Conquest of Granada*:

Well mayst thou make thy boast whate'er thou art!
Thou art the first e'er made Almanzor start.
My legs
Shall bear me to thee in their own despite:
I'll rush into the covert of thy night,
And pull thee backward, by thy shroud, to light;

---

4 *The Second Part of Absalom and Achitophel*, lines 526-39.

Or else I'll squeeze thee, like a bladder, there,
And make thee groan thyself away to air.

(The Ghost retires.)

So thou art gone! Thou canst no conquest boast:
I thought what was the courage of a ghost.—
The grudging of my ague yet remains:
My blood, like icicles, hangs in my veins,
And does not drop;—Be master of that door,
We two will not disturb each other more.
I erred a little, but extremes may join;
That door was hell's, but this is heaven's and mine.

*(Goes to the other door, and is met again
by the Ghost.)*

Again! by Heaven, I do conjure thee, speak!
What art thou, spirit? and what dost seek?[5]

But it is not enough to say that Dryden's experience in the theatre gave his verse a dramatic quality. Donne's poetry is essentially dramatic, but his speaking voice is unlike Dryden's; and the dramatic quality of Shakespeare's verse, too, is often very different from that of Dryden's. Shakespeare's characters can muse, wonder, exalt, weave delicate fancies, explore the depths and heights of passion, or give voice to gentle irony: often they speak to or for themselves; their utterances frequently have the quality of private or intimate speech. Dryden's dramatic verse almost always develops the rhythms of public speech. His characters most commonly speak so as to drive home a point, to appear forceful, or impressive, or clear, to someone else. They declaim rather than talk: their utterances seldom leave the level of heroic splendour on which the plays move.

Given the nature of the heroic play, Dryden's success lay in the extent to which he could sustain the heroic elevation without sacrificing the vitality and flexibility of natural speech rhythms. It was here, without doubt, that the "plain and natural, and yet majestic" style of the poetry of statement was born: in the need, for instance, to give precision and liveliness, and a degree of naturalness, to the interminably lofty debates about love and honour that are one of the staple materials of the heroic play. Dryden himself speaks of

5 "Almanzor and Almahide; or, The Conquest of Granada" (1672), Part Two, Act IV, iii, *The Works of John Dryden*, ed. Sir Walter Scott and George Saintsbury (18 vols.; London: 1882-92), IV, 188-89.

the matter, as part of his defence of rhyme: "The scenes which in my opinion most commend it," he writes concerning rhyme, "are those of argumentation and discourse, on the result of which the doing or not doing of some considerable action should depend." And again: ". . . in the quickness of reparties (which in discoursive scenes fall very often) it has so particular a grace, and is so aptly suited to them, that the sudden smartness of the answer, and the sweetness of the rhyme, set off the beauty of each other."[6] Prose, he says, is not to be used in serious plays because "it is too near the nature of converse". Verse, on the other hand, while it may lack the immediate realism of prose, is

nearest the nature of a serious play; this last is indeed the representation of Nature, but 'tis Nature wrought up to higher pitch. The plot, the characters, the wit, the passions, the descriptions, are all exalted above the level of common converse, as high as the imagination of the poet can carry them, with proportion to verisimility.[7]

Nevertheless, despite the exalted nature of the discourse, the verse must seem to have the "negligence of prose", and must not be made to sound "so unnaturally as no man would in ordinary speaking".

Here again Dryden was striving for the advantages of both prose and poetry. The central core of the discourse, or argument, was to be presented without loss of clarity: Professor Sutherland, for instance, has shown how Dryden "simplifies" a passage from Shakespeare's *Troilus and Cressida*, by dispensing with all but the most obvious metaphors, by which means he "brings the passage closer to the language of discourse".[8] At the same time the elevation, needed to raise the "admiration" that for Dryden was the object of the heroic play, was achieved through the development of the formal rhythms of the rhymed couplet, without abandoning, however, the vigour of natural speech. This combination of a prose clarity and naturalness, raised by verse to a more than ordinary level of imaginative intensity and interest, lies behind the success of all Dryden's poetry of statement.

6 Dryden, "Epistle Dedicatory to 'The Rival Ladies'" (1664), *Essays of John Dryden*, ed. W. P. Ker (2 vols.; Oxford: Clarendon Press, 1900), I, 7-9.
7 Dryden, "An Essay of Dramatic Poesy" (1668), *ibid.*, I, 100-101.
8 See James Sutherland, *Preface to Eighteenth Century Poetry* (Oxford: Clarendon Press, 1948), p. 15.

One group of poems which, in point of time and occasion, belong with the heroic plays, but which in character bridge the gap between Dryden's dramatic and non-dramatic poetry, are his Prologues and Epilogues, especially those composed for delivery from the stage of the Restoration theatre. These are as peculiarly his own as anything that Dryden wrote. In them he is striving to gain and control the attention of an unruly audience: and nowhere in his poetry are we made more aware of the presence of an audience. We have only, I think, to compare these dramatic prologues with his more formal ones (those, for example, addressed to the University of Oxford or to the Duchess of York) to realize this. Nowhere is it more apparent than here that Dryden's poetry is conceived, not in his own soul, but in the presence, imagined at least, of a living, breathing audience (in this case often a shouting, brawling, vociferous audience), and that he writes not for his own satisfaction but for what he hopes will be theirs.[9] These poems are permeated with the rhetorical spirit, and they use words with a wonderful effectiveness in bringing a subject to life.

One would not expect to find in these Prologues and Epilogues even the degree of subtlety achieved in poems like *Absalom and Achitophel*; nor are they likely to rely on Dryden's usual unobtrusiveness of effect. With an audience such as they were written for, often inclined to admire its own wit more than what it ostensibly came to hear, the poet must work in a manner that is forceful and unsubtle, at least until he has gained the attention of his listeners. Here are the lines that open the Prologue to one of Dryden's own plays, *The Assignation: or, Love in a Nunnery*:

Prologues, like Bells to Churches, toul you in
With Chimeing Verse; till the dull Playes begin:
With this sad difference though, of Pit and Pue;
You damn the *Poet*, but the *Priest* damns you.[10]

There is no attempt at a flow of verse here: every line has at least one strong medial pause, and each one except the first is strongly endstopped. Each line makes use of this fragmen-

9 For an account of the Restoration theatre audience see Allardice Nicoll, *A History of English Drama 1660-1900* (6 vols.; Cambridge: Cambridge University Press, 1952).
10 Prologue to *The Assignation: or, Love in a Nunnery* (1673), lines 1-4.

tation to accent the hammerlike blows of "like Bells to Churches", "the dull Playes begin", and "of Pit and Pue": blows that have no particular significance in themselves but that lead up to the forceful, obvious wit of the climactic line. Here energy is conserved by being concentrated at either end of the line. All but one of the six strong stresses in the line are distributed among the first two and final three syllables, and they are separated by a pause placed amidst three weak syllables. The result is two strong, antithetic, balanced statements:

You damn the *Poet*, | but the *Priest* damns you.

Into this antithetic structure is concentrated the forcefulness of direct address in the repeated "you", made more effective by its transposed placement at either end of the line; of the repeated "damn"; and of the juxtaposition of *"Poet"* and *"Priest"*, with its alliteration of the plosive p sounds already built up in the preceding lines. But for all their rhetorical blacksmithing the lines retain their note of the speaking voice and the animation it brings. They are written to be spoken by an actor, speaking familiarly with an audience.

Dryden can, indeed, achieve a remarkable naturalness and ease of expression. "A fastidious delicacy, and a false refinement, in order to avoid meanness," Joseph Warton declared, "has deterred our writers from the introduction of common words, but Dryden often hazarded it, and it gave a secret charm and a natural air to his verses."[11] Despite his frequent adherence to a deliberately elevated and rather stereotyped poetic diction, Dryden probably more than any other English poet used (or, more truly, appeared to use) the language really spoken by men. Even in the heroically declamatory style of *Absalom and Achitophel* there is a colloquial ease of expression, a comfortable familiarity between poet and reader:

Others thought Kings an useless heavy Load,
Who Cost too much, and did too little Good.
These were for laying Honest *David* by,
On Principles of pure good Husbandry.[12]

11 Joseph Warton, "Essay on the Genius and Writing of Pope" (London, 1756), *Eighteenth Century Critical Essays*, ed. Scott Elledge (2 vols.; New York: Cornell University Press, 1961), II, 717-63.
12 *Absalom and Achitophel*, lines 505-8.

Homely adjectives and phrases of this type abound, and they help give Dryden's verse its colloquial flavour; though there is often nothing that is particularly simple or homely about the words themselves—about the word "Husbandry", for instance. It is a commonplace (and obvious) enough word here, but only as part of the phrase "pure good Husbandry", following on the idea of "laying Honest *David* by", does it get the down-to-earth taste that is quite lacking in its use in these lines from *The Hind and the Panther*, where the tone is elevated rather than colloquial:

As where the lightning runs along the ground,
No husbandry can heal the blasting wound.[13]

And though Dryden's words and phrasing are characteristically natural, he avoids the self-conscious excesses of monosyllabic simplicity practised by Wordsworth, where the very naturalness becomes contrived and artificial. Indeed, by contrast with Wordsworth, Dryden theoretically objected to the cluttering effect of consonants in monosyllabic lines: "it seldom happens but a monosyllabic line turns verse to prose; and even that prose is rugged and unharmonious."[14] There are many such monosyllabic lines in Dryden's poetry, but they seldom serve towards or achieve simplicity. More frequently their purpose is far removed from that of imitating natural or simple speech, as in this line from the portrait of *Achitophel*, where the deliberate movement that results from the monosyllables is expressive of the speaker's deep contempt for his subject:

Would steer too nigh the sands to boast his wit.[15]

Because he must always have listened to the sound of his verse, because he had, as Wordsworth himself said, an "excellent ear", Dryden would never have allowed a desire for naturalness of diction to lead him into such a line as:

This morning gives us promise of a glorious day.[16]

To his contemporaries his verse must have sounded even more natural than it does today, and the common charge

---

13 *The Hind and the Panther*, I, lines 223-24.
14 Dryden, "Dedication of the 'Aeneis' ", Ker, *op. cit.*, II, 227.
15 *Absalom and Achitophel*, line 162.
16 W. Wordsworth, *Resolution and Independence*, line 84.

that his expression is inflexibly stiff would have been incomprehensible. He is always the conscious artist, but he demonstrates conclusively how artifice can be made to sound natural. Listen as he makes his "will and testament" as a playwright, in the Prologue to his last play, *Love Triumphant*. Almost every couplet exploits its formal structure to achieve a different kind of movement, but the whole thing has the spontaneity of natural speech:

He Dies, at least to us, and to the Stage,
And what he has, he leaves this Noble Age.
He leaves you first, all Plays of his Inditing,
The whole Estate, which he has got by Writing.
The Beaux may think this nothing but vain Praise,
They'l find it something; the Testator says:
For half their Love, is made from scraps of Plays.
To his worst Foes, he leaves his Honesty;
That they may thrive upon't as much as he.
He leaves his Manners to the Roaring Boys,
Who come in Drunk, and fill the House with noise.
He leaves to the dire Critiques of his Wit,
His Silence and Contempt of all they Writ.
To *Shakespeare's* Critique, he bequeaths the Curse,
To find his faults; and yet himself make worse:
A precious Reader in Poetique Schools,
Who by his own Examples damns his Rules.
Last for the Fair, he wishes you may be,
From your dull Critiques, the Lampooners free.
Tho' he pretends no Legacy to leave you,
An Old Man may at least good wishes give you.
Your Beauty names the Play; and may it prove,
To each, an Omen of Triumphant Love.[17]

The quality of these lines is an essential part of Dryden's whole achievement in the poetry of statement.

The power of Dryden's rhythms, serving rather to enliven and emphasize the statement than to articulate an independent meaning of their own, has the effect of limiting both the dialectical and imaginative possibilities of his lines. His meaning is vigorously clear rather than suggestively complex;

17 Prologue to *Love Triumphant; or, Nature will Prevail* (1694), lines 34-56.

and in this he provides a striking contrast with a poet like Donne, who often parades in his verse a succession of outwardly simple monosyllables, any of which are capable of receiving significant stress, and which may consequently allow a multiplicity of meanings, dependent on how they are read. This simple line of Donne's, for instance, has aroused a recent scholarly discussion:

So if I dream, I have you, I have you.[18]

Here the stress pattern can remain indeterminate because the meaning is not clearly stated. Dryden's verbal subtlety, however, is not of the sort that demands, or allows, penetrating analysis to extract deep implications from individual words; and even his structural subtlety does not generally depend on a tentative or ambiguous syntax, where the rhetorical or rhythmical stress determines the role of each individual word in the synthetic structure. It would be difficult, I think, to find many lines in Dryden's verse where the meaning could be materially altered at the choice of the reader by adopting a different manner of reading. Because his aim is to state clearly what he means, Dryden's rhythms can afford to be strong and energetic, rather than to hover in a subtly elusive way over a cluster of words of indeterminate meaning. His verse, as it were, reads itself.

Sound and rhythm can work in only one direction at a time; and, in poetry like Dryden's where rhythm is often the dominating element, this can have important consequences. Though the meaning with which the sound co-operates can be varied, the extent of this variation will be limited by the strength or resilience of the sound pattern. If, for argument's sake, Donne's line had occurred in a context which had set up a continuingly powerful rhythmic pattern resulting in a reading such as:

So if I dream, | I have you, I have you,

the effective range of meaning in the line would be considerably reduced. If the sound pattern is strongly vital in this way, then the sense may be strengthened but it will lose in subtlety and complexity: on the other hand, the more subtle

18 See the *Kenyon Review*, XVIII (1956), 411-77.

or complex the sense, the more the rhythm is likely to lose in vitality.

We have seen, for example, how in this line from the *character* of *Zimri*:

Was Chymist, Fidler, States-Man, and Buffoon,

the strong rhythmic movement draws attention away from the satiric potentiality of the silent intrusion of the incongruous word "States-Man" among the other trivial diversions of the courtier: the reader is denied the opportunity to dwell on the implications of individual words, which become submerged under the heavy stress pattern, and the meaning is consequently simplified.[19] The even rhythm of the line is no doubt intended to draw attention to the irony of a situation in which the activities of a statesman are no more important, no more deserving of stress, than those of the fiddler or buffoon. But in the full rhythmic context of the portrait, Dryden fails partially for the reason that he is trying to pack more meaning into the line than his poetic method will carry. By contrast, because his rhythmic movement is less insistent, Pope can achieve the kind of satiric finesse Dryden misses, with this line from the picture of Belinda's toilet in *The Rape of the Lock*, where there is a similar juxtaposition of incongruous objects:

Paint, patches, powder, bibles, billet-doux.

But in this passage Pope is not seeking at the same time to build up an overall satiric effect through a strongly significant rhythmic beat: on the contrary, his movement has all the delicacy of a miniaturist, in which every tiny detail is revealed. And failing a nice balance between the two, it would seem that a poet must seek either subtlety of meaning, or a relatively simple meaning that can be accentuated or animated by strong rhythmic effects. Dryden's genius, the secret of his poetry of statement, lies in the latter direction. His characteristic aim is to achieve vitality of expression rather than an equivocal richness of meaning, and this allows him a general freedom of operation in combining metrical accent with rhetorical stress, without the difficulties encountered in the line from the *Zimri* portrait. Because of the very

19 See above, p. 44.

nature of his perspicuity of expression, a close harmony between sound and sense is possible.

Dryden can thus give the significant word in a line or couplet dominance through sound as well as sense, because this is a rhythmically simple device, not involving any complexity or ambiguity of meaning. For instance, important words can be made to draw attention to themselves by their syllabic structure as well as by their meaning:

Did wisely from Expensive Sins refrain;[20]

or:

The Stamp and Coyn of their adopted Lord.[21]

Here the ironical words "Expensive" and "adopted" are nicely pointed by the sensitive articulation they demand. Similarly the very quality or pitch of sound can become outstanding, as the "dark" diphthong in "Owls" dominates this line from *MacFlecknoe*:

On his left hand twelve reverend *Owls* did fly.[22]

or as the insensitive sound reinforces the meaning of "Mug" by ironically echoing the m sound of "mighty" in:

He plac'd a mighty Mug of potent Ale;[23]

Even the proper name *Ogleby* gets an unexpectedly delicious quality from a masterly use of sound:

And Uncle *Ogleby* thy envy raise.[24]

But generally Dryden's sound and rhythm work, not to highlight an individual word or phrase, but to emphasize a significant structure, as they do in this couplet from the *character* of *Shimei* in *Absalom and Achitophel*:

Shimei, whose Youth did early Promise bring
Of Zeal to God, and Hatred to his King.[25]

Part of the significance of this second line comes not from the line by itself, but from its relationship to the larger meaning of the poem, where God and the King who rules by

20 *Absalom and Achitophel*, line 587.
21 *The Medall*, line 144.
22 *MacFlecknoe*, line 129.
23 *Ibid.*, line 121.
24 *Ibid.*, line 174.
25 *Absalom and Achitophel*, lines 585-86.

Divine Right are virtually identified. Rhetorically the line is unobtrusive but well formed, the suppression of the fourth metrical stress giving it two nicely balanced halves:

Of Zéal to Gód, | and Hátred to his Kíng.

The result is a clean, forcible statement, with the antithesis of "Zeal" and "Hatred" stated with sufficient clarity to give the underlying paradox of their association with God and King respectively the force of surprise, without however its being strong enough to risk claiming all the attention for itself. It is fully effective, both in itself as rhetorical statement, and, in the context of the poem, as poetry.

A rather different use of carefully structured rhythm for what might be described as rhetorical purposes is to be seen in these lines that round off one verse paragraph in *Religio Laici*, where Dryden has been arguing the case for reliance on the word of the Scriptures:

Unask'd their *Pains, ungratefull* their *Advice,*
Starving their *Gain,* and *Martyrdom* their *Price.*[26]

Here Dryden makes use of the convenience of couplet rhythm for stating logical propositions in a way that gives his argument an air of precision: that makes it, in fact, appear more logical than it really is. In this couplet each word in both lines, with the exceptions of the rhyme words and the compensating "and", is balanced by a word of equal syllabic length in the other line. The construction of each line is similar, both having a suppressed fourth stress that gives two more equally balanced halves, accentuated in the first line by the repeated "un":

Unásk'd their Páins, | ungrátefull their Advíce.

The tendency towards perfect balance in this context, ending a passage in which the movement has been rather loosely mediative, results in an overwhelming finality, and gives the couplet a portentous weightiness as the climax of the paragraph that makes us tend not to notice its considerable lack of logical relevance to what has gone before.

A couplet from *The Second Part of Absalom and Achitophel* will illustrate the difficulties involved in judgments

26 *Religio Laici*, lines 144-45.

that deny the quality of suggestiveness to Dryden's lines, but it also shows the strength attained by the rhythmic pattern:

The Midwife laid her hand on his Thick Skull,
With this Prophetick blessing—*Be thou Dull*.[27]

There is potentially a whole world of suggestiveness here, arising from the introduction of the midwife and Shadwell's "Thick Skull" into the context of an episcopal blessing, and from the juxtaposition of the idea of such a blessing and the blessing as it is actually pronounced—*"Be thou Dull"*. But none the less the suggestiveness arising from an incongruity of ideas and images is not the dominant quality of these lines. The reader is certainly aware of the incongruity, but he is discouraged from developing it, from dwelling on it for all it is worth, in the manner of poetry that depends primarily on this kind of suggestiveness. Rather is his attention drawn to other and more powerful elements associated with the sound and movement of the lines: elements that work to reinforce the direct statement rather than to add any element of oblique or indirect suggestiveness. Against the background of the normal poetic suggestiveness of the lines, sound and movement combine to give an image of slow, ponderous dullness surrounding Shadwell that is not to be achieved by the suggestiveness of the words alone, and in which this kind of suggestiveness plays only a minor role.

This mimetic quality of Dryden's rhythms finds its way at all levels into the structure and texture of his verse—from the crudely onomatopoeic effect of:

The Treble squeaks for fear, the Basses roar;[28]

to the richly suggestive quality that sound gives to this image from the lines *To the Memory of Mr. Oldham*:

Thy generous fruits, though gather'd ere their prime
Still shew'd a quickness; and maturing time
But mellows what we write to the dull sweets of Rime.[29]

"Still shew'd a quickness" is accelerated by its heavy stress at the beginning of the line, and by its brisk alliterative

27 *The Second Part of Absalom and Achitophel*, lines 476-77.
28 *MacFlecknoe*, line 46.
29 *To the Memory of Mr. Oldham* (1684), lines 19-21.

emphasis. Then the pause, and the succession of unstressed syllables leading to a slowly drawn-out vowel in "maturing", retard the flow of the verse. Similarly the run of alliterated monosyllables in "what we write" halts the movement, preparing for the heavy quality of "dull sweets".

There is an imaginative use of sound, too, in the formal patterning of *Absalom*'s response to the temptation offered him by *Achitophel*, where again, as in *Religio Laici*, the movement of the lines is made to reflect the "passions" of the speaker's mind. *Absalom*'s initial attitude is one of elaborate, almost over-elaborate, correctness: "what Pretense have I," he asks, "to take up Arms for Public Liberty?"

My Father Governs with unquestion'd Right;
The Faiths Defender, and Mankinds Delight:
Good, Gracious, Just, observant of the Laws;
And Heav'n by Wonders has Espous'd his Cause.[30]

Here the use of a pause after a weak syllable in the first, second, and fourth lines allows for the suppression in each case of the stress on the third foot of the metrical pattern, and for the consequent balancing of the two remaining pairs of strong stresses against each other:

My Fáther Góverns | with unquéstion'd Ríght.

The result is an exaggeratedly stilted rhythm, appropriately self-righteous in tone, until *Absalom*'s ambition and the attractiveness of *Achitophel*'s proposition commence to have their effect, and *Absalom* begins to waver from his first impeccable manner; whereupon the verse becomes more fluid and less strained—ironically, perhaps, more natural— and the formality of the stress pattern less dominant. *Absalom* is still protesting, but his protests have a different tone:

Why then shoud I, Encouraging the Bad,
Turn Rebell, and run Popularly Mad?
Were he a Tyrant who, by Lawless Might,
Opprest the *Jews*, and Rais'd the *Jebusite*,
Well might I mourn . . . &c.[31]

The actual meaning of the last line of this next passage

30 *Absalom and Achitophel*, lines 317-20.
31 *Ibid.*, lines 335-39.

from *Absalom and Achitophel* is not determined by its quality of sound, but the satire is considerably enriched:

With blandishments to gain the publick Love;
To Head the Faction while their Zeal was hot,
And Popularly prosecute the Plot.[32]

The word "Popularly" has an ironic flavour, both from its meaning and from the quality of enunciation it requires, as in this line, for instance:

On each side bowing popularly low.[33]

But, especially after the smoothly caressing sound of "blandishments", the awkwardness produced by the juxtaposition of polysyllabic words in the last line, combined with the clutter of cumbersome and explosive p sounds, lends the expression an air of false pomposity: the polysyllables, instead of providing dignity or elevation, tend rather to "topple over" into the ridiculous.

The ability of rhythm to cling closely to the experience behind it, to co-operate dynamically with the meaning it seeks to express, is seen in the carefully modulated and remarkably varied movement of these lines from *The Medall*:

Besides, their pace was formal, grave and slack:
His nimble Wit outran the heavy Pack.
Yet still he found his Fortune at a stay;
Whole droves of Blockheads choaking up his way.[34]

The purely literal content of these lines does not amount to very much, and it is not helped any by the unimpressive incipient image of the second line; while the directness of the last line is, if anything, to be deplored. Yet the isolated words are invigorated in their metrical combination by Dryden's mastery of rhythm, metre, caesura, and texture. Dryden does not (as in the more formally "correct" heroic couplet) place his caesura after the fourth or sixth syllable here, but in the first line uses three heavy pauses which invest the line with a haltingly natural intonation.

Besides, | their pace was formal, | grave | and slack.

32 *Ibid.*, lines 488-90.
33 *Ibid.*, line 689.
34 *The Medall*, lines 44-47.

The next three lines, by contrast, are without caesuras; but the last two are thickened in their texture, while the second moves briskly. Within these couplets Dryden manages the deft transition from a slow and heavy to an agile rhythm, and then reverts to a weightier movement that becomes strained and cluttered in the final line. Variations in texture, metre, and caesural pause co-ordinate to achieve this result: in the first couplet the stress pattern is kept strictly regular, and it is the texture and the pauses that work to produce the sudden switch in movement:

Besides, | their pace was formal, | grave | and slack:

His nimble Wit outran the heavy Pack.

In the first line the vowels tend to be appropriately dull and long ("Besides", "pace", "formal", "grave"), and the pauses after "besides" and "formal" work against the usual lightening effect of disyllabic words in the line. The monosyllabic "their pace was" also halts the flow of the verse by demanding for each a separate accent, however slight. By contrast, in the second line of the couplet, monosyllables are skilfully alternated with words of two syllables to fit effortlessly into the iambic stress pattern. The vowels in this line, too, are quick and sharp, rather than resonant: "his nimble wit".

In the next two lines a sensitive texture of sound makes metrical adjustment necessary:

Yet still he found his Fortune at a stay;

Whole droves of Blockheads choaking up his way.

In the first of these lines the word "Fortune" receives extra weight because of the heavy quality of its initial vowel and because it is joined alliteratively with the preceding "found". And the sound of the following line is so thickened by its texture that the verse refuses to be read smoothly or regularly. The cluster of stresses mimes the "choked" movement that Dryden is describing. The line is clogged by assonance ("Whole droves"); by consonance (especially in the words "Blockheads choaking", but the repetition of the v sound in "droves of" even leads the reader to falter and stumble over the preposition); and by the juxtaposition of brittle and thick consonants. Because the texture is so cluttered the line is difficult to articulate, the stresses accumulating within it; and in both lines Dryden uses a favourite device of a preposition placed in the normal position of the fourth stress, giving the end of the line a quality of release by at least partially suppressing this stress, thereby both relieving and accentuating the pressure created by the initial tense movement of the line. The sound resources of the verse are exploited in these ways, but all the time to intensify, to give vitality to, the stated meaning of the lines, weak as it may be in this particular case.

As he has done to some extent in the lines just discussed, Dryden can, by the use of "significant and sounding words", vitalize images otherwise lacking in depth. In this couplet from *MacFlecknoe* he makes inverted use of the oak image, conventionally employed for its connotations of permanence, magnificence, and royalty (in the *Aeneid* the stereotyped expression for oak is "royal plant"):

Thoughtless as Monarch Oakes, that shade the plain,
And, spread in solemn state, supinely reign.[35]

In common with most of Dryden's imagery, these lines do not achieve a truly concrete or sensuous quality, yet their sound and movement still enable the image to evoke a response that is not wholly intellectually abstract. Rhythm is an important ingredient in the vitality and suggestiveness of the couplet: it imparts to the verse a feeling of heavy insensitivity, of dull inertia. Consonance gives weightiness to "Monarch Oakes", while assonance emphasizes the slowness of "shade the plain", and alliteration serves to heighten the force of taut movement in "spread in solemn state", with its deflating echo in the slackening sound of "supinely".

But once again the sound of the verse is not to be divorced from its literal meaning. The image in these lines depends for its effectiveness upon a mock heroic use of the notion of grandeur and royalty, and its force of inversion is strengthened by the texture and movement of the verse. The determining factor, however, is still ultimately the meaning of the words.

35 *MacFlecknoe*, lines 27-28.

Essentially the deflation comes not from a mixture of "grand" and "inert" sounds, but from the bracketing of the elevated "Monarch Oakes" between the deflating words "Thoughtless" and "supinely". The auditory effects gained by inverting the initial foot with "Thoughtless" might be interpreted as intensifying a feeling of blind inertia: but only in that it co-operates in a strictly subordinate way with the meaning of the word itself. We have seen, in fact, how in the line:

Scatter'd his Maker's Image through the Land,

this inversion of the initial foot can invigorate and strengthen the movement. Similarly the slack vowel in "supinely" serves to enhance but in no way to determine the meaning.

To be carried away by the apparent ability of sound to determine meaning in poetry is always a danger, and nowhere more than in poetry like Dryden's, where sound is used to such good purpose, but where the controlling statement is also normally so strong. It is only rarely that we find Dryden using sound or rhythm to tamper with or to determine his sense: that is, using them for purposes of indirect suggestiveness rather than for the enrichment of the direct statement. One such example is to be found in this couplet from *The Medall*, where Dryden probably intended the dragging, listless movement of the second line to be incompatible with the explicit meaning, particularly as the passage in which it occurs is already underlined by a tone of heavy sarcasm:

Nor Faith nor Reason make thee at a stay,
Thou leapst o'er all eternal truth, in thy *Pindarique* way![36]

Here the suggestion of long-windedness and prolixity achieved by the fourteener contrasts with the mental agility inferred by the verb "leapst", and has a strongly ironic effect. The line reflects an undertone of sarcasm from its context, but its movement largely determines its immediate ironical force. Indirect auditory or rhythmic devices of this kind, however, are isolated rather than typical with Dryden. Generally he seeks to adhere closely to the sense expressed, without depending too strongly on any oblique or allusive quality of sound.

36 *The Medall*, lines 93-94.

In most of the passages discussed so far in this chapter, Dryden's rhythms operate within a strong framework of syntax where sense is closely followed. There are, however, some occasions when the rhythm does dominate at the expense of meaning: when the sense is largely undeveloped and syntax tends to be neglected or to become "a play of empty forms". In what can properly be described as poetry of statement these occasions are infrequent, though the portrait of *Zimri* does provide one rather special example where the emptiness of the syntactical structure is made to reflect the emptiness of *Zimri* himself. Examples of a rather different kind are furnished by the casual development of thought in the musical odes, and also the songs from the plays and operas, where the rhythm of the verse can determine emotional association in a strikingly explicit manner. The orchestration of sound in these poems masks the slightness of their content. Dryden presents a series of varied explorations in mood by changing the pace and sound of his verse, and in these transitions the actual meanings of the words become relatively insignificant. The words are not intended to be meaningless, but within the framework of a fluctuating rhythm their denotation is unimportant. In the following stanza from *A Song for St. Cecilia's Day* the last three lines are left "hanging", or syntactically disconnected:

But oh! what Art can teach
What human Voice can reach
The sacred ORGANS praise?
Notes inspiring holy Love,
Notes that wing their heav'nly ways
To mend the Choires above.[37]

Yet the hollow, deep sound of the repeated "Notes" is so onomatopoeically satisfying that we scarcely notice the syntactic laxity. Similarly the dynamic, turbulent movement of *Alexander's Feast*, despite its dramatic/narrative structure, depends more on sound than on sense for its progress. In both these odes syntax is not closely adhered to, and the progression is haphazard rather than logical. The sound dominates, rather than follows the meaning of the words.

Dryden's interest in sound is evidenced, too, by his attempts at opera, and particularly by his theorizing on the

37 *A Song for St. Cecilia's Day. 1687*, lines 42-47.

subject in his Preface to *Albion and Albanius,* an opera he produced in 1685. Here he gives critics a warning that could very well apply to criticism of all his poetry. After refusing to give rules for the writing of opera, which, he says, would then be used by the critics against himself, he writes: "if they will criticize, they shall do so out of their own fond; but let them first be assured that their ears are nice; for there is neither writing or judgement on this subject without that good quality."[38] Because of its musical demands, which are made doubly difficult to meet in English because of the prevalence of consonants and monosyllables, "thought" and "elevation of fancy" are not to be expected in opera. Sound is everything: "The chief secret is the choice of words; and, by this choice, I do not mean here elegancy of expression, but propriety of sound, to be varied according to the nature of the subject."[39] Dryden thought that "perhaps a time may come when I may treat of this more largely, out of some observations which I have made from Homer and Virgil, who, amongst all the poets, only understood the art of numbers ...", but unfortunately this time did not eventuate.

Dryden's operas, and his odes and songs, are not poetry of statement, in which a direct, logical meaning is dominant. But they are of some significance, because they display beyond question Dryden's interest in sound as an organic element in poetry, and also his ability to convey emotion through sound and rhythmical variation. And this is something he frequently succeeds in doing in the best of his non-lyrical poetry, though the effects he aims at there are less flamboyant and more part of a complex structure of sound and movement. Sound is an especially important ingredient in Dryden's verse, with often an emotional quality that can otherwise be lacking in the poet's perception. It was as if he "felt in metre". His perception of things may have been largely intellectual, but his feeling was for the movement of the words in which these things were expressed. To return to a phrase of Empson's quoted earlier, Dryden was perhaps not interested in the "echoes and recesses of words" in the way that Empson himself is, but he was interested in their

38 Dryden, "Preface to 'Albion and Albanius, An Opera'" (1685), Ker, *op. cit.,* I, 276-77.
39 *Ibid.,* I, 277.

immediate sounding qualities; and certainly he had an imaginative talent for the use of words that went beyond an interest simply in "the echoes and recesses of human judgement". It would be more accurate, too, to say that he "felt in metre" than, as Van Doren puts it, that he "thought in metre", for the rhythmical element in Dryden's poetry is essentially an affective rather than a rational one. His meaning is clear independently of sound: he does not depend on niceties of enunciation to establish what he is saying. The function of sound is to enliven and enrich the meaning imaginatively, to give it passion.

Thus it was part of Dryden's poetic development that he learned not only to give "significant accent" to his verse by adjusting the metrical stress as a reinforcement of meaning, but also to exploit rhythm so as to generate emotion. In his early attempts in the quatrain form he generally failed to make the sound of the verse contribute either towards emotional effect or articulated meaning. This is a typical stanza from his *Annus Mirabilis*:

To the pale foes they suddenly draw near,
  And summon them to unexpected fight:
They start like Murderers when Ghosts appear,
  And draw their Curtains in the dead of night.[40]

Here there is at best a certain technical competence, but the rhythm is flaccid; and when continued inertly stanza after stanza it becomes monotonous. By comparison with the *Heroique Stanza's* to Cromwell, Dryden did attempt in *Annus Mirabilis* to give coherence and continuity by frequently linking the quatrains either grammatically or rhetorically, but he still does not attain the ease and flow that is essential to his best style; nor, for that matter, the elevation needed for his heroic purpose in this poem. The lack of vitality of the quatrain form is not a fault in itself, if its tendency towards slackness is made to co-operate with the feeling of the verse: it harmonizes beautifully with the quiet gravity and reflective movement of Gray's *Elegy written in a*

---

40 *Annus Mirabilis: The Year of Wonders MDCLXVI. An Historical Poem* (1666), lines 737-40.

Country Churchyard. But Dryden needs here a majestic or a grandiloquent style, and the verse lacks the energy needed to raise itself to the heroic pitch required. Even the line:

They start like Murderers when Ghosts appear,

is incongruously inanimate. Dryden is not yet able to make his verse form harmonize with, and give vitality to, its statement.

In his poetic maturity Dryden learned not only to wield the heroic couplet as a semantically co-operating unit, but also to exploit the unusual amount of energy it tends to generate: the form becomes not simply a peg on which to hang the expression, but something dynamic and integrated. Thus the justly famed portrait of *Achitophel* in *Absalom and Achitophel* forms an obvious contrast with the stanza just quoted from *Annus Mirabilis.* Here all the energy for which Dryden has been so often praised is communicated to his indictment of Lord Shaftesbury, not as something random, but controlled, meaningful, figuring forth in the very movement of the lines the restless, turbulent power that constitutes both Shaftesbury's greatness and his menace to the safety of the State as Dryden sees it.

Of these the false *Achitophel* was first:
A Name to all succeeding Ages Curst.
For close Designs, and crooked Counsels fit;
Sagacious, Bold, and Turbulent of wit:
Restless, unfixt in Principles and Place;
In Power unpleas'd, impatient of Disgrace.
A fiery Soul, which working out its way,
Fretted the Pigmy Body to decay:
And o'r inform'd the Tenement of Clay.[41]

The formal pattern of the metre here is relatively regular, though not rigidly so. The broken but unbridled surge of movement, seemingly held with difficulty within the metrical bonds, until the final triplet when it escapes by forcing itself out into the extra line, is created by the discursive speech rhythms, which, more than the formal metre, the rhetoric of the passage is made to serve. The sound gives a concrete quality to a character described in abstract, moral terms: the first six lines contain no sensuous word or embellishing

41 *Absalom and Achitophel,* lines 150-58.

imagery, yet the quality of their sound gives them a sharp, almost tactile effect. This effect is produced by the strident sounds, by the fierce rhythmical energy, the intense, strong, metrical beat. The first two lines are without pause, and are hurled along to exaggerate the sharp rhymes of "first" and "Curst". In the next three lines the movement is disjointed, and the sound texture roughened, through an accumulation of consonants, except where the suppressed beats make the lines bound forward at the end almost with a quality of release. Plosive consonants are used, as they often are in Dryden's satire, to indicate grotesqueness—here the irrationality of a man who cannot be satisfied with the position he has justly won:

In Power unpleas'd, impatient of Disgrace.

The movement becomes almost a stutter: "In P . . . unp . . . imp. . . ." And the long vowel sounds and alliterative w's mime the very strain of the struggling soul in:

A fiery Soul, which working out its way, &c.

Dryden gains these things by tempering, at times by sacrificing, his "long majestic march" for mimetic purposes. The appeal is not only rational, to what is "stated": it is also affective.

It is often difficult in analyzing Dryden's rhythm to distinguish between what is purely rhetorical and what is poetic in the sense of a genuinely imaginative extension of the statement. This is only to be expected in view of the traditionally close relationship of poetry and rhetoric: poetry, Dante once declared, "is nothing else but a rhetorical composition set to music (*nihil aliud est quam fictio rethorica in musicaque posita*)".[42] Yet the fact that Dryden gives rhetorical emphasis through metrical stress should not be observed without noting how the metre can sensitize or give poetic meaning to words: what appears a purely rhetorical adjustment can often have something approaching an emotional quality. For example, in *MacFlecknoe* he writes:

In Prose and Verse, was own'd, without dispute
Through all the Realms of *Non-sense*, absolute.[43]

42 Dante Alighieri, *De vulgari eloquentia* (London: Dent, 1904), IV, 77.
43 *MacFlecknoe*, lines 5-6.

The pause in this second line, all the heavier for being placed so late in the line, isolates the word *"Non-sense"*, emphasizing the heavy stress that falls naturally on the syllable "non", and so intensifies its deflating effect. In this way metrical adjustment is made to coincide with semantic emphasis; yet the versification could also be said to give the word an emotional quality. *"Non-sense"* is enabled to acquire through its placement before the heavy caesura a dull, lifeless flavour appropriate to its meaning. And Dryden uses this same device of placing a pause after a word to allow emphasis to its leaden, insensitive tone again and again:

Mature in dullness from his tender years.[44]

That he till Death true dullness would maintain.[45]

And born a shapeless Lump, like Anarchy.[46]

While *David*, undisturb'd, in *Sion* raign'd.[47]

Some further examples of the emotional effect to be gained from metrical control are provided by those passages in Dryden's verse where metrical regularity is allowed to become obtrusive: because his usual impression is one of ease, in which the stress pattern is not obtrusive, instances of a noticeable metronomic beat are rare and tend to have a special purpose. This device has been seen already, used to give a special quality to the beginning of *Absalom's* reply to *Achitophel*; and in the following lines the hammering regularity of the metre focuses the mock heroic colouring:

Sh — alone, of all my Sons is he
Who stands confirm'd in full stupidity.
The rest to some faint meaning make pretence,
But *Sh* — never deviates into sense.[48]

The final appeal of the passage, as nearly always with Dryden, is to the overt content. The two words that determine its significance are "stupidity" and "sense", placed

44 *Ibid.*, line 16.
45 *Ibid.*, line 115.
46 *Absalom and Achitophel*, line 172.
47 *Ibid.*, line 42.
48 *MacFlecknoe*, lines 17-20.

climactically at the end of each couplet and made emphatic by the couplet closure and by the echo of the rhymes. Yet the insistently regular metre, in which the rhythm of formal speech fully coincides with a rigidly strong and regular stress pattern, determines the bland tone of Fleckno's almost ritualistic chant: his declamation acquires, because of the metronomic beat, the emotional quality of an incantation.

Similarly, in these lines from *The Medall*, the forced regularity of the metre underlines the tone of ironic emptiness:

Five daies he sate, for every cast and look;
Four more than God to finish *Adam* took.[49]

Here again the rhythm provides a tonal background rather than determines the result: the idea of pretentious emptiness is perhaps produced as much by the awkward dislocation of syntax in the delaying of the rhyme word "took" as by the metronomic beat. But in both these last examples the emotional contribution made by the ostentatious metrical regularity, as a background to the adjustment of the sense, cannot be denied.

While Dryden's prose and verse are both, at their characteristic best, what might be called "natural", the verse is invigorated through the quality of its sound to a much more considerable extent than is the prose. Yet Dryden does not, except in such less successful pieces as the *Aeneid*, use sound ostentatiously. His typical effect is a muted one: he generally does not exploit sound at the expense of sense (in the way, for instance, that Swinburne does), nor does the sound of his verse often deafen the sense (as it can do in some of Tennyson's poetry). Rhythm, rather than evaporating meaning, or accompanying a relatively neutral meaning, is intended to intensify it. The intellectual statement becomes transformed into poetry through the art of versification; but that art only exists to give vitality and expressiveness to the thing said.

Dryden's command of rhythm impresses by its effect of ease and naturalness. But even in his "plainest" passages

49 *The Medall*, lines 18-19.

subtlety of sound, like subtlety of meaning, is often covert rather than absent. His rhythm is no more rigid or "flat" than is the meaning of his words, yet both have the quality of precision that issues from sureness of control. Significantly, Dryden was the only master of the heroic couplet in the Augustan age who exhibited real versatility in other verse forms. He was the most considerable song writer in an age not much given to song, and his *A Song for St. Cecilia's Day*, for example, has both forcefulness and ease, where Pope's ode on the same theme appears stiff and restrained by comparison. This flexibility and control was reflected in Dryden's command of the heroic couplet. The couplet may, superficially, seem a stringent form that tends towards monotony of rhythm, just as free verse is often thought of as the form that lends itself to the greatest rhythmical variety. Yet, paradoxically, because of this very tightness of form, the heroic couplet can sustain a remarkable degree of variation within its tight framework, without losing its essential shapeliness: the "bones" of the structure can remain clear and continue to exercise a positive control, in spite of a fluidity of sense and a flexibility of movement. Precision is not necessarily attained at the expense of freedom of movement.

Dryden's typical heroic couplet was not as tightly strung and regular as Pope's, and in fact his liberal variations within the form might be seen as a regression from its characteristic development. In the hands of Pope, as well as other eighteenth century poets like Gay and Johnson, the heroic couplet assumed a more mechanically "correct" character, with sharply chiselled lines and symmetrical rhythms. At its best this formal patterning did not become oppressive or even obtrusive, and could be used, as it was by Pope, to develop minute and subtle effects not often equalled by Dryden. But its greater regularity resulted in a more dominant, as well as a more regular stress pattern. With poets like Pope variety of *texture* becomes a vital feature in the movement of the verse, while variations in metre and caesura are diminished in importance.

The gradations in Dryden's verse come from variations in metre and caesura, as well as in texture. The extreme compression and strict organization of Pope is not essential to his method. He learned during his apprenticeship as a dramatist to capture an elasticity of movement by varying his caesura in position and depth, without abandoning the closure of the couplet form; his concern for texture is evinced by his constant search for "significant and sounding" words; and though not sacrificing the drive and energy of the iambic pentameter line, he does not concentrate or dislocate his sense to fit the rigid dictates of his form, but believed in the fluidity and naturalness resulting from the significant variation of accent. He distributed his emphasis and varied his movement as the sense demanded, and "the result is the speaking voice". Herein lay the secret of his success, the thing that enabled him to build into his verse a great deal of artifice without the appearance of art. Because at his best he wrote in a way that sounded like a normal manner of speaking, because his verse does sound essentially like a poetry of statement, it is accepted as natural; and the art, the careful contrivance of rhythm and movement, achieves its purpose of enriching the statement all the more effectively because it can do so without being obtrusive.

Dryden could be called (as Euripides was by "Longinus") a poet by virtue of his composition rather than his ideas. His subject, and its essential statement in the poem, may be of prose and of the intellect. But while the strength and directness of the statement allows it to retain its full character as statement, it is yet coloured by a quality of sound that evokes a response not purely intellectual. It is above all in the sureness of his technique, in his intuitive "auditory imagination", that Dryden demonstrates the feeling for language that is essential to poetry. His verse transcends a wholly intellectual appeal, not because it attempts to transfuse emotion lyrically by an imaginatively controlled form of thought, but because it depends so strongly for its total effect on the emotive power of auditory suggestiveness.

chapter four

Imagery

Poetry conceived as imitation will result in poems that are themselves images of their subject: as *Religio Laici* is an image of the mental experience that lies behind the argument it seeks to present. But in the construction of these images or "imitations" Dryden makes relatively slight use of imagery in the usually accepted sense of the term: to go from his use of rhythm, from the sounding quality of his auditory imagination, to his use of imagery, is to be conscious of going from the "essence" of Dryden's poetry to something obviously more incidental to his poetic achievement. And yet an analysis of the function of the images in his poetry is essential to an appreciation of the nature of Dryden's art, if only because it demonstrates his limited dependence on what is most frequently regarded as a central element in poetic expression. For we rarely feel that Dryden is using imagery to give expression to a unique perception, to reveal an intuitive grasp of relationships too subtle or complex to be expressed directly, in the manner demanded by much post-Romantic poetic theory. Such a use of imagery has apparently little place in his poetry of statement.

The typical image in Dryden's poetry—in his more successful poetry, that is—is explicit, immediately perceived, yet strictly subservient to the thought it is intended to embellish: while it vitalizes the prose content it does not itself become palpable or sensuous. Its meaning for the poem

is readily paraphrasable, and has no tendency to expand
its significance as the image is contemplated. It is an image
that serves towards enriched and ornamented expression, not
ineffable expression.

One such typical image is contained in these lines from
Religio Laici:

While Crouds unlearn'd, with rude Devotion warm,
About the Sacred Viands buz and swarm,
The *Fly-blown Text* creates a *crawling Brood*;
And turns to *Maggots* what was meant for *Food*.[1]

This image could be described as matter-of-fact, clearly
defined, vivid, vigorous; yet undeveloped, non-visual, not
really memorable in a concrete or sensuous way. The attention of the reader remains less on the quality or detail of the
isolated image than on the literal meaning it is intended to
convey. The image is essentially an aid towards stating something in a vivid or emphatic manner. As a mode of expression it is used to adorn the thought: it is not in itself an
expression of the concept. It is metaphorical in form, but
only because Dryden is not really interested in exploring
the connexion between his image and the basic thought it
is identified with. More attention is given to the vigorous
statement of the image than to its imaginative development
—Dryden uses the image loosely to lend vividness to the
exposition of the thought, without indicating any neatly
developed chain of relationships between the material image
and the thought it adorns. The two are thus metaphorically
identified rather than related in the manner of a simile: the
image is explicit and organic, but not logical. And because
it remains undeveloped in this way the tone arising from
these lines from *Religio Laici* issues less from a perception
of this individual, concrete image than from a general disgust
conveyed by its deliberate lowness. Dryden is using here a
certain type of image, with conventionally accepted associations, rather than hazarding the imprecision of purely
emotive or sensuous imagery.

This "typical" image will serve to introduce the discussion
of Dryden's use of imagery by indicating the form of imagery
he habitually uses in his mature poetry, and its characteristic

---

1 *Religio Laici*, lines 417-20.

function in that poetry—particularly the limitations of that function. Some five years before he composed the image we have been discussing, Dryden wrote:

Imaging is, in itself, the very height and life of Poetry. It is, as Longinus describes it, a discourse, which, by a kind of enthusiasm, or extraordinary emotion of the soul, makes it seem to us that we behold those things which the poet paints, so as to be pleased with them, and to admire them.[2]

But this is theory rather than practice. And in its use of ideas drawn from "Longinus's" *Treatise on the Sublime*, moreover, it is theory that looks forward to the eighteenth century beginnings of Romanticism, rather than reflecting the poetic practice of the seventeenth century. The renewal of interest in the *Treatise on the Sublime* in the later seventeenth century was one aspect of a general movement in poetic ideas that was beginning to see the mental life of the poet himself as an important subject for poetry—a movement that was to result eventually in the shift from a "rhetorical" emphasis on the poet's audience to a "romantic" interest in his own feelings and passions: a shift from seeing poetry as a means of moving or teaching the reader to one of allowing the poet to express his own emotions. "Sublimity", as it is described by "Longinus", is the expression of an elevated soul, made possible by the perfection both of the soul and of art;[3] and as such it links together in the poem the resources of poetic language and the sensitivity of

2 Dryden, "The Author's Apology for Heroic Poetry and Poetic Licence" (1677), *Essays of John Dryden*, ed. W. P. Ker (2 vols.; Oxford: Clarendon Press, 1900), I, 186.

3 "Sublimity," says "Longinus", "is the echo of a great soul" ("On the Sublime", I, *Longinus on the Sublime*, trans. W. R. Roberts, Cambridge: Cambridge University Press, 1899, p. 43). "Of the five sources of sublimity two are constituents of the soul, while the other three are the verbal means of expressing the first two: There are, it may be said, five principal sources of elevated language. . . . First and most important is the power of forming great conceptions. . . . Secondly there is vehement and inspired passion. These two components of the sublime are for the most part innate. Those which remain are partly the product of art. The due formation of figures deals with two sorts of figures, the first those of thought and the second those of expression. Next there is noble diction, which in turn comprises choice of words, and use of metaphors, an elaboration of language. The fifth cause of elevation—one which is the fitting conclusion of all that have preceded it— is dignified and elevated composition" (*ibid.*, VIII, pp. 57-59). For a more detailed discussion of the place of "Longinus" in the poetic theory of the seventeenth and eighteenth centuries see K. G. Hamilton, *The Two Harmonies* (Oxford: Clarendon Press, 1963), pp. 180-83, and the bibliographical references listed therein.

the poet in a manner that has no parallel in the rhetorical approach to poetry of the tradition to which Dryden, almost always as a poet and fundamentally as a critic, essentially belongs.

Van Doren has rightly pointed to Dryden's failure to achieve or to understand the kind of poetic image associated with sublimity. As he says, the metaphor that Dryden brings forward from his own work to prove that he approximated the poetical image of "Longinus" is unfortunately a typically bad one:

Seraph and cherub, careless of their charge,
And wanton, in full ease now live at large:
Unguarded leave the passes of the sky,
And all dissolved in hallelujahs lie.

The image quoted is certainly not impressive, even though Dryden admits that he had some trouble finding it. It comes from his *State of Innocence and Fall of Man,* an opera composed in 1677 and not noted for its poetic qualities, which Dryden adapted from *Paradise Lost* after Milton had given him permission, as he said, to "tag his verses". Dryden himself reports one of his "well natur'd censors" as having remarked rather rudely that he had heard of "anchovies dissolved in sauce, but never of an angel dissolved in halle-lujahs": to which "mighty witticism" he scathingly retorted by pointing to the classical source of his image. This defence is itself significant, for it indicates something that is generally true of Dryden's imagery—the fact that it is often derivative, and not freshly struck out in the white heat of artistic creation. But his attempt at self-justification is also rather futile, and the dry common sense of his seventeenth century critic not inappropriate. Dryden never became skilled in producing that "willing suspension of disbelief" essential to the type of poetic image he thought he was producing here. His image does not generate the "transport" described by "Longinus" as the outcome of sublimity, and rational dissec-tion of it remains not only a possible but a natural reaction —with the unfortunate results indicated by his "well natur'd" critic.

But Van Doren is less justified when he takes the evidence of this obvious failure to use or understand the sublime image as "final proof that Dryden lacked discrimination in executing and judging figures of speech".[4] Dryden can and does use figurative language with considerable skill and discrimination, but rather in the service of that other type of imagery, also described by "Longinus" and classified by him as "rhetorical", whose aim he defines as "vivid description".[5] Despite his belief that he had mastered the poetic, transcendental type of image, Dryden's view of the nature of the imagination—the "image making" faculty—remains that of medieval and Renaissance faculty psychology, by which imagination is not able to be divorced from the reasoning intellect. "Imagination in a man, or reasonable creature," he says, "is supposed to participate of Reason", and even in imaginative writing the reason only plays at surrendering its control:

when that [imagination] governs, as it does in the belief of fiction, Reason is not destroyed, but misled or blinded. . . . Reason suffers itself to be so hoodwinked, that it may better enjoy the pleasures of the fiction: but it is never so wholly made captive, as to be drawn into a persuasion of those things which are most remote from possibility. . . . Fancy and Reason go hand in hand; the first cannot leave the last behind: and though Fancy, when it sees the wide gulf, would venture over, as the nimbler, yet it is withheld by Reason. . . .[6]

Imagination in a poet, he says, "is a faculty so wild and lawless, that like an high ranging spaniel, it must have clogs tied to it, lest it outrun the judgement".[7]

Man is essentially a "reasonable creature", and thus cannot make the surrender to the forces of imagination demanded of the poet who works through images and symbols, for to do so would be to surrender his nature as a man, the part of his being that raises him above the animals. Nor can this view of the imagination provide a basis for the unique, intuitive grasp of relationships or correspondences that is

4 Mark Van Doren, *John Dryden: A Study of his Poetry* (Bloomington, Indiana: Indiana University Press, 1946), p. 41.
5 ". . . you will be aware of the fact that an image has one purpose with the orators and another with the poets, and that the design of the poetical image is enthralment, of the rhetorical—vivid description" ("On the Sublime", XV, Roberts, *op. cit.*, pp. 83-84).
6 Dryden, "Defence of an 'Essay of Dramatic Poesy' ", Ker, *op. cit.*, I, 127-28.
7 Dryden, "Epistle Dedicatory to 'The Rival Ladies' ", *ibid.*, I, 8.

the essence of the sublime image. It serves rather to make of the imagination, and of the images the imagination produces, a means to an end: through the image the poet projects the idea convincingly, arrestingly, and in this projection the image is not made the focus of attention per se, but serves to embroider or enliven the thought without in any way lessening its immediacy or its definitiveness. The imagination, declared a contemporary of Dryden, "hath been bestow'd on man for the service of the understanding". And: "So often and whensoever the understanding is busied about anything the imagination also acts its part by presenting it with the image of the same thing or some other." The imagination, he says, using the image later echoed by Dryden, "always accompanies the understanding, as a Dog follows his master every where. . . ."[8]

Despite Dryden's own words, such a concept of the imagination is not likely to result in imagery that gives poetry "its very height and life"; imagery that of itself renders discourse poetic and without which it would no longer be poetry—which is what he seems to mean by the phrase in its context, and not simply that imagery helps add life, or liveliness, to the subject. It is a concept more likely to lead to the sort of ridicule Dryden himself suffered for years as a result of indulging in what would now be regarded as a mildly figurative line in his *Astrea Redux*, but which in his own time was seen as an offence against common sense:

An horrid Stillness first invades the ear.[9]

Martin Clifford used this line in 1687 to show that Dryden was frequently so concerned with the sound of his verse as to neglect the sense,[10] while twenty years after the line was

---

8 J(ohn) D(avies), trans., *Reflections upon Monsieur Des Carte's Discourse of a Method* . . . (London, 1655). For a more complete discussion, and also bibliographical references, concerning the fancy . . . wit . . . judgment set of notions so critical in Restoration poetry and criticism, see Hamilton, *op. cit.*, pp. 158-77.

9 *Astrea Redux. A Poem* (1660), line 7. Cf. Dylan Thomas's phrase from *A Refusal to Mourn the Death by Fire, of a Child in London*:
   Never until . . . . .
      . . . . . .
   . . . . all the humbling darkness
   Tells with silence the last light breaking.

10 Martin Clifford, *Notes upon Mr. Dryden's Poems in Four Letters* (London, 1687), p. 13.

written, a minor satirist, Alexander Ratcliffe, could still hope to raise a smile with the couplet:

Laureat, who was both learn'd and florid,
Was damned long since for silence horrid.[11]

And even Dr. Johnson, in his *Life of Dryden*, feels it necessary to attempt a justification of the line as not really being contrary to good sense.[12] In a poetry characterized by reasoned, orderly progression, this circumscribing of the imagination is most likely to result in a rhetorical use of imagery, serving to help transmit thought with "perspicuity", "energy", and "vividness", in the manner of the image from *Religio Laici* described earlier in this chapter as typical of Dryden, and it is here, as one part of the ornament that serves to make the poem's imitation more vital and delightful, rather than at the centre or essence of his poetry, that we should look for the contribution of imagery to Dryden's poetic achievement.

Dryden's use of imagery in his early poems was very much influenced by the decaying metaphysical tradition of the earlier part of the seventeenth century (the metaphysical tradition, that is, as it was to be seen in the work of poets like Cleveland), as well as by the young poet's self-conscious attempts to experiment with various kinds of poetry. This is especially apparent in his elegy *Upon the Death of Lord Hastings*, his earliest surviving poem, written while he was still a pupil at Westminster School. "Was there no milder way but the Small Pox", he asks concerning the death of Hastings:

The very Filth'ness of *Pandora*'s Box?
So many Spots, like nœves, our *Venus* soil?
One Jewel set off with so many a Foil?
Blisters with pride swell'd; which th'row's flesh did sprout
Like Rose-buds, stuck i' th' Lily-skin about.
Each little Pimple had a Tear in it,
To wail the fault its rising did commit:

11 Alexander Ratcliffe, *The Ramble, an anti-heroick poem* (London, 1682), p. 4.
12 Samuel Johnson, "Life of Dryden", in *Lives of the English Poets* (London, 1779), ed. G. Birkbeck Hill (3 vols.; Oxford: Clarendon Press, 1905), I, 334-35.

Who Rebel-like, with their own Lord at strife,
Thus made an Insurrection 'gainst his Life.
Or were these Gems sent to adorn his skin,
The Cab'net of a richer Soul within?[13]

Ruth Wallerstein has shown how both the kind and the extravagance of the imagery in this poem are related to Dryden's concept of the genre in which he was endeavouring to write;[14] though despite this it is plain that his lack of experience and poetic taste at this early stage of his career let him down. But leaving aside what he may have been trying to do, as well as the shockingly bad poetry of the result, a difference is apparent between the use of imagery here and the so-called typical image from *Religio Laici*. Unlike that image, the small pox image makes considerable progress within itself, much as we may wish it had not: it manages to get, for instance, from "Rose-buds" to "Insurrections", without returning from the figurative to the literal level. There is in this image, in fact, a good deal of the metaphysical poet's tendency to analyze and expand his imagery, focussing attention on the ramifications of the image itself rather than on its effectiveness in conveying or adorning an idea. Such imagery often gives the impression of probing the thought through the image, as if the image itself were a vehicle for exploration, although this is hardly true of the image from the Hastings poem.

The imagery of Dryden's *Annus Mirabilis* is even more profuse and varied, but as becomes an heroic poem it also tends more towards the straightforward Homeric simile, which is extended simply for the opportunity it offers for adornment. But here again, as with the metaphysical type of image, the result of this extension is to draw attention to the image, for what *it* has to offer, and away from the subject intended to be illuminated by it. These stanzas, describing the state of some of the British and Dutch ships after four days of battle, have certainly not the sheer badness of *Upon the Death of Lord Hastings*, but the kinship is none the less obvious:

13 *Upon the Death of Lord Hastings* (1649), lines 53-64.
14 See R. Wallerstein, *Studies in Seventeenth Century Poetic* (Wisconsin: Wisconsin University Press, 1950), pp. 115-42.

So have I seen some fearfull Hare maintain
  A Course, till tir 'd before the Dog she lay:
Who, stretch'd behind her, pants upon the plain,
  Past pow'r to kill as she to get away.

With his loll'd tongue he faintly licks his prey,
  His warm breath blows her flix up as she lies:
She, trembling, creeps upon the ground away,
  And looks back to him with beseeching eyes.[15]

> Later in his career, had Dryden used this image at all, he
> would have been content with the first two lines, or at most
> the first stanza: from this point onwards the image depends
> on development within itself, and not on a direct meta-
> phorical relationship to the state of the ships.
>
> In this earlier poetry, and particularly in *Annus Mirabilis*,
> Dryden sought to draw original imagery from a wide field.
> ". . . the proper wit of an Heroic or Historical poem," he
> tells us in the Preface to *Annus Mirabilis*, "I judge . . . chiefly
> to consist in the delightful imaging of persons, actions,
> passions, or things."[16] Thus references to many branches of
> natural philosophy, to both the old and the new science,
> abound, as do images drawn from classical poetry, especially
> Virgil's *Georgics*, while his use of nautical terms was an
> innovation that brought him a good deal of criticism. But
> his rather bungling attempts at the witty conceit in these
> early poems were evidence of his failure in the intuitive
> grasp of relationships that is the central faculty of the writer
> skilled in the creation of original imagery. In the *Religio
> Laici* image discussed earlier, it is the *type* of image rather
> than its effect per se that creates its "lowness". A parallel
> image from *Annus Mirabilis* illustrates Dryden's failure
> when he attempts to develop it in the manner of a witty
> conceit. Throughout the poem animal and insect imagery
> is used in a valiant attempt to be wittily original, and at the
> same time declamatory, but the result is often ludicrous
> rather than grandiloquent:

The wary *Dutch* this gathering storm foresaw,
  And durst not bide it on the *English* coast:
Behind their treach'rous shallows they withdraw,
  And their lay snares to catch the *British* Host.

15 *Annus Mirabilis*, lines 521-28.
16 Preface to *Annus Mirabilis*, Ker, *op. cit.*, I, 14.

So the false Spider, when her Nets are spread,
    Deep ambush'd in her silent den does lie:
And feels, far off, the trembling of her thread,
    Whose filmy cord should bind the strugling Fly.[17]

> The impression achieved here is not one of aptness, but of
> unintentional ingenuity, because Dryden has not yet found
> the "proper" context for the type of imagery at his disposal.
> The attempt to be original results only in idiosyncrasy,
> something that in his more mature verse Dryden generally
> learned to avoid. Much simpler, but more successful because
> it aims at a vivid but unspecific lowness, leaving the detail of
> meaning to the statement, is his description of the sects in
> *The Hind and the Panther*:

A slimy-born and sun-begotten Tribe:
Who, far from steeples and their sacred sound,
In fields their sullen conventicles found:
These gross, half animated lumps I leave;
Nor can I think what thoughts they can conceive.
But if they think at all, 'tis sure no high'r
Than matter, put in motion, may aspire.
Souls that can scarce ferment their mass of clay;
So drossy, so divisible are They,
As wou'd but serve pure bodies for allay:
Such souls as *Shards* produce, such beetle things
As onely buz to heav'n with ev'ning wings;
Strike in the dark, offending but by chance,
Such are the blind-fold blows of ignorance.
They know not beings, and but hate a name,
To them the *Hind* and *Panther* are the same.[18]

> Here there is no sense of ingenious striving for effect. Image
> shades into statement and back into image almost imper-
> ceptibly, the imagery serving only to colour and vivify the
> passage without defeating the purpose of the statement by
> dominating it. In his later work, the startling image, like the
> incongruous one, is most frequently used by Dryden for
> purposes of deflation, through its position in a context
> normally precise and unobtrusive.
>   In his mature work, too, though he resembles the meta-
> physical poets in that his images are normally explicit,

---

17 *Annus Mirabilis*, lines 717-20.
18 *The Hind and the Panther*, lines 311-24.

Dryden differs from them in that he usually avoids their habit of drawing logical but cluttering analogies between the idea and the image. His imagery[19] tends rather to be a sudden projection into the analytical and logical development of the poem's argument, presented as an undeveloped metaphor rather than as the more logical simile.[20] One image from *Absalom and Achitophel* that does have some of the "witty" quality of the typical metaphysical image (of Donne's analogy, for instance, between the parted lovers and the legs of a pair of compasses in *A Valediction: Forbidding Mourning*) is contained in these lines:

Mistaken Men, and Patriots in their Hearts;
Not Wicked, but Seduc'd by Impious Arts.
By these the Springs of Property were bent,
And wound so high, they Crack'd the Government.[21]

The meaning of this image has to do with the Whig party's playing on the fears of the property owners that Charles, and particularly his brother James if and when he became King,

---

19 The editors of the California edition of Dryden would apparently not agree with all that I have said on the subject of Dryden's imagery. Commenting on the imagery of *Annus Mirabilis*, they write: "Dryden's mind was rich and curious, and as a gifted poet he was aware of the multiple implications in word or image. Even in 1666 he was exploring the unexpected capacity (or shall we say ambiguity?) of imagery. For example the figure in lines 91-92 is accepted by Van Doren as suitably heroic; but Dryden was at the same time using the figure as a pleasantry in *Secret Love*. Again, the simile in stanza 59 strikes Van Doren as a ridiculous illustration to set against the dignity of the first two lines; but Dryden was using the sober image of the lofty Belgian ships as part of the roisterous comedy of *Secret Love*" (E. N. Hooker and H. T. Swedenborg Jr., *et al.*, eds., *The Works of John Dryden*, California: University of California Press, 1954, I, 266-67). I am inclined rather to agree with Van Doren: in *Annus Mirabilis* these images remain simply heroic, and in the case of stanza 59 rather ridiculous as well. The fact that Dryden can also use them for comic purposes is, I think, rather an indication of their superficiality than of any ambiguous quality: because they are so much "on the surface" they will fit equally well into widely different contexts; and Dryden's use of them in these different contexts is rather an indication of his tendency to repeat imagery than of any deep realization of its potentiality for multiple implications.

20 Ernest Tuveson, in an article on Pope's *Essay on Man*, has noticed this quality in the images of *Religio Laici* and attributed it to the underlying thesis of the poem that reason is inadequate in matters of faith, in consequence of which the logically developed image would be out of place—by contrast with Pope who makes use of the more sustained type of metaphor. It is true that *Religio Laici* has this type of imagery, but it is perhaps too typical of Dryden's use of imagery elsewhere to be anything more than a happy coincidence that in this poem his poetic method and his immediate needs should have been so well suited. (See Tuveson, "An Essay on Man" and "The Way of Ideas", *ELH*, XXVI (1959), 368-86.)

21 *Absalom and Achitophel*, lines 497-500.

intended to interfere with property rights. It is a vividly expressive image, and one that is more concrete and original than most of Dryden's imagery in this particular poem, or in any other poem written in what might be described as his more successful style. But compared with Donne's compass image it remains undeveloped, and much of its effectiveness comes from the mimetic sound effect of the climactic "Crack'd the Government". As an image it is again no more than a momentary injection of figurative vividness into the discursive movement of the narrative.

The value of this type of imagery in poetry that is itself discursive in nature, demanding primarily a logical, analytical response from the reader, is that its force lies in its tonal significance, in its appeal to the emotions rather than to the intellectual faculty of reason. A logically developed image, on the other hand, would attract attention to itself in a way that would impose an extra strain on the reader's intellectual comprehension. And, in addition, an analytic image in such a context would add to, rather than alleviate, the prosaic quality of the verse; as happens in this passage from Dryden's *Threnodia Augustalis*, describing the elation of the Duke of York as his brother King Charles rallied temporarily from what was to be a fatal illness:

His manly heart, whose Noble pride
Was still above
Dissembled hate or varnisht Love,
Its more than common transport cou'd not hide;
But like an *Eagre* rode in triumph o're the tide.
Thus, in alternate Course,
The Tyrant passions, hope and fear,
Did in extreams appear,
And flasht upon the Soul with equal force.
Thus, at half Ebb, a rowling Sea
Returns and wins upon the shoar;
The watry Herd, affrighted at the roar,
Rest on their Fins a while, and stay,
Then backward take their wondring way:
The Prophet wonders more than they,
At Prodigies but rarely seen before,
And cries a *King* must fall, or Kingdoms change their sway.[22]

22 *Threnodia Augustalis: A Funeral-Pindarique Poem* (1685), lines 130-46.

This is a dreadfully dull poem, and the imagery, elaborate as it is, does nothing to alleviate the dullness. It simply transfers the discursive, analytical movement from the structural statement to the image: Dryden has even to add a learned footnote to tell us what an *Eagre* is, as he had seen it on the River Trent, a fortunately rare attempt by him to develop imagery based on his own observation of nature. Dr. Johnson, whose judgment of the *Threnodia* was that it was "not among his happiest productions", also noticed this weakness of the imagery, particularly when Dryden tried to develop it: "He seems to look around him for images which he cannot find, and what he has he distorts by endeavouring to enlarge them."[23] And for comparison, take these lines from *The Medall*:

God try'd us once; our Rebel-fathers fought;
He glutted 'em with all the pow'r they sought:
Till, master'd by their own usurping Brave,
The free-born Subject sunk into a Slave,
We loathe our Manna, and we long for Quails;
Ah, what is man, when his own wish prevails!
How rash, how swift to plunge himself in ill.[24]

Here the statement remains generally on the literal level; and neither latent nor explicit figurative elements interrupt the argument, but they do lend it some life.

Dryden's preference for the compressed metaphor, where the image and the direct meaning coalesce, rather than for the logically developed simile, should not be wrongly interpreted: the fact that his best imagery is imaginative rather than logical in its way of working must be kept within the context of the limited role given to imagery in his poetry. Metaphor has often been considered the essence of the suprarational, or purely imaginative in poetry; the means by which the poet expresses in a single perception something that has multiple and inexhaustible implications. Thus William Empson takes a single line from a Shakespearian sonnet:

Bare ruined choirs, where late the sweet birds sang,

and draws a chain of implicit relationships contained within

23 Johnson, "Life of Dryden", Hill, *op. cit.*, I, 438.
24 *The Medall*, lines 127-33.

the "simple" expression.[25] Many of Shakespeare's metaphors are of this type: though they take effect instantaneously, their figurative quality is suggested or concealed, the images being melted into the language. They are, in fact, the kind of poetical images that apparently Dryden would have liked to think he could write, although significantly he protested against the over-figurative quality of Shakespeare's language, against his obscuring of expression through metaphor.

Dryden's tendency to use strong, active verbs itself has a leaning towards imagery, or latent imagery, and here, too, the image itself is unobtrusive, because it has become melted into the language of common speech. But its use by the poet is not necessarily indicative of any extraordinary perception or originality. Metaphors can become so closely ingrained into the common language that we pass over them without recognizing them as such, though these submerged metaphors, even when used to make a direct statement, may be made to colour it with the subtlety and expressiveness of an implied comparison. Dryden's poetry is rich in this type of expression. For instance, this line from *MacFlecknoe* where he is describing the school for actors:

Where unfledg'd Actors learn to laugh and cry,[26]

and this one from the portrait of *Achitophel*:

To that unfeather'd, two Leg'd thing, a Son,[27]

both contain latent bird images that serve to enliven the verse though they may virtually escape notice. Yet it could be idle to suppose that such relatively moribund and dead metaphors repay close analysis; that they are meant to be "revived" in the verse. It may be tempting to declare that the verbs in these two lines from *The Medall*:

The free-born Subject sunk into a Slave,[28]

and:

How rash, how swift to plunge himself in ill,[29]

25 See W. Empson, *Seven Types of Ambiguity* (London: Chatto & Windus, 1947), p. 2.
26 *MacFlecknoe*, line 76.
27 *Absalom and Achitophel*, line 170.
28 *The Medall*, line 130.
29 *Ibid.*, line 133.

have an integral and meaningful connexion with other
strands of water imagery in the poem. But in reading the
energetic sweep of the verse, while the words do appear
vividly expressive and their repetition has some cumulative
effect, we are scarcely conscious of any depth of figurative
implication. For a similar reason, the shift away from personification in these lines from the opening paragraph of
Religio Laici is barely perceptible.

So pale grows *Reason* at *Religions* sight
So *dyes*, and so *dissolves* in *Supernatural Light*.[30]

Logically the verbs "*dyes*" and "*dissolves*" clash, but the
figurative element is so muted as to render the illogicality
scarcely noticeable. The latent image colours the verse, but
does not demand or repay close analysis.

Dryden's typical metaphors certainly lack Shakespeare's
wealth of implication: they do not really expand or deepen
what is being said. The basic statement is merely embellished
by imagery, and from the resultant metaphor the figurative
element in the language can at will be extracted, leaving the
meaning more or less intact. Dryden's verse is paraphrasable,
not because his imagery is logically developed, but because
in stating the basic meaning it can virtually be dispensed
with. If it may be said that poetry either vivifies (or relieves)
its statements through imagery, or thinks in images, then
Dryden's does the former, Shakespeare's the latter. Dryden
would tend to use the irrational metaphor because he
bestowed little thought on its development into a simile:
Shakespeare would exploit the indefinable richness of metaphorical language because the relationships he wished to
express were, by their very nature, elusive and inexhaustible.

An image from *The Medall* will serve to reiterate some
of what has been said thus far about Dryden's use of imagery,
and will also indicate the subordinate role that purely visual
imagery can play in relation to the auditory potentialities
of his lines:

30 *Religio Laici*, lines 10-11.

But this new *Jehu* spurs the hot mouth'd horse;
Instructs the Beast to know his native force;
To take the Bit between his teeth and fly
To the next headlong Steep of Anarchy.[31]

> Much of Dryden's imagery is derivative rather than original,
> and very likely the use of the Biblical allusion here as a
> poetic image is not his own invention—he uses it again later
> in very much the same way in these lines from *The Hind
> and the Panther*:

Or like wild horses sev'ral ways have whirl'd
The tortur'd Text about the Christian World;
Each *Jehu* lashing on with furious force,
That *Turk* or *Jew* cou'd not have used it worse.[32]

> In *The Medall* the image occurs in a rather dull patch of
> political moralizing, and it serves to give life to its tediously
> abstract argument. The effect again is not one of visual
> elaboration, where the details of the image become the focus
> of attention, but rather one that gives vivid expression to a
> general notion of disaster and destruction. The figurative
> language adorns the concept expressed, but never itself be-
> comes truly sensuous. Thought and image are fused in a
> metaphorical way rather than being linked logically: the
> abstract is not related to the concrete but is identified with
> it, as in:

To the next headlong Steep of Anarchy.

> The image is thus very similar in function and form to that
> discussed previously from *Religio Laici*. Where suggestive-
> ness enters the lines, it does so through the sound and move-
> ment of the verse rather than from the allusive or associative
> qualities of the image itself. If the image vitalizes the
> thought, it is the rhythm, the mimetic sound pattern, that
> animates the image. The effect is auditory rather than imagi-
> natively extensive in a visual or concrete way. It is the
> rhythm that images the "headlong rush", gathering momen-
> tum because of the absence of caesuras, the enjambment of
> the second couplet, and the alliteration of the third line,
> where the rapidity and closeness of the metronomic beat

31 *The Medall*, lines 119-22.
32 *The Hind and the Panther*, II, lines 118-21.

combine with the repeated t sounds to give a "galloping"
quality to the line:

To take the Bit between his teeth and fly.

In this relationship between explicit meaning and expressive sound the figurative quality of the image plays a strictly
subordinate role, the stronger emotional overtones coming
from the rhythm and not from the poet's perception of the
image. Such a use of imagery may be contrasted with that of
a poet like Donne, who relies heavily on the potentiality of
the image itself, and very little on the resources of sound,
to reinforce the figurative quality of his language.

This is not to belittle Dryden's use of imagery, but merely
to illustrate the strictly organic role it generally plays in his
poetry. The image is made to form part of a meaningful
whole in which the direct statement, and also the rhythm or
pattern of sound, are frequently more important elements.
This can happen even when Dryden uses imagery that is
more than usually precise and concrete—in these lines, from
The Medall, a sensitive use of alliterative echo and of heavy
polysyllables claim an attention for themselves that is largely
independent of the image:

And, like white Witches, mischievously good;
To his first byass, longingly he leans.[33]

Here the image of the white witches who aim at good ends
by mischievous and devious means is taken up in a second
image of the bowl that uses its bias to reach the white ball by
a circuitous route thereby circumventing the obstacles presented by the bowls already on the green: Shaftesbury is
equally devious, although his aim is to achieve greatness by
evil means. The image is a reasonably good one, though not
altogether logically realized—the element of *contrast* between the image and Shaftesbury seems to have been overlooked. But the lines are striking because of their expressive
sound. Alliteration and soft consonants in the first line give
it a "whispering" or fleeting quality appropriate to its image.
Liquid sounds after the caesura in the second line combine
with the strong stress on the first syllable of "longingly" to

33 *The Medall*, lines 62-63.

impart to it a heavily clinging movement that gives an emotional quality to the image and is indeed its dominant element. Compare the strength of this with a line that makes a similar use of "bias" and "leans", but without the assistance of "longingly":

But, when to Sin our byast Nature leans;[34]

and similarly "longingly" can be much less influential in a less carefully structured line:

Nor did his Eyes less longingly behold.[35]

　　To return to the original lines from *The Medall*, the sound pattern invests both lines with a strongly figurative quality in which the complicated image plays only a subordinate role. Maynard Mack is right when he points to the way in which the strict heroic couplet can concentrate and subdue imagery. But Dryden masters this rigidity of form rather than is mastered by it, making the sound and movement of his verse operate in a positive way to give vitality and meaningfulness to his expression. The strong formal pattern compresses thought and imagery in one way, but adds to it in another: while it limits the associative quality of the image by denying it latitude for loose expansion, it adds suggestiveness beyond the image's mere literal content through its reverberations of sound.

　　When Dryden's imagery lacks this expressiveness of sound it rarely impresses in standing alone. Even in poems like *Annus Mirabilis* where there is a greater striving for pictorial imagery, the images that succeed best are those mainly notable for their expressive sound. Compare, for instance, the "hound and hare" image quoted earlier, in which sound is virtually a neutral element, with this one:

The wild waves master'd him, and suck'd him in,
　And smiling Eddies dimpled on the Main.[36]

But the role of sound in its relation to Dryden's imagery is perhaps to be seen most clearly if the two portraits of Shaftesbury, the one from *Absalom and Achitophel* and the

34 *Absalom and Achitophel*, line 79.
35 *Aeneid*, Bk. 9, line 487.
36 *Annus Mirabilis*, lines 375-76.

other from *The Medall*, are placed side by side. Both employ imagery widely, but the latter uses "lower", more crudely robust images (in the manner of Butler's *Hudibras*), while the former, except in the direct and cruel couplet about Shaftesbury's son, uses a more dignified and impersonal type of image, in keeping with Dryden's professed ideal of the nature of satire. This excerpt begins the Shaftesbury portrait from *The Medall*:

A Martial Heroe first, with early care,
Blown, like a Pigmee by the Winds, to war.
A beardless Chief, a Rebel, e'r a Man:
(So young his hatred to his Prince began.)
Next this, (How wildly will Ambition steer!)
A Vermin, wriggling in th'Usurper's Ear.
Bart'ring his venal wit for sums of gold
He cast himself into the Saint-like mould;
Groan'd, sigh'd and pray'd, while Godliness was gain;
The lowdest Bagpipe of the squeaking Train.[37]

The cluster of five or more independent images in these lines approaches theoretically the notion of a collocation of images produced by free association, sometimes thought of as a necessary quality of poetic expression. But here the free association obviously does not produce poetry. The lines have at best a certain vitality, but their directly abusive quality, their lack of restraint, makes them inferior, both as satire and as poetry, to the finesse of the other portrait from *Absalom and Achitophel*. And the imagery in these lines from *The Medall* has almost to stand alone: it does not adorn a basic literal meaning, but rather attempts to express its meaning through direct description. It is not easy to extract a non-figurative meaning. The lines are not of the kind that can be easily paraphrased in the manner of the first image discussed from *Religio Laici*. Most of all, Dryden does not in this passage really exploit the sound resources of his verse: an effect of harshness or "ruggedness" is the most that is achieved.

By contrast the opening sentence of the *Achitophel* portrait in *Absalom and Achitophel*, contains only a single image, that in the final three lines:

37 *The Medall*, lines 26-35.

Of these the false *Achitophel* was first
A Name to all succeeding Ages Curst.
For close Designs, and crooked Counsels fit;
Sagacious, Bold, and Turbulent of wit:
Restless, unfixt in Principles and Place;
In Power unpleas'd, impatient of Disgrace.
A fiery Soul, which working out its way,
Fretted the Pigmy Body to decay:
And o'r inform'd the Tenement of Clay.[38]

These lines are strongly expressive of the restless, turbulent
power of Shaftesbury, that Dryden saw as his chief menace
to the State, and, as was suggested in an earlier chapter, it
is the fierce rhythmical energy that carries the strongest
reflection of this power. In the final three lines that contain
the image, the broken but unbridled surge of movement
finally forces itself out of the metrical bonds into the extra
line, and the figurative quality of the rhythm becomes at
least as important as any visual quality. The passage is
satirical: its purpose is to attack Shaftesbury. But it is also
in a way a magnificent tribute to Shaftesbury's power. It is
satire that works by enhancing its victim, by showing him as
a worthy opponent, someone whose strength makes it all the
more necessary he should be subdued; and it is satire that
seeks to gain by giving the appearance of fairness, of an
ability to see the good as well as the bad, the strengths as
well as the weaknesses of its victim. Whereas in *The Medall*
Dryden hurls everything he can lay hand to into the attack,
in *Absalom and Achitophel* he concentrates on the theme of
rebellion and the restless ambition that lies behind it. The
major burden of his satiric purpose is carried by the statement, reinforced by the imaginative quality of the rhythm.
The image in these lines gives indirection and distance to
the attack. Because Dryden seeks to turn the greatness, the
power, of Shaftesbury to his own advantage, it is important
that he give dignity and importance to his victim, and the
image serves partly towards a more "elevated" tone. Rather
than being simply colourful or vivid, its appeal is to a strongly
intellectual background: "Pigmy" is, or was, a learned word
of Greek origin, and in the context of the relationship of
the body and the soul, the notion of "inform'd" is reminiscent

38 *Absalom and Achitophel*, lines 150-58.

of Aristotelianism, while the "Tenement of Clay" was a conventional and highly respectable description of the body. Without this elevating effect of the image to flavour it, the crude vigour of the rhythm would lose some of its complex satiric power.

It is clear that Dryden succeeds in his attack on Shaftesbury in *Absalom and Achitophel* partly because of his control of imagery. The imagery is not allowed to gain ascendancy, but has rather a subdued and indirect role in the total meaning of the passage. When the imagery does become more central, more directly structural in his poetry, as it does in the portrait from *The Medall*, Dryden is less satisfactory than when his images are strongly yoked to a non-figurative meaning and developed as part of the development of that meaning. His best imagery is an organic feature of his verse, but it is seldom directly expressive, simply as imagery. Significantly, *Absalom and Achitophel*, though it is an heroic poem, contains no genuinely heroic simile. The images never seem to have been elaborated for their own sake. When Dryden does attempt this kind of simile—in *Annus Mirabilis*, for instance—his efforts are usually more heroic than the results. Indeed an important part of Dryden's poetic progress from his elegy *Upon the Death of Lord Hastings* through *Annus Mirabilis* to *Absalom and Achitophel* and *Religio Laici* (and also an important part of the development of his poetry of statement), is a movement away from a central dependence on imagery to a strictly subordinate use of it. This is not a progress that is uniformly sustained, but deviations from it, even though they do not always go as far as "angels dissolved in hallelujahs", are generally unfortunate.

The *Achitophel* portrait comes within the bounds of the poetry of statement because rhythm and, more indirectly and to a lesser extent, imagery, serve only to give an added flavour and intensity to the statement. Dryden does, however, particularly in his lighter satire, use an evaluative kind of image, where the figure can be said to adjust the sense rather than merely to adorn it. There is what might be called the "inverted" image, for instance, that is evaluative by being

wittily deflating. Here the power of the imagery depends on
its incongruity or inappropriateness. It is in fact parallel to
the witty deflation produced by simple verbal juxtaposition
that was noticed earlier in this study, and relies on a similarly
implicit—though obvious—incongruity in a context of overt
normality. A good example of such an image is provided by
this couplet from *MacFlecknoe*:

About thy boat the little Fishes throng,
As at the Morning Toast that Floats along.[39]

Here what at first might appear a descriptive image is, in
fact, a deflatingly evaluative one. Its power and its humour
lie in the outwardly bland identification of the inane Shadwell with the scraps of waste food or, more likely, floating
excrement,[40] pursued by a retinue of "little Fishes"; and in
this satiric process whatever concrete quality the image has
tends to be lost.

Dryden, as this last couplet shows, was at least occasion-
ally capable of producing the immediately vivid, concrete
image, but generally, as here, he was not interested in
developing it for this quality: except when, as happens in
some of the images from *Annus Mirabilis* or *Threnodia
Augustalis* noticed earlier, he has nothing else to do, and
then the result is generally disastrous. These lines from the
portrait of *Corah* in *Absalom and Achitophel* are unusual
for their use of direct descriptive detail:

Sunk were his Eyes, his Voyce was harsh and loud,
Sure signs he neither Cholerick was, nor Proud:
His long Chin prov'd his Wit; his Saintlike Grace
A Church Vermilion, and a *Moses's* Face.[41]

But here again the description and its accompanying images
are evaluative in a way that is abstract rather than concrete,
and dependent on an inversion of the actual statement. The
description itself is direct but mainly commonplace: sunken
eyes, loud voice, long chin; and the last line depicts *Corah*
as the priest of stage comedy, whose red-painted face is

39 *MacFlecknoe*, lines 49-50.
40 Pope, in his note to *Dunciad* A, Bk. II, lines 65-71, refers to these lines and
appears to equate the "Morning Toast" with "Corinna's Cates"—that is,
floating excrement from the sewers.
41 *Absalom and Achitophel*, lines 647-50.

ironically seen as shining like the face of Moses returning from Sinai. But this detail is presented less as an image than for the opportunity it offers for the empty cliches, the meaningless remarks about character, that help express the shallowness and hypocrisy seen by Dryden as surrounding Titus Oates, the original of *Corah*:

Erect thy self thou Monumental Brass.[42]

As with *Achitophel*'s physical deformity, the actual physical detail provided by the image tends to be overlooked.

In *MacFlecknoe* the evaluative type of image based on ironic inversion is sustained, and the accumulation exaggerates the mock-heroic tone:

In his sinister hand, instead of Ball,
He plac'd a mighty Mug of potent Ale;

. . . . . .

His Temples last with Poppies were o'erspread,
That nodding seem'd to consecrate his head:
Just at that point of time, if Fame not lye,
On his left hand twelve reverend *Owls* did fly.
So *Romulus*, 'tis sung, by *Tyber's Brook*,
Presage of Sway from twice six Vultures took.[43]

This is the kind of suggestiveness to be achieved by a bland inversion of values. It is simply illogical rather than alogically connotative. Imagery of this type serves as an indirectly ironical way of expressing absurdities, and it succeeds by at once recognizing and ignoring the Augustan ideals of clarity, precision, reason, and order. Dryden's comic wit differs from the typical metaphysical wit in that it achieves a nice balance of incongruous differences rather than building on neat and ingenious correspondences: it relies on surprising oppositions and not on startling reconciliations. Where the metaphysicals would tend to bind together dissimilar things by strenuous analogies, Dryden would use them for deflation by silent, but obviously ironical juxtaposition; and the unstrained, explicit, precise quality of his statement advertises this heterogeneity in a way that more vague or nebulous verse

42 *Ibid.*, line 637.
43 *MacFlecknoe*, lines 120-21 and 126-31.

would not. Passages like those we have been looking at still have the characteristics of the poetry of statement, but their satiric purpose leads to what is rather "inverted" statement.

The traditional, derivative, and repetitive nature of Dryden's imagery can mean that his verse is often thick with allusions, potentially rich in their power of reference. Yet in spite of this potential richness his poetry could not be said to rely on a referential and allusive quality for its total meaning, as does—to take an extreme example—such a poem as *The Waste Land*. Because the "Jehu" image from *The Medall* discussed earlier is primarily a framework for more dominant auditory effects, a recognition of its Biblical source is relatively unimportant. Even echoes from other poets tend to be self-contained in their implications:

Swift was the Race, but Short the Time to run,[44]

whether or not an echo of Chaucer is intended, is so elemental that it carries its own significance. And though the average seventeenth century reader of Dryden would have recognized the covert allusion to Cowley's *Davideis* in these lines from *MacFlecknoe*, Dryden's couplet contains its own adequate implications:

Where their vast Courts the Mother-Strumpets keep,
And, undisturb'd by Watch, in silence sleep.[45]

A knowledge of Cowley's epic would reinforce the power of mock heroic deflation here; but Dryden's own words, the elevated "vast Courts" and "in silence sleep", have enough specious dignity of their own to set against the intrusion of the "Mother-Strumpets" and the "Watch". The verse does not depend for its final significance on the doubtful factor of outside reference. It is self-contained, both semantically and atmospherically, and its allusiveness, though not an irrelevant quality, is not vitally important.[46]

44 *Absalom and Achitophel*, line 837.
45 *MacFlecknoe*, lines 72-73.
46 George Williamson (*The Proper Wit of Poetry*, London: Faber & Faber, 1961) has pointed to other similar allusions to Cowley in Dryden's work. In each case, however, the "wit" is essentially in Dryden's version itself, and virtually independent of any quality of allusion.

A rather similar situation, too, is provided by these lines from the section of *Religio Laici* dealing with the "opinions of the several sects of philosophers":

Thus, *anxious Thoughts* in *endless Circles* roul,
Without a *Centre* where to fix the *Soul*,[47]

which it has been suggested depend on a multiple irony involving

the fact that the pagan philosophers, seeking in their pride by purely natural means to fathom the great mystery of Deity, end up rolling in circles without a centre: an ironic mocking resemblance to the nature of God, whose centre, as Nicholas of Cusa says, is everywhere, and whose circumference is no where.

Dryden could certainly have intended this allusion to Nicholas of Cusa, but again the self-contained quality of the verse—the very effectiveness of *"anxious Thoughts"* and *"endless Circles"* to express the first part of this interpretation—inhibits the effectiveness of any deeper allusiveness. It has already been suggested in another connexion that Dryden's verse is not often of the sort that can allow for richness and complexity in more than one direction at a time.[48] This must, I think, be taken as one of the characteristics—or limitations—of the poetry of statement. It would seem, for example, something of a contradiction to speak in terms like Eliot's of the "satisfying completeness" of Dryden's statement and at the same time put any strong emphasis on its quality of allusiveness.

Where Dryden does use images dependent on allusion, the allusion is generally more important for the structure of the poem than for the enrichment of the image itself. Such allusive images resemble his use of "charged" words, in that, within the context of the particular poem, they depend on repercussions *beyond* themselves, rather than on reverberations *within* themselves. For instance, the many images in *Absalom and Achitophel* depending on allusion to *Paradise Lost* and to the Bible are not simply incidental. The rebels are clearly identified with the fallen angels, and this makes their fall from grace all the more significant:

47 *Religio Laici*, lines 36-37.
48 See above, pp. 71-74.

Some had in Courts been Great, and thrown from thence,
Like Fiends, were harden'd in Impenitence.[49]

Similarly it is not accidental that the part played by *Achitophel* in helping to tempt the people to rebellion should be associated with a tree:

Disdain'd the Golden fruit to gather free,
And lent the Croud his Arm to shake the Tree.[50]

These Miltonic and Biblical echoes have their significance in the allegorical framework of the poem. They provide an imaginative background of reference by which to evaluate the events. But this evaluation depends as much or more on a strong structure of ideas within the poem as it does on the quality of the images and allusions themselves. The discursive argument remains the essence of the poem, whose appreciation depends primarily on an intellectual understanding of Dryden's statement of his political and social beliefs, which the images serve to embellish rather than to express.

It would in fact be possible to trace repetitive structures in the actual framework of Dryden's own imagery, but such a study would be mechanical rather than illuminating; except for the unobtrusive structuring effect achieved by the repetition of latent images within individual poems. D. W. Jefferson has traced the metaphysical element in Dryden's imagery (using the term "metaphysical" in its ontological sense rather than in the "extra-natural" sense intended by Dr. Johnson in his references to the poetry of the earlier seventeenth century).[51] But significantly Jefferson concentrates his attention on a pattern of motifs in which he examines the philosophical subject matter rather than the figurative framework of expression: for example, Dryden is found to use repeatedly imagery concerned with matter, the body, and the soul. The emphasis is on the strong intellectual content of the basic idea, and not on the figurative skill or imaginative perception of the image—in images like this one from *Annus Mirabilis*:

(Vast bulks which little souls but ill supply.),[52]

---

49 *Absalom and Achitophel*, lines 144-45.
50 *Ibid.*, lines 202-3.
51 D. W. Jefferson, "Aspects of Dryden's Imagery", *EC*, IV (1954), 20-41.
52 *Annus Mirabilis*, line 280.

which has some of the same weightiness of intellectual content we have noticed in the *Achitophel* portrait, and where
the interest is less on the figure than on the *idea* it introduces.

But whether or not there is any such underlying intellectual pattern in his imagery, Dryden does not, I think, enrich
his expression simply through the repeated use of images, in
the manner of poets like T. S. Eliot or Yeats, but rather
seems to repeat them from sheer expediency. For example,
cramped development is several times expressed in terms of
retarded plant growth:

The *wiser Madmen* did for *Vertue* toyl:
A Thorny, or at best a barren soil.[53]

Michal, of Royal blood, the Crown did wear,
A Soyl ungratefull to the Tiller's care.[54]

Or, had the rankness of the Soyl been freed
From Cockle, that opprest the Noble seed.[55]

Such images do not illuminate each other. Their repetitive
quality serves as a guide for the poet in his composition,
rather than as an aid for the reader in his appreciation. They
are merely indicative of the repetitive nature of much of
Dryden's imagery. He is not indeed beyond repeating the
same image without so much as a change of wording. The
line:

Drawn to the dregs of a Democracy,

occurs both in *Absalom and Achitophel* and in *The Hind
and the Panther*,[56] and it was not even original to Dryden
in the first place. Apparently he remembered it from Marchmont Needham's contribution to the memorial volume to
Hastings, which begins:

It is decreed we must be drain'd (I see)
Down to the dregs of a Democracie.

53 *Religio Laici*, lines 31-32.
54 *Absalom and Achitophel*, lines 12-13.
55 *Ibid.*, lines 194-95. The image here, of course, is not simply one of retarded
growth, but of healthy growth impeded by a too vigorous growth of
poisonous plants. The reference is probably to Matthew 13:24ff, the Parable
of the Tares.
56 Lines 227 and 211 respectively.

Although it must be conceded that Dryden made better use of the image, it gains nothing for his poetry from its mere repetition.

The images of retarded plant growth quoted in the preceding paragraph probably owe their origin to the Bible, and certainly they are traditional rather than original. Many of Dryden's images are similarly embedded in tradition, so that they might be said to absorb their traditional associations. The use of the oak to symbolize monarchy, grandeur, and permanence; of the circle to indicate perfection; of light to represent spiritual illumination; of palms to signify victory; and of laurels to convey the notion of prestige in poetry: these are so grounded in convention that Dryden can employ them with perfect ease, avoiding any effects of eccentricity or extravagance. Animal images in his poetry have their prototype in classical satire, and as we have seen at the beginning of this chapter their use provided Dryden with a convenient type of image to give a tone of "lowness" to his verse. Dryden, in fact, helped to inaugurate the neo-classical habit of employing certain types of images for certain themes, and of using stereotyped means of description. Such images suited his poetry of statement admirably, because they could play their part in giving it an imaginative richness, without drawing an undue amount of attention away from the statement.

Probably the most sustained and deliberate use of imagery in any of Dryden's poetry is in the Pindaric ode *To the Memory of Mrs. Anne Killigrew*. This poem, too, is certainly as uneven in quality as anything Dryden ever wrote, and a comparison of the splendidly successful first stanza with the almost equally flat and unsuccessful sixth stanza will provide an opportunity to bring together and reiterate some of the more important points of this discussion of his use of imagery. In the first stanza of the poem Dryden has avoided altogether the predilection for an inert, fustian type of image, such as characterized earlier poems like *Annus Mirabilis* and the *Heroique Stanza's* on Oliver Cromwell—images that added nothing vital by way of either embellishment or suggestion, being simply tacked on to the statement, like this one from the *Heroique Stanza's*:

And made to battails such Heroick haste,
As if on wings of victory he flew.[57]

Instead the stanza is beautifully sustained both rhythmically and syntactically. Its first fifteen lines form one complete, unbroken sentence, and imagery takes its place within this enveloping framework:

Thou Youngest Virgin-Daughter of the Skies,
Made in the last Promotion of the Blest;
Whose Palmes, new pluckt from Paradise,
In spreading Branches more sublimely rise,
Rich with Immortal Green above the rest:
Whether, adopted to some Neighbouring Star,
Thou rol'st above us, in thy wand'ring Race,
    Or, in Procession fixt and regular,
    Mov'd with the Heavens Majestick Pace;
    Or, call'd to more Superiour Bliss,
Thou tread'st, with Seraphims, the vast Abyss:
What ever happy Region is thy place,
Cease thy Celestial Song a little space;
(Thou wilt have Time enough for Hymns Divine,
    Since Heav'ns Eternal Year is thine.)
Hear then a Mortal Muse thy Praise rehearse,
        In no ignoble Verse;
But such as thy own voice did practise here,
When thy first Fruits of Poesie were giv'n;
To make thy self a welcome Inmate there:
    While yet a young Probationer,
        And Candidate of Heav'n.[58]

The figures employed here are not startlingly intrusive, and they do not absorb attention at the expense of the total design of the stanza. Some individual words and phrases are "conceited" ("Promotion", "adopted to", "Inmate", "Probationer", "Candidate"), but the conceits are unobtrusive rather than extravagantly elaborated. Through compression

57 *Heroique Stanza's, Consecrated to the Glorious Memory of his most Serene and Renowned Highnesse Oliver, Late Lord Protector of this Commonwealth,* (1659), lines 51-52.
58 *To the Pious Memory of the Accomplisht Young Lady Mrs. Anne Killigrew, Excellent in the two Sister-Arts of Poesie and Painting. An Ode* (1686), lines 1-22.

Dryden manages to avoid the effects of idiosyncrasy which such expressions would be likely to gain in more flamboyantly metaphysical verse. Though the concept itself may be extravagant, the degree of elaboration contained in its expression is restrained. Similarly, in these lines, the central image of the stanza is stated without being unduly or ostentatiously elaborated:

Whose Palmes, new pluckt from Paradise,
In spreading Branches more sublimely rise,
Rich with Immortal Green above the rest:

The image here achieves "decorum", in that it exploits a traditional association between "palms" and "victory", and in being confined to only three lines of verse. Also restrained is the image that follows, with its reference to Anne Killigrew's "Star", which anticipates the star imagery of the ninth stanza of the poem.

In this opening stanza of *To the Memory of Mrs. Anne Killigrew* Dryden has employed figurative expression as a means of embellishing his statement. But it is a statement that is controlled, made coherent and complete, not by the embellishing imagery, but by syntax and rhythm. Despite the richness of its imagery, the perfection of the stanza is essentially a perfection of statement, not of imagery. And in keeping with this subsidiary role, the images are themselves lacking in amplification, though they serve to amplify the thought. Dryden does not here elaborate on his means of elaboration. And this is in accord with the neoclassical tendency to use certain *types* of imagery, rather than degrees of elaboration, in order to amplify or "illustrate" the subject matter. Dryden usually succeeds best when he adheres to this neoclassical precept. In stanza six of the ode he deviates from it, using the conceit in a more self-conscious fashion, thereby allowing it to become intrinsically extravagant:

Born to the Spacious Empire of the *Nine*,
One would have thought, she should have been content
To manage well that Mighty Government:
But what can young ambitious Souls confine?
    To the next Realm she stretcht her Sway,
        For *Painture* neer adjoyning lay,
A plenteous Province, and alluring Prey.

A *Chamber of Dependences* was fram'd,
(As Conquerors will never want Pretence,
   When arm'd, to justifie the Offence)
And the whole Fief, in right of Poetry she claim'd.
The Country open lay without Defence:
For Poets frequent In-rodes there had made,
   And perfectly could represent
The Shape, the Face, with ev'ry Lineament;
And all the large Demains which the *Dumb-sister* sway'd,
   All bow'd beneath her Government,
   Receiv'd in Triumph wheresoe're she went.[59]

> Here there is none of the perfection of statement, none of
> the overriding control of rhythm and syntax that articulates
> the opening stanza of the poem. Instead articulation is
> attempted through a more sustained type of imagery. In these
> lines Dryden is not using the figure as a means of embellish-
> ment, but rather is embellishing it as an end in itself. By
> contrast with the first stanza he *does* "elaborate on his means
> of elaboration". The image becomes the organic structure
> of the stanza. Where in the earlier stanza images had been
> briefly employed and then submerged under the enveloping
> control of the beautifully modulated rhythm, here attention
> is focussed on the quality of the image itself, on the means
> of amplifying the statement rather than on the statement
> itself. The image fails, becomes as mediocre as Anne Killi-
> grew's poetry and painting in fact were, because Dryden is
> not often skilled in handling the heroically sustained image,
> or the image which by continued elaboration attempts not
> to adorn but to take the place of discursive statement. And
> it fails, too, because the need to sustain a greater degree of
> elaboration leads Dryden away from his dependence on the
> use of certain traditional types of images for certain themes,
> into an attempt to develop witty and original correspon-
> dences in the manner of the metaphysical poets.
>
> *To the Memory of Mrs. Anne Killigrew* is obviously not
> a poem of statement in the manner that *Religio Laici* is. It
> is of an entirely different poetic "kind", and Dryden would
> probably have had a clearer realization of this difference
> than most twentieth century critics, for whom the concept of
> the poetic genre is a less lively issue. But a study of this
> poem will reveal that, though Dryden does not necessarily

59 *Ibid.*, lines 85-105.

set out to write poems of statement, his genius as a poet, irrespective of the form in which he is writing, is seen at its best when he preserves the relationship between poetic expression and discursive statement that is seen most clearly in poems like *Religio Laici*. Thus even in a poem such as this Pindaric ode, where the need for continuous elevation imposed by his concept of the genre makes a heavy demand on imagery, Dryden succeeds only when his images are muted, controlled, subordinated to other more continuous and powerful elements in the poetry.

And, indeed, any discussion of Dryden's use of imagery will inevitably be of a rather negative nature, because the attempt to exalt its function in the total poetic meaning is doomed to failure: just as, to take the other side of the picture, criticism based on the failure of Dryden's imagery to perform basic functions in his verse it is not intended to perform (its failure, for instance, to give the poetry a concrete, sensuous quality), however justified it may be in itself, is likely to be irrelevant or inadequate for a full appreciation of his achievement in the poetry of statement.

A more just estimate of the role given to imagery by Dryden at his best is achieved by placing "Longinus's" claim that a figure is always more effective "when it conceals the very fact of its being a figure" alongside Van Doren's remark about the imagery of *Religio Laici*: "Metaphors unobtrusively clinch a point before the reader is aware advantage is being taken of him." Van Doren's observation is made in passing, but it deserves greater emphasis than he gives it: it points to the fact that images in Dryden's poetry are often not obvious, but are rather something taken up for the moment as a means of vitalizing thought, effective without being obtrusive as images: that they combine with the statement to manifest meaning with such clarity and immediacy that attention is directed away from their figurative quality towards this meaning. This oratorical type of image is not only the most common in Dryden's mature poetry, but also the most successful, because it is best suited to the needs of the poetry of statement. Its purpose and its effect is to give an imaginative quality to an essentially rational statement, and not to transcend the statement or to transform it into the expression of a purely imaginative apprehension of its subject.

Finally, to clinch this matter of the relative importance of imagery in Dryden's poetry, we might look at this couplet from his contribution to *The Second Part of Absalom and Achitophel*. The reference is to the unfortunate Shadwell, or *Og*, as he appears in the poem:

A Double Noose thou on thy Neck dost pull,
For Writing Treason, and for Writing dull.[60]

The first line is figurative and quite innocuous. The second line is superb—pure vintage Dryden—and nothing could state more directly or precisely exactly what it means; or be further from the flat or prosaic.

60 *The Second Part of Absalom and Achitophel*, lines 496-97.

chapter five

Amplification

Chaucer, according to Dryden, "wanted the modern art of fortifying".[1] It is not unexpected that an "Augustan" age should think of the writers of the past as "barbarous", no matter how highly they may have rated their genius. But none of Dryden's historical criticism, not even his criticisms of Shakespeare, is more likely to damn him in twentieth century eyes than his failure to appreciate the quality of simplicity in the work of Chaucer. But what was it he thought to be lacking in Chaucer, and what are the implications of his attitude to Chaucer for his own poetic method?

If we wish to be severe with Dryden, we can do as A. E. Housman has done, and seek to find an answer to these questions by comparing Dryden's version of Chaucer's *Tales* with their originals. We can, for instance, see Chaucer's:

The smiler with the knife under the cloke,

become in Dryden's version:

Next stood Hypocrisy, with Holy leer;
Soft smiling and demurely looking down,
But hid the dagger underneath the Gown.[2]

Housman's criticism of passages like this one is certainly

1 Dryden, "Preface to 'Fables, Ancient and Modern'" (1700), *Essays of John Dryden*, ed. W. P. Ker (2 vols.; Oxford: Clarendon Press, 1900), II, 256.
2 See A. E. Housman, *The Name and Nature of Poetry* (Cambridge: Cambridge University Press, 1933), pp. 24-25. Dryden's lines are from Bk. II of *Palamon and Arcite: or, The Knightes Tale*.

justified. But the implication that all "amplification" in poetry is automatically bad is more open to question: it overlooks the fact, for instance, that Chaucer's own verse, like almost all medieval poetry was amplified, in accordance with the precepts of such medieval arts of poetry as the *Nova Poetria* of Geoffrey of Vinsauf, and that the difference between Chaucer's lines and Dryden's is the difference between good and bad amplification. Despite Housman, amplification remains a poetic method that has produced some fine poetry, and one that is virtually essential to a poetry that seeks to be an art of enriched or adorned statement. "No subject matter is prescribed [for poetry]," declared one Renaissance writer on poetic theory, "unless perhaps in general it should be what can be adorned in the treatment."[3]

Amplification is, however, essentially a poetic method belonging to the rhetorical tradition of poetry, and as such is largely unfamiliar and often uncongenial to the twentieth century reader; as it obviously is to Housman. C. S. Lewis has referred to this difficulty arising from a lack of sympathy with the rhetorical tradition in his history of sixteenth century English literature:

While Tudor education differed by its humanism from that of the Middle Ages, it differed far more from ours. Law and rhetoric were the chief sources of the difference. . . . In rhetoric, more than in anything else, the continuity of the old European tradition was embodied. Older than the Church, older than Roman Law, older than all Latin literature, it descends from the age of the Greek Sophists. Like the Church and the law it survives the fall of the empire, rides the *renascentia* and the Reformation like waves, and penetrates far into the eighteenth century. . . . Nearly all our older poetry was written and read by men to whom the distinction between poetry and rhetoric, in its modern form, would have been meaningless. The "beauties" which they chiefly regarded in every composition were those which we either dislike or simply do not notice. This change of taste makes an invisible wall between us and them . . . we must reconcile ourselves to the fact that of the praise and censure which we allot to medieval and Elizabethan poets only the smallest part would have seemed relevant to those poets themselves.[4]

3 R. Kelso (trans.), "Girolamo Fracastoro Navgerius, sive de poetica dialogvs", *Univ. of Ill. St. in Lang. & Lit.*, IX (1924), No. 3, p. 58.
4 C. S. Lewis, *English Literature in the Sixteenth Century Excluding Drama* (Oxford: Clarendon Press, 1954), pp. 60-61.

What Lewis says here remains equally true for the neo-classical literary tradition and for Dryden. And an illustration of the result of this lack of sympathy for the rhetorical attitude, as it affects an appreciation of Dryden, might be provided from Mark Van Doren's study of his poetry:

The distinction made by Longinus between true sublimity and "amplification" reflects directly upon Dryden and scarcely to his credit: "The sublime is often conveyed in a single thought, but amplification can only subsist with a certain prolixity and diffuseness." Dryden spent energy on both his figures and his heroic declarations; but the effect is one of words rather than things.[5]

The particular words of the *Treatise on the Sublime*, here given a strongly derogatory flavour by Van Doren's translation as "a certain prolixity and diffuseness" are rendered by a classical scholar with perhaps less of an axe to grind as "a certain magnitude and abundance".[6] Also, although "Longinus" does associate sublimity with intensity, as distinct from amplification, he does not necessarily associate intensity with poetry and amplification with oratory. This is a much later development, perhaps as late as the nineteenth century. In medieval and Renaissance times, and at least until the early eighteenth century, rhetorical amplification continued to be closely associated with poetry; and, although at times it degenerated into a complicated means of rendering expression more luxuriant and profuse, it continued to be thought of as the primary means of achieving poetic elevation.

Dryden thus inherited a long continuing tradition that invested verse with a deliberately poetical quality by means of the art of formal eloquence. Amplification, defined by Thomas Wilson in his *Arte of Rhetorique* (1553) as "a figure in Rhetorique which consisteth most in augmenting, and diminishing of any matter, in divers ways", was a conscious device which sought (to use the definition provided by the OED), "the extension of simple statement by all such devices as tend to increase its rhetorical effect, or to add importance

5 Mark Van Doren, *John Dryden: A Study of His Poetry* (Bloomington, Indiana: Indiana University Press, 1946), p. 41.
6 W. Rhys Roberts (trans.), *"Longinus" on the Sublime* (Cambridge: Cambridge University Press, 1899), sec. VII, p. 77.

to the thing stated". The thought was to be "illustrated",
that is to say rendered illustrious, by formal embellishment.

It is certainly true that this amplification could become
simply a diffusely prolix addition to the statement of the
verse, and that in Dryden's case many of his attempts to be
grandiloquently "poetical" can be dismissed as mere verbiage.
But there is another view of amplification: a view expressed
for us by the sixteenth century Italian literary theorist
Girolamo Fracastoro, to whom the art of ornamentation is
something much closer to the imaginative expression of
experience than would be required for the merely extrinsic
adornment of the subject matter: "But when I think of
simply beautiful language I wish to be understood in this
way: that this beauty harmonizes with the subject under
discussion and is appropriate to it and its different attributes,
and is not merely beautiful in and for itself".[7] The ornaments of poetry are for Fracastoro the very life and truth of
the subject matter with which the poet deals:

For if you mean [by ornaments] whatever is added to the bare
object, certainly it will be enough to use ordinary speech in
explaining things, for the other refinements of style are not necessary. And similarly, if columns and peristyles and other things
are added to houses, they will be extraneous, for the barest structure will serve the purpose of a house, which is to protect us from
cold and storm. But, indeed, if we consider objects as they should
be, and look for perfection, these additions will not only not be
extraneous but essential. Or ought we to think splendid garments
extraneous because poor ones are sufficient. Do you not see that
just as perfection and ornament are a real part of the things which
nature produces, so they are of the things which art produces?
What perfection and beauty are, only the greatest artists know;
and if you take them away from the subject, assuredly you have
somehow taken away life itself. Therefore what the painters and
the poets add to things for perfection is not extraneous, if we
mean by "thing" not the bare object such as common artificers,
or those who are controlled and restricted by some purpose make,
but the object perfected and given life.[8]

Fracastoro belongs to the same rhetorical tradition of
poetry as does Dryden, and his words are quoted here, not
so much as those of an individual critic, but as providing a

7 Kelso, op. cit., p. 64.
8 Ibid., p. 68.

representative expression of the possibilities offered by the view of poetry belonging to this tradition. For it is the neglect of these possibilities that is most likely to be harmful to an appreciation of Dryden. It is true that, as Van Doren says, Dryden's more obvious attempts at verbal decoration often do become ludicrous, and that he is generally more satisfying when he writes more plainly. Yet Van Doren neglects to consider the possibility that Dryden's very "plain-ness" is frequently more apparent than real: that it is often a stylized bareness that uses rhetorical figures in a concealed or unobtrusive manner. And there is also a danger in the summary dismissal of even Dryden's more obviously elevated vein. While his verse can be consistently more appealing when it gives the appearance of plainness, an antipathy for its consciously poetic elements can lead to a neglect of things that are genuinely worth while.

Fallacious, too, is the treatment of amplification as a device related to the poet, rather than as something integrally connected with the subject matter; and Van Doren and A. E. Housman could both be accused of failing to realize this in their criticism of Dryden. What is quite within the bounds of propriety as the illustration of the subject of a poem may indeed be verbiage if it is thought of in terms of the expression of an attitude towards the subject. But the seventeenth century does not seem to have been particularly interested in the poet himself, or in his attitudes and emotions as such. Its interest was in the poet's ability to create delightful imitations of nature, and amplification demanded not a "state of mind" in the poet, but rather an "illustrious" subject matter—a subject matter that required and could sustain formal embellishment. The fact that Dryden's verse is not lyrical should not prompt the judgment that it should be so, or that it fails when its treatment of the subject is not lyrical. Poetry as "the expression of a fine personality" does not belong to the rhetorical tradition, and "fine writing" to Dryden would rather be the "expression of an important subject", its art being that of relating embellished treatment to illustrious objects. Amplification should not be confused with lyricism or a state of mind in the poet: its consideration should be centred on the subject matter and on the poetical treatment of that subject matter.

In his own critical writings Dryden showed that he fully realized the basic need to integrate treatment and subject matter. Copiousness and elaboration were to be applied in strict accordance with the demands of sense: "Thus in poetry the expression is that which charms the reader, and beautifies the design, which is only the outlines of the fable. 'Tis true the design must of itself be good; if it be vicious, or, in one word, unpleasing, the cost of the colouring is thrown away upon it."[9] Ornament could not thus, of itself, make the poem. "Expression" and "colouring" are useless unless the design of the poem is itself pleasing. And, too, Dryden obviously realized the dangers of overwrought treatment. "Some parts of the poem," he says, "require to be amply written, and with all the force and elegance of words; others must be cast into shadows, that is passed over in silence, or but faintly touched."[10]

Theoretically Dryden would avoid indiscriminate copiousness: that type of expression which can be dismissed as mere prolixity. Amplification ideally demanded a suitable design and was to be executed only in strict accordance with that design. Propriety and decorum were to be observed at all times, and this leads to an attack on the indulgence in epigrammatic wit simply for its own sake:

'Tis not the jerk and sting of an epigram, nor the seeming contradiction of a poor antithesis (the delight of an ill-judging audience in a play of rhyme), nor the jingle of a more poor paronomasia; neither is it so much the morality of a grave sentence, affected by Lucan, but more sparingly used by Virgil; but it is some lively and apt description, dressed in such colours of speech, that it sets before your eyes the absent object, as perfectly, and more delightfully than nature.[11]

And again, in the Preface to the *Fables* he declared that the "thoughts remain to be considered; and they are to be measured only by their propriety; that is, as they flow more or less naturally from the persons described, on such and such occasions".[12] But none the less he clearly reveals his allegiance to the idea of poetry as an art of ornamentation:

9 Dryden, *A Parallel of Poetry and Painting* (1695), Ker, *op. cit.*, II, 148.
10 *Ibid.*, p. 151.
11 Dryden, "Preface to 'Annus Mirabilis' ", *ibid.*, I, 14-15.
12 Dryden, "Preface to the 'Fables Ancient and Modern' ", *ibid.*, II, 256.

'Tis true, that to imitate well is a poet's work; but to affect the
soul, and excite the passions, and, above all, to move admiration
(which is the delight of serious plays), a bare imitation will not
serve. The converse, therefore, which a poet is to imitate, must
be heightened with all the arts and ornaments of poesy; and must
be such as, strictly considered, could never be supposed spoken
by any without premeditation.[13]

The "art of fortifying" is thus basic to Dryden's poetic
method and inspiration. At one extreme it is responsible for
the extraordinarily extravagant and startling imagery of the
elegy *Upon the Death of Lord Hastings* where the whole
work positively exudes the Renaissance ideal of a poem as an
art object that is to be given richness and elevation by continuous ornament: although it should be remembered that
the splendour of the first stanza of *To the Memory of Mrs.
Anne Killigrew* also belongs to this end of the scale. But at
the opposite end of the scale, where Dryden may seem to be
writing most plainly, where his design seems least contrived,
there can still be unobtrusive amplification. While Dryden's
characteristic statement in this plain style lacks the compression and organization that gives a more formal stylization
to Pope's couplets, his ease and artlessness can be more
apparent than real. A certain element of stylization seems
essential to the rhetorical pattern of neoclassical wit, where
the poet follows a "pattern of thought", rather than allowing the sense to develop naturally.[14] Often the colloquialness
for which Dryden has been praised (and which Housman
said was his "true vein") actually emerges only in single
words and isolated phrases, flavouring the verse without
dominating the essentially stylized expression. In the portrait
of *Zimri*, for instance, in *Absalom and Achitophel*, it has
been seen how the first ten lines serve loosely to elaborate
the one quality of *Zimri*'s "variousness", though syntactically
the lines are tightly knit, and linguistically the expression
has a colloquial vitality. The passage was found on analysis
to be disciplined and stylized, even amplified, concealing
the lack of matter under an artificially contrived manner

13 Dryden, "Defence of an 'Essay of Dramatic Poesy'", *ibid.*, I, 113-14.
14 George Williamson has examined the strength of this tendency in "The
Rhetorical Pattern of Neo-classical Wit", *MP*, XXXIII (1935), 55-81.

that imaged the emptiness of *Zimri* himself, though the artifice remains unobtrusive, so that the surface impression is simply one of condensation and haste.

Instances of this submerged type of amplification can be multiplied: Dryden is often tenuous in meaning where his expression appears deceptively compact. Without adopting a stiffly formal rigidity he can none the less loosely elaborate his verse, and the result has been accepted by Van Doren and Housman as "plain". The art becomes concealed and the effect is one of artlessness. The rhetorical doublet in this line from *Absalom and Achitophel*, for example, is made barely perceptible by the unifying texture of the line, and the expression could be termed vital and plain:

As ever tried th'extent and stretch of grace.[15]

Similarly this parallel construction from the portrait of *Barzillai* in the same poem might appear neatly compressed:

Oh Narrow Circle, but of Pow'r Divine,
Scanted in Space, but perfect in thy Line![16]

The phrase "Scanted in Space" is, after the "Narrow" of the first line, strictly unnecessary. The antithetical construction is most prone to this type of amplification, and in Dryden's usage the style carries the addition so easily as to be almost unnoticed. The following couplet from *Absalom and Achitophel* has a typically colloquial ease:

Not weigh'd, or winnow'd by the Multitude;
But swallow'd in the Mass, unchew'd and Crude.[17]

Yet the sense is not closely developed, and the logical progression in the second line is negligible.

In the beautifully restrained elegy *To the Memory of Mr. Oldham* there seems scarcely an unnecessary word either semantically or structurally, yet this effect is not one achieved

15 *Absalom and Achitophel*, line 46.
16 *Ibid.*, lines 837-38.
17 *Ibid.*, lines 112-13.

by concentrating wholly on simplicity and economy. A number of the key words in the following lines are strictly repetitive, and the idea they elaborate is varied in expression rather than expanded in meaning:

For sure our Souls were *near ally'd*; and thine
Cast in the *same* Poetick mould with mine.
One *common* Note on either Lyre did strike,
And Knaves and Fools we *both* abhorr'd *alike*:
To the *same* Goal did *both* our Studies drive,[18] &c.

The effect is muted, and the repetition becomes emphatic rather than monotonous or merely irritating, a tribute to Dryden's apparent unselfconscious simplicity of expression. Indeed it would seem that only verse that has this apparent extreme simplicity can unobtrusively carry such repetition. Compare with Dryden's, for example, these lines from Wordsworth's *The Solitary Reaper*:

Behold her, *single* in the field,
Yon *solitary* Highland lass!
Reaping and singing *by herself*
. . . . .
Alone she sits . . .

In lines like these the repetitions, far from adding diffuseness, seem to add to the concision and completeness of the statement.

Another way of amplifying unobtrusively is by parallel figurative expression, as in these couplets from the portrait of *Achitophel*, where the second line is simply an adorned repetition of the first:

Great Wits are sure to Madness near ally'd;
And thin Partitions do their Bounds divide:[19]

or:

But wilde Ambition loves to slide, not stand;
And Fortunes Ice prefers to Vertues Land.[20]

The artistic tact of this sort of amplification becomes apparent if it is compared with many of the quatrains of *Annus*

18 *To the Memory of Mr. Oldham* (1684), lines 3-7. My italics here.
19 *Absalom and Achitophel*, lines 163-64.
20 *Ibid.*, lines 198-99.

Mirabilis where the last two lines also serve to adorn the first two, but in a much more obvious manner:

On high-rais'd Decks the haughty *Belgians* ride,
  Beneath whose shade our humble Fregats go:
Such port the *Elephant* bears, and so defi'd
  By the *Rhinocero's* her unequal foe.[21]

In these lines from *Religio Laici* logical development is virtually non-existent when Dryden employs for purposes of amplification another rhetorical device—*interpretatio*—by which different ways of saying the same thing are presented:

How can the *less* the *Greater* comprehend?
Or *finite Reason* reach *Infinity*?
For what cou'd *Fathom* GOD were *more* than *He*.[22]

Here each line presents a new facet of the same idea in the typical manner of the balanced co-ordinate sentence. The lines serve as a static climax to a long verse paragraph, and amplification gives the expression the required emphasis; but, like the other examples, this passage demonstrates Dryden's ability to amplify or stylize his statement while yet retaining a quality of conciseness and plainness. Though the expression could be said to follow a pattern of thought, rather than the strict sense, it has not the feeling of discipline or repetitiveness.

There can be this element of stylization in even the most apparently unadorned and tersely expressed couplet. The following two lines from *Absalom and Achitophel* contain no obvious figures, no parallelism or antithesis, no imagery or "fanciful" diction:

Whose differing Parties he could wisely Joyn,
For several Ends, to serve the same Design.[23]

Yet stylization enters here through an unobtrusive but none the less careful use of balance: "differing Parties" is closely linked with "several Ends" in meaning, and "differing" and "several" serve to counterbalance the contrasting word "same"; while "wisely Joyn" also has its place in the pattern

21 *Annus Mirabilis*, lines 233-36.
22 *Religio Laici*, lines 39-41.
23 *Absalom and Achitophel*, lines 493-94.

by continuing the form of the adjective-noun series that gives a quadrilateral shapeliness and symmetry to the couplet. But despite this stylization of expression the meaning of the couplet could not be described as loosely repetitive. The sense is tersely expressed, yet to classify this terseness merely as plain is to ignore the careful discipline of the lines.

Another form of stylized amplification is to be found in the series of adjectives that Dryden often inserts into his lines without their becoming a particularly noticeable feature of them. He is more frequently remembered for his vitally energetic verbs rather than for his adjectives, but the latter can be an important element in the harmony of his verse. In the lines *To the Memory of Mr. Oldham*, for example, a pattern of noun-adjective combinations reticulates quietly through the elegy: "common Note", "either Lyre", "early ripe", "maturing time", "abundant store", "advancing Age", "harsh cadence", "rugged line", "dull sweets". These adjectives are appropriate and usually expressive enough, but certainly are not deep or sensuous in the manner of epithets used by Keats or Hopkins. The adjective-noun combination has been suggested as the most effective unitary phrase in verbal rhythm,[24] and here they lend themselves to the smooth harmony of the verse and to the "satisfying completeness" of its statement.

The unobtrusive kind of amplification illustrated by these various passages is of great importance in the poetry of statement. It helps give the expression the dignity and elevation it needs as poetry, helps raise it above the level of common speech, without noticeably interfering with its character as direct statement. And such amplification, too, by expanding the statement makes room within its structure for the rhythmic and figurative elements necessary for the development of the poem's imaginative dimension. Yet for all this, amplification did mean for Dryden a more consciously poetic style of embellishment, and not simply a means of expanding in a closely disciplined way a restrained and tersely organized mode of expression. A distinctively poetic style of amplification appears intermittently throughout Dryden's work, sometimes to its advantage though not infrequently to its detriment.

---

24 See Morris Croll, "The Cadence of English Oratorical Prose", *SP*, XVI (1919), 1-55.

Amplification of this kind is particularly to the fore in poems such as *To the Memory of Mrs. Anne Killigrew* and the *Aeneid*, where Dryden's concept of the genre in which he was writing demanded continuous elaboration and ornamentation. In *To the Memory of Mrs. Anne Killigrew* the idea of the Pindaric ode as a form to be developed in an elevated manner is combined with the demands of epideictic oratory, the oratory of display, which among other things sought by rhetorical amplification to add lustre to what was already of itself illustrious. The result was for Dr. Johnson "the noblest ode our language has produced", and the poem does undoubtedly achieve the formal metrical beauty that Dryden was striving for: the varied cadences, the "ordered irregularity" of the Pindaric form, are in some stanzas managed with perfect artifice. Yet the rhythm never takes fire from within as it does in the portrait of *Achitophel*, nor lends significance to changing patterns of mental experience, as it does in *Religio Laici*. The perfection of the ode, when indeed it does achieve perfection, is a purely external and formal one. In literal prose meaning the poem adds up to very little. It is the *treatment* of the illustrious subject, not the content of the statement, that provides the fabric of expression.

In these circumstances, where amplification becomes not so much embellishment as the very stuff of which the poetry is made, success depends on the poet's ability to integrate the ornament into some sort of organic unity. We have seen in the previous chapter how in *To the Memory of Mrs. Anne Killigrew* Dryden both succeeds and fails in his attempts to use imagery as a primary means of ornament: succeeds when the imagery is articulated by means of a finely controlled rhythmic and syntactical development, into which it becomes merged, and fails when the attempt is made to provide articulated structure through the sustained development of the image itself. But amplification can also be achieved without imagery, by means of the elaboration of the thought itself.

In the portrait of *Achitophel* we saw how Dryden employed the philosophic notion of Aristotle's *forms* in these lines:

A fiery Soul, which working out its way,
Fretted the Pigmy Body to decay:
And o'r inform'd the Tenement of Clay.

In stanza two of *To the Memory of Mrs. Anne Killigrew* a rather similar concept is elaborated:

But if thy Præxisting Soul
Was form'd, at first, with Myriads more,
It did through all the Mighty Poets roul,
    Who *Greek* or *Latine* Laurels wore,
And was that *Sappho* last, which once it was before.
    If so, then cease thy flight, O Heav'n-born Mind!
Thou hast no Dross to purge from thy Rich Ore:
    Nor can thy Soul a fairer Mansion find,
    Than was the Beauteous Frame she left behind:
Return, to fill or mend the Quire, of thy Celestial kind.[25]

These lines contain a philosophical idea rather than an image. Though certain words, such as "Mansion", contain latent images, Dryden's concern here is an intellectual rather than an imaginative or figurative one. The ornamentation is not inertly diffuse, but dynamically meaningful. Dryden states elaborately, in terms of Platonic philosophy, that Anne Killigrew comes of poetic stock by reincarnation from Sappho, that she is too pure to suffer further reincarnation, and that when she has ceased listening to the poem that is now addressed to her she must return to the host of heavenly singers. Because of the wealth of intellectual interest here, amplification becomes not only justifiable but necessary. The idea is not statically or superficially elaborated, but is elaborately developed. The comparison with the lines from the portrait of *Achitophel* is profitable, because where these are merely descriptive, using the philosophic concept as an instrument for achieving elevation while the forward movement of the lines is ensured by other means, in the lines to Anne Killigrew the philosophic idea itself becomes a means of progression. The thought is itself elaborately stated, and the elaboration is not something decoratively overlaid.

Unfortunately Dryden could not always sustain, either within this ode itself or elsewhere, these ideals of figurative restraint and dynamically developed thought that in the first two stanzas of the ode allow him to achieve his purpose of maintaining continuous elevation and adornment without losing control. Above all he is seldom successful when he attempts to make poetry from nothing, or from nothing

25 *To the Memory of Mrs. Anne Killigrew*, lines 29-38.

more than a general idea of epic elevation: as he tries to do throughout his *Eleonora*, a poem composed, as Van Doren put it, "for a fat fee", in honour of the late Eleonora, Countess of Abingdon, and obviously modelled on Donne's *Anniversaries*. Dryden wrote in his dedicatory letter to the poem:

Doctor Donne, the greatest wit, 'tho not the greatest poet of our nation, acknowledges, that he had never seen Mrs. Drury, whom he has made immortal in his admirable *Anniversaries*. I have had the same fortune, tho' I have not succeeded to the same genius. However, I have follow'd his footsteps in the design of his panegyric: which was to raise an emulation in the living, to copy out the example of the dead.[26]

What Dryden apparently did not realize was that although Donne had not known Elizabeth Drury he did have something to say about other things—about the decay of the world and the state of man's soul in it. In writing *Eleanora* Dryden had nothing to say, and he tries to raise a poetic structure with no basis at all. Although he calls it a "pane-gyrical poem", *Eleonora* has not even the sense of form given by the concept of the Pindaric ode to lend it the support that *To the Memory of Mrs. Anne Killigrew* has. The poem consists of a continuous series of hyperboles and conceits, that never get off the ground because there is no basic foundation or framework on which they can be raised up: no underlying strength of statement, no dynamically organized syntactical progression such as articulated the images of the first stanza of *To the Memory of Mrs. Anne Killigrew*, no elaborate development of thought. Here is a random sample of the result, probably Dryden's dullest poem, though Dr. Johnson apparently thought it had some merit.

> Now, as all Vertues keep the middle line,
> Yet somewhat more to one extreme incline,
> Such was her Soul, abhorring Avarice,
> Bounteous, but, almost bounteous to a Vice:
> Had she giv'n more, it had Profusion been,
> And turn'd th' excess of Goodness, into Sin.
>   These Vertues rais'd her Fabrick to the Sky;
> For that which is next Heav'n, is Charity.

26 Dryden, "Dedicatory letter prefixed to 'Eleonora'", *The Poems of John Dryden*, ed. J. Kinsley (4 vols.; Oxford: Clarendon Press, 1958), II, 583.

But, as high Turrets, for their Ay'ry steep
Require Foundations, in proportion deep:
And lofty Cedars, as far, upward shoot,
As to the neather Heav'n they drive the root;
So low did her secure Foundation lye,
She was not humble, but Humility.[27]

The same fate befell Dryden's attempts at embellishment
in his translations—other than his translations from the
classical satirists, where his undoubted vein for satire mainly
kept him out of danger by keeping him occupied—and it is
here that his efforts towards amplification have met with the
least praise. Any discussion of Dryden's translations is difficult because they are translations, and consequently owe
something both to their originals and to their author's theory
of translation. Dryden's theory of translation, though it
tended to vary as between the translation of classical and
medieval authors, was generally that of paraphrase, where
"the author is kept in view by the translator, so as never to
be lost, but his words are not so strictly followed as his sense;
and that too is admitted to be amplified, but not altered".[28]
The general results of this method are summarized by Frost
in his study of Dryden's art of translation, when he says that
he

allowed the European cultural tradition to serve as a matrix for
his own creation; consulted the desires and expectations of late
seventeenth-century readers; treated the literal sense of his authors
with such liberties "as no Dutch commentator will forgive me";
and always kept one eye on the more "untranslatable" aspects of
his originals, the other on the esthetic requirements of his own
new-minted poetry.[29]

Dryden's translations, therefore, can to a large extent be
safely treated as original poems; and this certainly applies
to what is our immediate concern—amplification—which, as
Dryden himself said, was to be regarded as a legitimate function of the translator.

In translating both Virgil and Chaucer Dryden seems
frequently to have found himself in much the same position

27 *Eleonora: A Panegyrical Poem* (1692), lines 82-95.
28 Dryden, "Preface to the translation of 'Ovid's Epistles'" (1680), Ker, *op. cit.*,
I, 237.
29 William Frost, *Dryden and the Art of Translation* (New Haven: Yale University Press, 1955), p. 58.

as he was in with *Eleonora*, with nothing in his original that he could grasp as a basis for his own poetry; and this, combined with his attitude to translation, meant that he was under constant temptation to expand his material. Master as he was of the unobtrusively stylized statement, Dryden showed little skill in that type of delicate, almost evanescent suggestiveness captured by both Virgil and Chaucer in much of their poetry. Though he speaks in the Dedication of the *Aeneis*, referring to Virgil, of "the sober retrenchments of his sense, which always leave somewhat to gratify our imagination, on which it may enlarge at pleasure",[30] he himself lacked this talent. He could render plain statement poetically, but not understatement. Effects that in his original were no more than suggested become in Dryden's version irritatingly obvious. For instance, Mary Hill, after painstakingly tracing an Ovidian pattern of rhetorical balance in Chaucer, is forced to admit to the nebulous quality of her findings. "No two persons," she says, "would agree exactly as to the passages to be included in an assemblage of balanced passages in Chaucer's poetry, and the same person might not always hold the same opinion in regard to a particular passage...."[31] Such elusiveness is not characteristic of Dryden's mode of expression. Though he praised Chaucer for his representation of the death of *Arcite*, and criticized Ovid for the "false wit" he would have used on such an occasion, when he himself comes to render this particular passage from *The Knightes Tale* he is apparently unable to avoid such stylized elaborations as:

.... but I lose my Breath
Near Bliss, and yet not bless'd before my Death.[32]

Because the real nature of this intangible element in his original eludes him, more often than not in Dryden's version it becomes mere embroidery, and his failures are the more frequent because the means he employs are usually mechanical rather than carefully considered. By the time he came to write the *Fables* he was an old man with many years of

30 Dryden, "Dedication of the 'Aeneis' ", Ker. *op. cit.*, II, 223.
31 Mary A. Hill, "Rhetorical Balance in Chaucer's Poetry", *PMLA*, XLII (1927), 846-47.
32 *Palamon and Arcite: or, The Knightes Tale, From Chaucer. In Three Books* (1700), Bk. III, lines 798-99.

writing behind him, and by his own confession he wrote with great facility. Versification had become a habit with him. And similarly in the *Aeneid* he appears often to be more absorbed with the technique than with the matter. Thus amplification easily became the "prolixity and diffuseness" which Van Doren identifies it with. And the worst excesses occur when he loosely elaborates his imagery without making it organic to the statement it embellishes (as it is in the first stanza of *To the Memory of Mrs. Anne Killigrew*), or when there is nothing progressive in the expanded expression of the thought (as there is in stanza two of the same poem). When either of these situations occurs the embellishment fails to harmonize with other elements of the verse, and becomes as a result an overwrought excrescence.

Such amplification as the expansion noted by Van Doren of the one word "huntyng" in Chaucer's *Knightes Tale* into four lines of pictorial imagery in Dryden's *Palamon and Arcite* would tend to confirm the common opinion that Dryden "coarsened" Chaucer:

A Sylvan Scene with various Greens was drawn,
Shades on the Sides, and on the midst a Lawn:
The Silver *Cynthia*, with her Nymphs around,
Pursu'd the flying Deer, the Woods with Horns resound.[33]

Here the verse lapses, somewhat irritatingly, into a conventional piece of Augustan description that is strongly reminiscent of the meretricious scene painted at the end of stanza six of *To the Memory of Mrs. Anne Killigrew*, as well as of hundreds of similar descriptions in neoclassical verse. The figurative language is inanimately laid on from without. Certainly it is traditional, and thus avoids any effect of idiosyncrasy; but it is *too* conventional, and so becomes devitalized. The means of decorating the verse through imagery become mechanical rather than carefully controlled.

But Dryden does not always fail in this kind of amplified description. Of his rendering of Boccaccio's tale of *Theodore and Honoria*, for instance, Van Doren says that the story "whirls on without an interruption or a couplet out of place. The effect is single; Dryden nowhere stops merely to heap up words or to paint an impossible, unnecessary scene";[34] and

33 *Ibid.*, Bk. II, lines 619-22.
34 Van Doren, *op. cit.*, p. 231.

this is despite the fact that one brief sentence from Boccaccio
can be amplified to this:

Alone he walk'd, to please his pensive Mind,
And sought the deepest Solitude to find:
'Twas in a Grove of spreading Pines he stray'd;
The Winds within the quivering Branches plaid,
And Dancing-Trees a mournful Musick made.
        . . . .
While list'ning to the murm'ring Leaves he stood,
More than a Mile immers'd within the Wood,
At once the Wind was laid; the whisp'ring sound
Was dumb; a rising Earthquake rock'd the Ground;
With deeper Brown the Grove was overspred:
A suddain Horror seiz'd his giddy Head,
And his Ears tinckled, and his Colour fled.
Nature was in alarm; some Danger nigh
Seem'd threaten'd, though unseen to mortal Eye.[35]

This is quite different from the inanimate piece of description amplified from Chaucer, but not because it is particularly original or imaginatively conceived simply as description. It succeeds because here the embellishment does not
have to stand alone, to articulate itself: it is caught up in, and
becomes part of an atmosphere of courtly romance and
supernatural horror pervading the whole story, and more
importantly, it becomes part of the narrative flow of the
verse. The directness and objectivity of Boccaccio's stories
enabled Dryden to transform them into something more to
his taste and something that he could get on with; and in
Theodore and Honoria he makes the heroic couplet a narrative instrument of great power and speed.[36]

35 *Theodore and Honoria, from Boccace* (1700), lines 76-80 and 88-96.
36 It is interesting to examine the manner in which Dryden has achieved
narrative speed and continuity in *Theodore and Honoria*, not so much in
spite of the limitations of the heroic couplet as by exploiting its narrative
potentialities. He does not, as might be expected, make wide use of run-on
lines. There is much more enjambment in the argumentative and meditative
passages of *Religio Laici*, and where run-on lines do occur in *Theodore and
Honoria* this tends to be in those parts where the forward movement of the
narrative is stilled for the moment. Instead, Dryden has made positive use
of what has been described as the "returning clink" of the heroic couplet,
which is generally accepted as having a fragmenting effect: but here the
weight of emphasis is generally in one way or another kept off the end of
the line, so that the rhymes are not obtrusive, but are still definite enough to
allow the narrative to "rattle along" over them with the same impression of
speed—to use the best illustration I can think of—as is achieved by a train
passing over regularly spaced gaps in the rails.

A similar power of statement is to be found in Dryden's translations of the Roman satirists, and particularly those of Juvenal. Satire was Dryden's bent, and the zest with which he carried out this work of translation was perhaps one of the main causes of his later reputation for immorality. "Mr. Dryden . . . ," wrote one of his co-translators in this project, "who distributed the work among us and gave it us to do, has reserved the sixth Satire for his own hand; and I can fully assure you, to his honour, that the original has lost none of its shamelessness through him."[37] However this may be, the work referred to here, the Sixth Satire of Juvenal, "a bitter invective against the fair sex", is certainly Dryden's most sustainedly powerful piece of translation, where all his tendency to elaboration is completely absorbed into the strength of his statement. The opening lines are not the strongest, but for this reason perhaps they are more open to quotation:

In *Saturn's* Reign, at Nature's Early Birth,
There was that Thing call'd Chastity on Earth;
When in a narrow Cave, their common shade,
The Sheep the Shepherds and their Gods were laid:
When Reeds and Leaves, and Hides of Beasts were spread
By Mountain Huswifes for their homely Bed,
And Mossy Pillows rais'd, for the rude Husband's head.
Unlike the Niceness of our Modern Dames
(Affected Nymphs with new Affected Names:)
The *Cynthia's* and the *Lesbia's* of our Years,
Who for a Sparrow's Death dissolve in Tears.
Those first unpolisht Matrons, Big and Bold,
Gave Suck to Infants of Gygantick Mold;
Rough as their Savage Lords who Rang'd the Wood,
And Fat with Akorns Belcht their windy Food.[38]

As Van Doren says, "the largeness of these lines is not specious". It is a largeness working through the very texture and movement of the lines. The triplet, for example, is a conventional means to elevation, but here it has a grandeur that is as strong and simple as the cavemen it depicts—its first

37 Letter of March 1693, Stepney to Leibnitz, in J. M. Kemble, *State Papers and Correspondence* (London: 1857), p. 121.
38 *The Sixth Satyr of Juvenal* (1693), lines 1-15.

line, for instance, with its succession of firm monosyllables, independent, but still not awkward:

When Reeds and Leaves, and Hides of Beasts were spread.

However, as with description, exposition or declamation can become merely prolix when amplification serves only to expand the expression without becoming an imaginative extension of the thought contained by it. Thus Chaucer's simple line:

Alas, that day that I was bore!

becomes inflated, to Housman's great indignation, in an attempt to be suitably grandiloquent, into:

Curs'd be the Day when first I did appear;
Let it be blotted from the Calendar,
Lest it pollute the month and poison all the Year.[39]

Perhaps it would be possible to link these lines with Job's blasphemous curse: "Let the day perish wherein I was born ... let it not be joined unto the days of the year, let it not come into the number of the months ... let them curse it that curse the day, who are ready to raise up their mourning." But this is doubtful justification for the bombast of the passage. Dryden is a heavily derivative poet, and the words of Job were very likely in his mind as he wrote; but his verse, though very often thick with allusions of this type, cannot be said to gain a great deal from this allusive quality. The sources are not completely irrelevant, but they are generally unimportant. The poetry, by its nature, offers its own direct explanation of itself, and on this level the lines from *Palamon and Arcite* remain empty verbiage.

Very often Dryden's renderings change (Housman would say rather mutilate) their originals beyond recognition. Thus Chaucer's simple words in *Arcite*'s dying speech to *Emily*:

But I biquethe the servyce of my goost
To you aboven every creature,
Syn that my lyf may no longer dure,

are transformed, by some strange process as "officious" as the shade they depict, into:

39 *Palamon and Arcite*, Bk. II, lines 89-91.

But to your Service I bequeath my Ghost;
Which from this mortal Body when unty'd.
Unseen, unheard, shall hover at your Side;
Nor fright you waking, nor your Sleep offend,
But wait officious, and your Steps attend.[40]

The insensitive, matter-of-fact quality of Dryden's rendering
is emphasized by its juxtaposition with the delicate restraint
of Chaucer's original lines. Similarly, what is perhaps the
best known single line in Virgil's *Aeneid*:

Sunt lacrimae rerum et mentem mortalia tangunt,

becomes six lines in Dryden's version, of which only the last
has any of the quality of the original:

. . . . O Friend! ev'n here
The Monuments of *Trojan* Woes appear!
Our known Disasters fill ev'n foreign Lands:
See there, where old unhappy *Priam* stands!
Ev'n the Mute Walls relate the Warrior's Fame,
And Trojan Griefs the *Tyrians* Pity claim.[41]

The effect of passages like these is certainly one of "words"
rather than of things. The style resembles the declamatory
vein of Dryden's heroic plays, in that, to use the words of Dr.
Johnson, it tends "to fill the air" rather than to awaken ideas.
The thought is not grand enough to sustain its overwrought
treatment. Take what happens to these four relatively straightforward lines from Virgil, effective simply because they are
straightforward:

Musa, mihi causas memora, quo numine læso
quidve dolens regina deum tot volvere casus
insignen pietate vivus, tot adire labores
imulerit, tantæne animis cælestibus irae?

This requires eight lines from Dryden:

O Muse! the Causes and the Crimes relate;
What Goddess was provok'd, and whence her Hate;
For what Offense the Queen of Heav'n began
To persecute so brave, so just a Man!

40 *Ibid.*, lines 781-85.
41 Dryden, *Virgil's Aeneis*, Bk. I, lines 644-49.

Involv'd his anxious Life in endless Cares,
Expos'd to Wants, and hurry'd into Wars!
Can Heav'nly Minds such high resentment show,
Or exercise their Spite in Human Woe?[42]

Dryden himself speaks of the difficulty of translating Virgil, whom he describes as "the plague of translators". "I . . . must confess to my shame," he says, "that I have not been able to translate any part of him so well, as to make him appear wholly like himself. For where the original is close, no version can reach it in the same compass."[43] And though he complains of Caro that he "commonly allows two lines for one of Virgil, and does not always hit the sense", the same could be said of himself. In the passage just quoted the doubling of length is almost entirely in the service of a more complex rhythmical structure: where Virgil uses one word or one idea Dryden must use two, in order to achieve the balanced structure on which so much of the rhetorical effectiveness of the couplet depends. The result is a general air of impressiveness, but one that blurs rather than contributes to the specific purpose of the passage. Compare, for instance, the effect of Virgil's direct question with that of the elaborate structure of Dryden's final couplet, which draws more attention to itself than it does to the question it asks. And, unlike many of the passages discussed in earlier chapters, the effects of sound and movement achieved here by the elaboration of the expression have no special significance, beyond that of epic elevation, in the organic structure of the verse.

The Renaissance ideal of poetry as an art object richly ornamented comes, in passages like these, to be too mechanically applied by comparison with the intrinsic nature of poetic ornament envisaged by Fracastoro, and achieved by Dryden himself in *Religio Laici*, *Absalom and Achitophel*, and elsewhere. L. D. Proudfoot, in his recent study of Dryden's *Aeneid*, cites the *Laöcoon* episode from the second book as an example of striking technical resourcefulness in what is nevertheless an unmistakably bad passage. ". . . the reader," he says, "recoils from the vehemence of its intentions

---

42 *Ibid.*, Bk. I, lines 11-18. The total number of lines in Dryden's version of the *Aeneid*, as compared with the original, is a fair indication of its wordiness throughout.
43 Dryden, "Preface to 'Sylvae: or, The Second Part of Poetical Miscellanies'" (1685), Ker, *op. cit.*, I, 256.

upon him, and the grossness of the means."[44] This comes close to the point. The means are "gross" because they are aimed only at a general epic elevation, resulting in an equally general tone, in which any subtle variations and niceties of meaning or emotion are lost under the heavy-handed ornament. And if such passages fail as poetry, they also fail as statement: while their ornament fails to provide a coherent and significant imaginative dimension for the poem, at the same time it blurs the pattern of narrative or exposition.

There is to the modern reader a certain insensitivity, a certain mechanical quality, about the elaborately "fortifying" devices of these translations. This type of aureate splendour can become irritatingly repetitive because the means of decoration are rather stereotyped. But it should none the less be remembered that the generalized, diffuse quality of this diction and imagery was eminently suited to Dryden's own age, and that such stereotyped expressions served to remove traces of idiosyncrasy from the verse of poets for whom originality was not the standard for poetic composition. In fact, the honestly historical critic would have to allow some defence for this type of amplification. The *Aeneid*, often condemned for its "impure verbiage", provided a "storehouse of devices" for poets for more than a century, and Dryden could be said to have been the one who popularized an "aureate" diction originating in the work of poets like Sylvester and Sandys, and also Milton. Certainly Housman's typically extravagant claim that this type of poetical expression consisted of "always using the wrong word instead of the right" cannot be admitted. Stereotyped means of embellishing the verse could also be "decorous" means of ornament— decoration according with the neoclassical notion of "rightness". Dryden's "finny fish" and "ambrosial dew" delighted his contemporaries, however much the modern taste might recoil from them.

And if this is not enough for the modern reader, as it may well not be, the risk mentioned earlier of neglecting what is really worthwhile by concentrating on what is obviously bad might be recalled. Amplification, if it could ruin the delicacy of Chaucer, could also be responsible for turning a few

44 L. D. Proudfoot, *Dryden's "Aeneid" and its Seventeenth Century Predecessors* (Manchester: University of Manchester Press, 1960), p. 256. I am indebted to this interesting study for some of the examples used here.

neutral words from Boccaccio's tale of *Cymon and Iphigenia*: "They, hearing this brought a great many people from the town to the seaside, and took Cymon and his companions prisoners . . .", into the superb satire on the Rhodian militia that T. S. Eliot so rightly praised:

The Country rings around with loud Alarms,
And raw in Fields the rude Militia swarms;
Mouths without Hands, maintain'd at vast Expense,
In Peace a Charge, in War a weak Defence:
Stout once a Month they march, a blust'ring Band,
And ever, but in times of Need, at hand:
This was the Morn when, issuing on the Guard,
Drawn up in Rank and File, they stood prepar'd
Of seeming Arms to make a short essay,
Then hasten to be Drunk, the Business of the Day.
 The Cowards would have fled, but that they knew
Themselves so many, and their foes so few;
But crowding on, the last the first impel,
Till overborne by weight, the *Cyprians* fell.[45]

Dryden has taken the opportunity here to indulge in some satire on the militia of seventeenth century England, but the passage is also true amplification—detail added to the narrative to give it greater verisimilitude. The problem of the poet is "to ornament the invention and so enrich it that it is not merely depicted in its own colours, but fully shaped"; and he must "use such adjuncts in a manner that makes them appear natural rather than placed there by art".[46] The Rhodian militia are not strictly necessary to the story. Boccaccio told it satisfactorily without mentioning them, and it might be argued that this passage is an irrelevant intrusion into the narrative. But Dryden makes their presence so real, so immediate, because of them the rest of the story becomes more real. They are an embellishment, but one that truly enriches the story and becomes part of it. There is here what the neoclassical critic would have called a "perfect synthesis" of story and ornament.

45 *Cymon and Iphigenia, from Boccace* (1700), lines 399-412.
46 *Dialogi di Messer Alessandro Lionardi, della inventione poetica* (Venice, 1554). Lionardi is another of the sixteenth century theorists who, like Fracastoro, gives expression to commonly held views of poetry based on the Renaissance interpretation of Aristotle's *Poetics*. His *Dialogues* are more fully discussed in K. G. Hamilton, *The Two Harmonies* (Oxford: Clarendon Press, 1963), pp. 69-71.

And against Dryden's failures in the *Aeneis*—against passages like the *Laöcoon* episode—might be placed lines such as these:

Now, when the Rage of Hunger was appeas'd,
The Meat remov'd, and ev'ry Guest was pleas'd;
The Golden Bowls with sparkling Wine are crown'd,
And through the Palace the chearful Cries resound.
From gilded Roofs depending Lamps display
Nocturnal Beams, that emulate the Day.
A Golden Bowl, that shone with Gems Divine,
The Queen commanded to be crown'd with Wine;

. . . . . .

'Twas *Bitias* whom she call'd, a thirsty Soul;
He took the Challenge, and embrac'd the Bowl:
With Pleasure swill'd the Gold, nor ceas'd to draw,
'Till he the bottom of the Brimmer saw.
The Goblet goes around: *Iopas* brought
His Golden Lyre, and sung what ancient Atlas taught:
The various Labours of the wand'ring Moon,
And whence proceed th'Eclipses of the Sun.
Th'Original of Men and Beasts; and whence
The Rains arise, and Fires their Warmth dispence;
And fix't and erring Stars dispose their Influence.
What shakes the solid Earth, what Cause delays
The Summer Nights and shortens Winter Days.
With Peals of Shouts the *Tyrians* praise the Song;
Those Peals are echo'd by the *Trojan* Throng.[47]

This is still more Dryden than it is Virgil; and being Dryden it is still "fortified". But here there is no sense of gross striving for extrinsic or general effects. The passage is organically as well as technically successful, reflecting the atmosphere and mood of the gathering in every word and movement. The scene is not only enriched but is made a living reality by means of the poetic ornament.

To be fair to Dryden, as well as allowing for the reiteration of some of the main points of this chapter, the discussion of his "art of fortifying" will be concluded with a study of the amplification in one of his most beautiful passages, the exor-

47 *Aeneis*, II, lines 1011-18 and 1034-48.

dium to *Religio Laici,* for these eleven lines have been universally praised, while much of his fortification has waned in its appeal. This passage, aptly described by Landor as "hymnlike", forms with its concluding alexandrine a distinct unit of expression within the poem:

Dim, as the borrow'd beams of Moon and Stars
To *lonely, weary, wandring* Travellers,
Is *Reason* to the *Soul*: And, as on high,
Those rowling Fires *discover* but the Sky,
Not light us *here*; So *Reasons* glimmering Ray
Was lent, not to *assure* our *doubtfull* way,
But guide us upward to a *better* Day.
And as those nightly Tapers disappear
When Day's bright Lord ascends our Hemisphere;
So pale grows *Reason* at *Religions* sight;
So *dyes*, and so *dissolves* in *Supernatural Light*.[48]

Here Dryden relies for amplification both on imagery and on the development of thought, the two elements that were the basis for the amplification in stanzas one and two respectively of *To the Memory of Mrs. Anne Killigrew*. And the two are closely interwoven, in as much as the image around which the passage is built is essentially an intellectual one, and is developed in rigid accordance with the thought it embellishes, as well as being organically fused with the thought. Thus in the opening couplet the inset simile may be strictly unnecessary, but this superfluity is overcome by the manner in which the image is made to seem contained even within the core of the thought: "Dim ... Is *Reason* to the *Soul*". This basic identification between thought and image prevents the latter from becoming an excrescence, and it is sustained throughout the passage, in the notion of "*Reasons* glimmering Ray" and in the concluding two lines:

So pale grows *Reason* at *Religions* sight;
So *dyes*, and so *dissolves* in *Supernatural Light*.

The verse is, as it were, "inlaid" rather than "overlaid", and the integration of the image with the thought gives the concept added magnificence without the image becoming in itself visually obtrusive. It is hard to see, indeed, why George Saintsbury should write of "the actual picture of the cloudy

48 *Religio Laici*, lines 1-11.

night sky and the wandering traveller".[49] The expression is vivid, but nevertheless, like most of Dryden's imagery, it is intellectually abstract rather than concrete in quality: it is an illustration, but in the strictly technical sense of an embellished statement. Moreover the thought itself is not inertly elaborated, but becomes dynamically meaningful: as the sentence unwinds the meaning accumulates, and the sense demands to be closely followed. The image and the thought are thus made to develop logically together, each helping to articulate the other.

With such a strong intellectual content, the image itself must not be allowed to become a source of distraction. The concept of the guiding light of reason, as well as being neatly analogous and inlaid in its development, is traditional and familiar in nature, and thus it avoids those effects of idiosyncrasy to which Dr. Johnson objected so strongly in the imagery of the metaphysical poets, and which mar stanza six of *To the Memory of Mrs. Anne Killigrew*. For instance, a poet like Donne would very probably have been unable to resist a "Sun"—"Son" pun in the line:

When Day's bright Lord ascends our Hemisphere.

Similarly the conceit of the "nightly Tapers" is muted, as are the conceits in the first stanza of *To the Memory of Mrs. Anne Killigrew*, and not extravagantly elaborated in the manner of this description of the "heavenly fire extinguisher" from *Annus Mirabilis*:

An hollow chrystal Pyramid he takes,
   In firmamental waters dipt above;
Of it a brode Extinguisher he makes,
   And hoods the flames that to their quarry strove.[50]

So, too, the personification of *"Reason"* growing pale at *"Religions* sight" is briefly stated and connected vitally with the developing concept, unlike many of the personifications in Augustan poetry—so muted is it, in fact, that, as we saw earlier, the shift from personification to more direct statement in the last line of the paragraph is likely to pass unnoticed.

The imagery, particularly the light imagery, of these lines

---

49 George Saintsbury, *John Dryden* (London: Macmillan Co., 1881), p. 93.
50 *Annus Mirabilis*, lines 1121-24.

from *Religio Laici* succeeds because it does harmonize in this
way with the idea it elaborates. Where it is emotionally
vivified, this is because of the sound of the verse. The flagging
movement in the line:

To *lonely, weary, wandring* Travellers,

is vividly expressive because of its mimetic movement, and
not because of the intrinsically evocative power of the image.
Dryden's success here, on the imaginative level, is, as nearly
always, very largely a rhythmical one. Isolated words are
sensitized because of the sound of the verse: the word "glimmering" seems to quiver because of its sensitive position before the rhyme word, and the same impression is achieved
with "doubtful", which also demands a slightly hesitating or
lingeringly emphatic pronunciation. "Dim" is strengthened
because of its isolation and its heavy stress. But these evocative effects achieved through sound belong to the subject,
to the idea, not to any emotional perception expressed
through imagery. The imagery is not emotionally perceived
(as is the light imagery of Shelley or Vaughan). But this is an
irrelevant consideration. The image is not intended to stand
alone, or to be a sublime expression of the state of mind of
the poet. Amplification should not be confused with notions
of sublimity.

The diction of these lines achieves the "plain and natural,
and yet majestick" style that Dryden in his Preface to the
poem declared he was aiming at. None the less the passage
is ornamental rather than rigidly structural or utilitarian in
its use of words. Dryden succeeds here with a fortified diction
because it is not purely mechanical. There are no "briny
waters", "sylvan scenes", or "crystal streams". "Dim" and the
Tennysonian "glimmering" are probably the only words that
would strike the modern reader as at all consciously poetic.
All the words, too, tend to be structurally integrated within
the framework of the poem. The adjective "borrow'd" relates
to the verb "was lent" and anticipates other "mercenary"
diction in the poem ("poverty", "celestial wealth", "fine",
"money") ; "Dim" is part of the light image; "Travellers" is
fused with "assure our doubtfull way" and with "guide".
Even the epithet "rowling" is not elaborately poetic and is
echoed in the relatively unadorned line a little later in the
poem:

Thus, *anxious Thoughts* in *endless Circles* roul.

Similarly the many variants on the light image are delicately and unobtrusively executed: "borrow'd beams", "rowling Fires", "glimmering Ray", "nightly Tapers", "Day's bright Lord", "*Supernatural Light*". There is nothing purely mechanical about these phrases, as in stereotyped poetic diction. But the words themselves are lacking in real suggestiveness: they do not acquire that depth of implication that absorbs attention and demands close inspection. The only possible exception, and that a doubtful one, is the verb *"assure"*, which in its context:

. . . . So *Reasons* glimmering Ray
Was lent, not to *assure* our *doubtfull* way,

can, in relation to "lent", have legal connotations that fit in with a consistent use of legal and commercial terminology throughout the poem, as well as retaining the more general meaning of "to make a thing certain or secure", which is implied by the use of "our *doubtfull* way". Moreover the word *"assure"* could also have the specifically theological meaning of "to give a subjective certainty of one's salvation". Yet this type of verbal analysis can easily be carried too far. Dryden may not, and probably did not, intend this degree of subtlety. Even his most poetic expressions are relatively lacking in depth of implication. Amplification does not generally combine with intensity, and "Longinus's" distinction between the two does seem to have some validity, whether what is opposed to intensity be seen as "prolixity and diffuseness" or "magnitude and abundance".

As well as forming a beautifully controlled and self-contained unit, the opening lines of *Religio Laici* are not, as a whole, an extraneous ornament or addition to the argument of the poem. In the first place the imagery and diction are structurally significant in the total framework. It has been seen how such words as "borrow'd" and "was lent" anticipate other mercenary terms throughout the poem. Similarly the light imagery indicates the "natural light" of reason (the Cartesian *lumen naturale*), which is briefly referred to at several points later in the poem; so, too, the "way" is a well-known Christian concept, again referred to unobtrusively in other passages. This subdued type of repetition abounds in the amplification of *Religio Laici*, but unlike the often irritating repetitions in the *Aeneid*, it is not generally an over-obvious feature of the poem. It is not unlikely that certain patterns of diction and imagery should emerge in a poem as long as this; and a good deal of Dryden's repetitions are fortuitous or mechanical rather than meaningful. But the unostentatious structural effect of this type of repetition as it is to be found in *Religio Laici* cannot rightly be overlooked. It is part of the careful artistry of composition typical of Dryden's more successful attempts to amplify his verse.

From another point of view, too, this exordium plays a role in the poem that goes beyond that of merely extrinsic embellishment. It is true that its tone of exultation contrasts strongly with the later more purely intellectual and logical progression of the verse; and also that, superficially, the argument that reason is inadequate in matters of faith might seem to invalidate the poem's whole rational argument. But in these eleven lines Dryden is not committing the fallacy of reasoning that reason is inadequate: he is *stating* that "Dim . . . Is *Reason* to the *Soul*" (the copular form corresponds to that of the Aristotelian logical proposition) as an unquestionable premise. The opening is closely developed, but it is developed in the manner of an illustration, not as a proof; and this premise or illustration is so vital to the argument of the poem that amplification is fully justified on the grounds of decorum. Elaboration gives the concept of Reason's fallibility the required emphasis, preparing for the tone of scepticism that permeates the whole poem and is implicit in the changing patterns of its argument.

The study of Dryden's amplification of these lines from *Religio Laici* has inevitably taken us back over some of the ground covered in previous chapters, and it thereby serves to indicate the central role of amplification in Dryden's concept of poetic discourse. Diction, rhythm, and imagery are each developed, not alone but as part of a pattern of embellishment of the subject matter that to him is the essence of poetry. He wrote of his translation of the *Aeneid*:

For what I have done, imperfect as it is for want of health and leisure to correct it, will be judged in after-ages, and possibly in the present, to be no dishonour to my native country, whose language and poetry would be more esteemed abroad, if they were better understood. Somewhat (give me leave to say) I have added to both of them in the choice of words, and harmony of numbers, which were wanting, especially the last, in all our poets, even in those who, being endued with genius, yet have not cultivated their mother-tongue with sufficient care; or, relying on the beauty of their thoughts, have judged the ornament of words, and sweetness of sound unnecessary.[51]

> Dryden's first concern as a poet is with words and sounds as the ornament of thought: as what, to use the traditional metaphor of poetry as a "speaking picture", enables the poet to develop his subject, to give it life and reality, as the painter's colours allow him to develop his design.
>
> In translating the *Aeneid*, this concept of his art led Dryden too frequently into an attempt to improve on his original; and, as Proudfoot says, "an inclination to improve on Virgil is rarely a wise one". And in much of his more gilded verse ornamentation becomes mechanical and stereotyped as the need for continuous embellishment overrides his artistic judgment. But the opening lines of *Religio Laici* serve as a testimony to the beauty of effect that Dryden's amplification could achieve. They succeed because here, as usual in his opening lines, he composed with great care, concealing his art beneath an organic surface. Dryden is generally more satisfying, at least to the twentieth century, when he shows "more matter and less art"—when he obeys such an injunction as that of Lionardi:

Art ... should be concealed and hidden as much as possible, so that the verses and invention seem born rather than made. . . . Just as in the judicial oration it appears that the cause itself rather than the great artificer makes the proof, so the poets should accompany their ideas with brief words, so that they be not empty and loquacious, following their vein or emotion, when invention is lacking.[52]

> Dryden is frequently "empty and loquacious"—in *Eleonora*, for instance, where invention was lacking simply because he had nothing to say; or in his translations of Virgil and Chaucer, where failure to grasp the intangible quality of his originals left him without material.
>
> But the devices of amplification are still present in the

51 Dryden, "Postscript to the Reader, annexed to the 'Aeneid' ", Ker, *op. cit.*, II, 241.
52 Lionardi, *op. cit.*, pp. 49-50.

"invention" of even such an apparently simple poem as the beautifully restrained elegy in memory of Dryden's fellow poet, John Oldham. Of *To the Memory of Mr. Oldham* it can truly be said that the "great artifice" is hidden beneath brief words. To nothing that he himself wrote more than to this is his praise of the *Pastorals* of Theocritus so apt: "A simplicity shines through all he writes: he shows his art and learning by disguising both":

Farewell, too little and too lately known,
Whom I began to think and call my own;
For sure our Souls were near ally'd; and thine
Cast in the same Poetick mould with mine.
One common Note on either Lyre did strike,
And Knaves and Fools we both abhorr'd alike:
To the same Goal did both our Studies drive,
The last set out the soonest did arrive.
Thus *Nisus* fell upon the slippery place,
While his young Friend perform'd and won the Race.
O early ripe! to thy abundant store
What could advancing Age have added more?
It might (what Nature never gives the young)
Have taught the numbers of thy native Tongue.
But Satyr needs not those, and Wit will shine
Through the harsh cadence of a rugged line.
A noble Error, and but seldom made,
When Poets are by too much force betray'd.
Thy generous fruits, though gather'd ere their prime,
Still shew'd a quickness; and maturing time
But mellows what we write to the dull sweets of Rime.
Once more, hail and farewell; farewell thou young,
But ah too short, *Marcellus* of our Tongue;
Thy Brows with Ivy, and with Laurels bound;
But Fate and gloomy Night encompass thee around.[53]

To the Memory of Mr. Oldham is more successful, as a complete unit, than the more grandiose *To the Memory of Mrs. Anne Killigrew*, where amplification is only intermittently under the control of an integrated artistic purpose. The elegy, indeed, might be regarded as the epitome of the poetry of statement. Here there is the structural, organic use of words and images, the naturalness of expression, the unobtrusive dominance of significant rhythm, the conscious

53 *To the Memory of Mr. Oldham.*

artifice that builds so skilfully as to be almost unnoticed, the control and articulation that bends all these things towards an effect of clarity and precision, that are to be found whenever Dryden's verse is successful as poetry of statement: that is when, like the lines *To the Memory of Mr. Oldham* it transcends the empty verbiage that is an ever-present pitfall for poetry conceived as a form of discourse that is, as Dryden himself said, "to be heightened with all the arts and ornaments of poesy", and becomes a true imitation of its subject.

chapter six

The Poetry of Statement and Literary Theory

Pope's *Essay on Man* is sometimes referred to as if it were the same kind of poem as *Religio Laici*; and its character as statement is emphasized by Pope himself in the Preface to the poem when he writes:

This I might have done in prose; but I chose verse, and even rhyme, for two reasons. The one will appear obvious; that principles, maxims, or precepts so written, both strike the reader more strongly at first, and are more easily retained by him afterwards: The other may seem odd, but is true, I found I could express them more *shortly* this way than in prose itself; and nothing is more certain, than that much of the *force* as well as *grace* of arguments or instructions, depends on their conciseness. . . .

But whether or not Pope was aware of what he was doing, the *Essay on Man* frequently transcends or overwhelms the literal statement in a way that leads the reader to respond less to a philosophical concept rationally expressed than to a purely imaginative apprehension of the idea of cosmic order. The imaginative dimension of the poem stands in the way of the effectiveness of the argument as such by drawing attention to itself: the lines frequently excite the imagination rather than inform the understanding.

This is not true of *Religio Laici*, or of the general method of the poetry of statement. The arguments of the "honest Layman", like the portrait of *Achitophel* or the caricature of Shadwell, achieve their own poetic reality as part of a "fiction" to which the imagination of the reader can respond. In their own way they illustrate the process by which statement is transformed into poetry. But *Religio Laici, Absalom and Achitophel*, and *MacFlecknoe* all present something more than an imaginative apprehension of a theological argument or a political or literary quarrel: as poems they are not wholly or even primarily the imaginative transformation of their subject.

In a way, the structure of poems like *Religio Laici* is the opposite of that of formal allegory. Allegory presents its subject primarily at the imaginative level, the "real" meaning deriving from this and having no existence in the poem except what is reflected from the allegory. Dryden's poems, even ostensible allegories such as *Absalom and Achitophel* or *The Hind and the Panther*, present their meaning directly at the level of discursive statement, the truly imaginative dimension deriving from the manner of the statement and serving only to give it greater richness and vitality. As poems they are "imitations of men in action": they make statements about men and in the dynamic pattern of the statement the subject becomes part of an image, or imitation, of a wider, more vivid, more vital reality. The supra-rational quality of these poems comes from no verbal dimension independent of, transcending, or counter to the statement, but from a poetic extension of it; from a reflection imaged in the statement's own pattern of sound and movement. It is as though the flat, neutral, prosaic statement is seen both in itself, and simultaneously reflected in a glass that has the property of seeming to bring it to life, without distorting it, or destroying its clarity and precision as statement.

In such a formulation as this the idea of a poetry of statement begins to have more meaning. Accurate statement is the province of logical or scientific discourse, of the strictly prosaic use of words; simply persuasive or effective statement is rhetoric; only discourse that in and through its manner of statement reflects, or images, or (since a seventeenth century poet is the centre of attention) that imitates a dynamic reality in such a way that the subject seems actually to live, may properly be called poetry of statement. It is poetry that seeks to lose none of the qualities of clear, precise, definitive statement, but yet strives to gain something more than this from the special resources of invention and language available to the poet.[1]

This view of the poetry of statement would serve to bring it closer to modern concepts of the nature of poetry than either Bateson's: "The Augustan achievement was by shearing words of their secondary and irrelevant association to release the full emphasis of their primary meanings"; or Eliot's: ". . . the lack of suggestiveness is compensated by the satisfying completeness of the statement." It is a view that allows for the limited and subordinate role played in this type of poetry by imagery and by the suggestive power of words, while still emphasizing elements recognizably poetic instead of, or at least in addition to, such things as clarity and precision, energy and completeness, that belong essentially to prose; and it is consequently a view that runs less danger of inadvertently labelling the poetry of statement as not poetry at all but prose. At the same time it remains a view that would be completely within the range of Renaissance concepts of poetry as an art of imitation, dependent on ornament to transcend the resources of everyday discourse: and there is a limit to the extent to which its interpretation can be made to accommodate itself to twentieth century ideas of what poetry should be, without at least the risk of distorting the poet's intentions. The modern reader of *Religio Laici* might well feel that its tone of scepticism, of the common sense of the layman "weary of the warring theologians", is the most important thing about it, and that for him it exists to give expression to the attitudes reflected by this tone. But to succumb to any such feeling would be anachronistic; for in terms of Renaissance theory this tone is but one part of the poem's ornament, and the poem could not be said to exist for the sake of its ornament. It exists for the sake of its effect on an audience, for its ability to give a particular kind of pleasure that will cause men to accept its subject as true or real, and all parts of the ornament are means towards this end.

1 The distinction made here between the poetry of statement and rhetoric is admittedly a narrow one; and, indeed, I think it would be true to say that such poetry is rhetoric which uses a special means to persuasion. For a discussion of the traditionally close relationship of poetry to rhetoric up to the end of the seventeenth century, see K. G. Hamilton, *The Two Harmonies* (Oxford: Clarendon Press, 1963), pp. 45-94.

To this extent, at least, the statement—what the poem manifestly says—must be important.

In *Religio Laici* the main part of the ornament comes from the reflection of the minds of the protagonists as they develop their argument. And it is the ornament that makes *Religio Laici* a poem instead of a theological discourse in verse: it is the ornament that gives it the delightfulness that will move men to moral action. But Dryden would think of himself as writing the poem in order to present an argument, not as using an argumentative form of verse in order to reveal, through its ornament, his personal feelings, or the workings of his own mind: just as he wrote the lines on Shaftesbury to discredit the Whig leader and win favour for the King. The moral purpose of *Religio Laici* is clearly stated in the Preface to the poem; while of the other great ratiocinative poem, *The Hind and the Panther*, Dryden also speaks in a manner that makes it clear that it too was a poem intended to sway public opinion. And his readers would receive his work with the same attitude. One has only to browse through the spate of panegyrics, poems, and pamphlets in reply to *Absalom and Achitophel* and *The Medall* to realize this. There is little concern to be found for the goodness or badness of the poems as poetry, only for the rightness or wrongness of the cause. For instance, in one such poem, *A Key (with the Whip) to open the mystery and iniquity of the poem call'd "Absalom and Achitophel"* (1682), Dryden's "libel" is said to be "all Bad Matter, beautifi'd (which is all that can be said) with good Meeter". In the phrase "poetry of statement" both parts are important. If Dryden had simply wished to make statements, as a good member of the Royal Society and of its committee for improving the English tongue, he would have written in plain, unadorned prose, of which he was indeed a master. But he was also too much in the tradition of poetry as one of the great arts of communication, closely related to logic and rhetoric, and with a didactic and moral purpose, to see the statements made by poetry as unimportant, as existing merely to provide the opportunity for a display of poetic ornament.

There were times when Dryden professed to place delight first in the aims of poetry. "I am satisfied if it cause delight," he wrote, "for delight is the chief, if not the only, end of poesy; instruction can be admitted but in second place, for

poesy only instructs as it delights."[2] The precedence is, however, rather one of time—poetry instructs, but only because it
also delights, and therefore the delight must come first. Thus
on another occasion Dryden declared that "pleasure was not
the only end of poesy"; and that "even the instructions of
morality were not so wholly the business of a poet, as that the
precepts and examples of piety were to be omitted".[3] Dryden
writes, as he says, firstly to entertain, but he also regards
poetry as having a clear public and moral function. Of his
lifelong desire to write an epic poem, he says: "This, too, I
had intended chiefly for the honour of my native country, to
which a poet is particularly obliged."[4] And he speaks of "that
kind of poetry which excites to virtue the greatest of men"
as being "of the greatest use to human kind".[5] Poetry, he says,
"must resemble natural truth, but it must be ethical".[6]
Dryden in fact, clearly regards himself as filling the position
of the public orator, "armed with the power of verse"[7]—as
being one skilled in what Quintilian described as *ars bene
dicendi*, the art of speaking well in a moral as well as a
technical sense. Verse, and indeed all the ornaments of
poetry, are ultimately means to this end. And, even in so far
as he might be led towards writing poetry for its delightfulness alone, Dryden would expect the delight to be found in
the poem as a whole, in the appropriateness, the "decorum"
of its total organization, and not in one of its parts.

This emphasis on Dryden's essentially rhetorical attitude
to poetry results here in a concentration on his conscious
intentions—on what he *thought* he was doing when he wrote
poetry rather than on what he was actually doing. These
things may not always be the same, for much in the poetry of
any age is likely to be independent of conscious intention.

2 Dryden, "A Defence of an 'Essay of Dramatic Poesy'", *Essays of John
Dryden*, ed. W. P. Ker (2 vols.; Oxford: Clarendon Press, 1900), I, 113.
3 Dryden, "Preface to 'Tyrannick Love; or, The Royal Martyr'" (1670), *The
Works of John Dryden*, eds. Scott-Saintsbury (18 vols.; Edinburgh: 1882-92),
III, 349.
4 Dryden, "A Discourse concerning the Original and Progress of Satire", Ker,
op. cit., II, 38.
5 Dryden, "Epistle Dedicatory to the Duke of York prefixed to 'Alamanzor and
Almahide: or, The Conquest of Granada'" (1672), Scott, *op. cit.*, IV, 11.
6 Dryden, "A Defence of an 'Essay of Dramatic Poesy'", Ker, *op. cit.*, I, 121.
7 Dryden, "A Discourse concerning the Original and Progress of Satire",
ibid., II, 22. Further evidence of this rhetorical attitude on Dryden's part
is provided by Lilian Feder, "John Dryden's use of Classical Rhetoric",
PMLA, LXIX (1954), 1258-78.

Nevertheless, a knowledge of these consciously held attitudes is necessary for a full and proper understanding of the poetry written in their light; and the analysis of Dryden's poetry of statement contained in the foregoing chapters has shown how closely its nature is in fact related to its rhetorical purpose.

Susanne Langer is one of the most influential of the present-day "aesthetic" critics who have followed the lead of Croce in opposing directly the idea that poetry can be a form of discourse in any way similar to discursive prose. For her the difference is an absolute one, based on a difference in the "laws" controlling the two forms. She writes:

Since every poem that is successful enough to merit the name of "poetry"—regardless of style or category, is a non-discursive symbolic form, it stands to reason that the laws which govern the making of poetry are not those of discursive logic. They are "laws of thought" as truly as the principles of reasoning are; but *they never apply to scientific or pseudo-scientific (practical) reasoning.* They are, in fact, the laws of imagination. As such they extend over all the arts, but literature is the field where their differences from discursive logic become most sharply apparent, because the artist who uses them is using linguistic forms, and thereby the laws of discourse, at the same time, on another semantic level . . . the laws of imagination . . . are obscured . . . by the laws of discourse.[8]

It is only in the eighteenth century, in the work of writers such as the Italian philosopher and forerunner of Croce, Giambattista Vico, and with the breakdown of faculty psychology, that views having any affinity with this begin to

8 Susanne Langer, *Feeling and Form: A Theory of Art Developed from Philosophy in a New Key* (London: Routledge & Kegan Paul, 1953), p. 203. Parts of Miss Langer's argument are very similar to what Leonard Welsted had to say in the eighteenth century in his attacks on neoclassicism. (See his "Dissertation concerning the perfection of the English tongue, and the state of Poetry, &c.", London, 1724, *Critical Essays of the Eighteenth Century 1700-1725*, ed. W. H. Durham, New Haven: Yale University Press, 1915, esp. pp. 367-68: "Reason operates differently, when it has different Things for its Object; poetical Reason is not the same as mathematical Reason; there is in good Poetry as rigid Truth, and as essential to the nature of it, as there is in a Question of Algebra, but that Truth is not to be prov'd by the same Process or way of Working; Poetry depends much more on imagination, than other Arts, but it is not on that account less reasonable than they.")

appear. For the seventeenth century the imagination, important as it still may be for poetry, is thought of always as the
servant of the rational judgment, and consequently it could
have no laws except those imposed on it by the judgment.
The imagination, Dryden was quoted earlier as saying, "is a
faculty so wild and lawless that like an high ranging spaniel
it must have clogs tied to it, lest it outrun the judgement".
And the "clogs" tied to the imagination in poetry like
Dryden's might, indeed, be seen as the "statement". The poet
must have something rational to say—and be intent on saying
it—before he can safely venture into the realms of imagination.[9] Certainly we have seen what frequently happens when
Dryden has nothing rational to say: his words "fill the air",
imaging only their own emptiness, either intentionally as in
the *Zimri* portrait, or unintentionally as in *Eleonora* and a
good deal of the *Aeneid*.

But to return to Miss Langer, the following passage from
her *Feeling and Form* (1953), while it may confirm as belonging to poetry some of the qualities that have been found in
poems like *Religio Laici*, also serves to illustrate how the
emphasis can be placed too far in one direction for what she
has to say to fit comfortably on a seventeenth century poem.
The second paragraph particularly shows the widening gap:

all poetry is a creation of illusory events, even when it looks like
a statement of opinions, philosophical or political or aesthetic.
The occurrence of a thought is an event in a thinker's personal
history, and has a distinct qualitative character as an adventure, a
sight or a human contact; it is not a proposition, but the entertainment of one, which necessarily involves vital tensions, feelings,
the imminence of other thoughts, and the echoes of past thinking. Poetic reflections, therefore, are not necessarily trains of
logical reasoning, though they may incorporate fragments, at least,
of discursive argument. Essentially they create the semblance of
reasoning; of the seriousness, strain, and progress, the sense of
growing knowledge, growing clearness, conviction and acceptance
—the whole experience of philosophical thinking.
Of course a poet usually builds a philosophical poem around

9 The same attitude seems to lie behind Dante's demand, so completely
foreign to present-day ideas of the nature of poetic expression, that when
the poet writes "under cover of a figure or of a rhetorical colour", he
should do so "not without indeed some reason, but with a reason which
it were possible afterwards to make clear in prose". (Dante Alighieri, *La
Vita Nuova*, XXV, trans. Dent (London: Dent, 1906), p. 99.)

an idea that strikes him, at the time, as true and important; but not for the sake of debating it. He accepts it and exhibits its emotional value and imaginative possibilities. Consider the Platonic doctrine of transcendental remembrance in Wordsworth's *Ode: Intimations of Immortality*: there are no statements pro and con, no doubts and proofs, but essentially the experience of having so great an idea.[10]

> It is because it reveals so clearly the truth of what Miss Langer says in the first of these paragraphs that *Religio Laici* achieves the quality of poetry conceived as imitation. The "thought" of the poem comes to us, not as something flat, detached from life, but as "an event in the thinker's personal history ... a human contact". The poem does create "the semblance of reasoning; of the seriousness, strain and progress, the sense of growing knowledge. . . ." But to move from this to the notion that Dryden went to the subject of *Religio Laici* without any idea of debating it, or that he took up the King's cause against Shaftesbury primarily for the sake of exhibiting its emotional possibilites, is difficult enough for the twentieth century reader to accept. To the seventeenth century reader, nurtured on Renaissance rhetorical poetics, it would have been quite incomprehensible: just as incomprehensible as it would have been for the nineteenth century to see the odes of Wordsworth, Shelley, and Keats as being similar in nature and purpose to the Great Ode of the early eighteenth century—as being "artistic constructions designed to the end of amplifying the wonders respectively, of immortality, wind, and nightingales". And in the portrait of *Achitophel*, too, there is a wider semblance of reality than seems to be provided for by Miss Langer. The portrait glows with the poet's own anger and indignation, and part of its richness comes from this. But only part: it is still an imitation, not of Dryden "experiencing" anger against Shaftesbury, but of the man himself. The violence and turbulence of sound and rhythm are an image, not of Dryden's anger, but of *Achitophel*'s power and force. Miss Langer's view of art is too personal, too much devoted to the artist as the centre of interest, to be adaptable to poetry that is essentially centred on the statement that it sets itself to enrich. If there can be no room for "statements pro and con, no doubts and proofs", obviously there can be little room for

10 Langer, *op. cit.*, p. 219.

Dryden. In the process of becoming poetry, philosophical statement may reveal imaginatively, as it does in *Religio Laici*, the "experience of having . . . an idea", but if the poem ceases to concentrate on the statement in order to develop, for its own sake, this expression of the experience, then it ceases to be poetry of statement.

Another prominent modern critic whose theories show something of the twentieth century difficulty with Dryden is Northrop Frye. Frye begins with a distinction, not between poetry and prose (a distinction which he believes has no reality and results only from a lack of proper terminology), but between "imaginative" literature on the one hand, and what he calls "descriptive" or "assertive" writing on the other. He speaks of the three main rhythms of discourse, related to the "three main areas of the trivium": philosophy with its discursive rhythms based on the unit of the proposition, which comes within the department of logic, poetry with its figurative rhythms based on the arranging and patterning of verbal symbols, which belongs to rhetoric, and history with its narrative rhythms, which is part of the province of grammar:

literature being hypothetical unites the temporal event with the idea in conceptual space. On the one side it develops a narrative interest which borders on history; and on the other a discursive interest which borders on philosophy, and in between them is the central interest of imagery.
We may thus distinguish three main rhythms of literature and three main areas of it, one in which the narrative controls the rhythm, one in which the discursive interest controls it, and a central area in which the image controls it. This central area is the property of poetry; parietal ones belong to prose which is used for both hypothetical and descriptive purposes.[11]

Apart from his linking of poetry and rhetoric (the reason for which in the context of his argument is not easy to understand), Frye is interesting for the central position he gives to rhythm. A poem such as *Religio Laici* might be said to be based on what he would call the proposition as its rhythmic unit, the propositions forming not only the basis of its argu-

11 Northrop Frye, "Levels of Meaning in Literature", *KR*, XII (1950), 251.

ment but also that of both the metrical and syntactical patterns, whose interaction determines the total rhythmic movement of the poem and gives it its distinctive character. This type of rhythm, however, Frye says is characteristic of discursive prose, which he describes as "a recurring effort to isolate the propositional rhythm". Elsewhere he does mention the danger of "a strong narrative or didactic interest in poetry which tends to infuse poetry with the word order of prose, just as conversely euphuism or figured prose tends to become 'poetic' "; and this danger would obviously beset a poem that purported to present a discursive argument. However, there is more than this needed to explain the poetic quality of *Religio Laici* or to fit it to Frye's formula. Considered as poetry, according to Frye, the poem must aim to be not "an organization of propositions" but rather "a figuration of images": but in so far as the poetry of statement, and *Religio Laici* in particular, has been shown to image anything, it does so primarily through the pattern of its discursive rhythms. The images of the "honest Layman" and of the turbulent *Achitophel* are similar in this respect: each puts forward statements, or "propositions", which become poetry by being reflected, or imaged, in the pattern of sound and rhythm. Once again it would seem that any attempt to make absolute distinctions between poetry and prose (or between poetry and something else that is not poetry) based on differences in their essential structure as discourse is likely to break down in face of the poetry of statement.

In some respects, however, Frye is closer to seventeenth century ideas than are views of the kind represented by Susanne Langer: as when he speaks of literature (distinguished from poetry which is only part of literature) as serving to unite, by virtue of its being "hypothetical", "the temporal event with the idea in conceptual space". Beneath the rather frightening terminology, if one is intrepid enough to attempt to penetrate it, there may be something here that is close to Renaissance Aristotelianism[12]—to the concept of poetry as an imitation resting on factual history but given verisimilitude, actuality, by means of poetic ornament. Applied to *Religio Laici*, it may be another way of saying that as a poem it expresses the philosophical or theological

12 There are, at times, quite striking affinities between Frye's attitudes to literature and those expressed in Sidney's *Apologie*.

idea ("the idea in conceptual space"), not simply in or by itself, but as a living mental state, an idea experienced by the poet, or by individuals created by him in the poem ("the temporal event", the event in time). This is to repeat what has already been said, that the poem, as poetry, is not merely a theological argument, effectively organized and persuasively presented, but an argument transformed, given life and action in time, as the expression or image of a reasoning mind, and made thereby into something that belongs neither to philosophy nor to history, but to poetry—not "what Alcibiades did or suffered", but "how a person of given character will on occasion speak or act, according to the law of probability or necessity".[13] "I have," said Dryden of his Horatian Epistle *To my Honor'd Kinsman John Driden*, "not only drawn the features of my worthy Kinsman, but have also given my own Opinion, of what an Englishman in Parliament ought to be: & deliver it as a Memorial of my own Principles to all posterity."[14] And he has done these things not so much directly as by letting us see a living example of them in his "imitation" of one such Englishman.

Yet to see this poem, or *Religio Laici*, in such a light is still to stop short of Miss Langer's limitation of poetry to the expression of the experience of having an idea. The emphasis remains on the poem as the expression of the idea itself, and not on the expression of the poet's experience of having the idea. This is a distinction that may seem difficult to make, but one that involves a difference of emphasis vitally important for an understanding of seventeenth century poetry. And again it is a difference to be explained at least in part in terms of the seventeenth century view of the imagination. The emphasis of Francis Bacon, for instance, in writing about poetry, is on the "inventive" power of the imagination, but his invention is essentially a joining together of objects in the external world:

Poesy, in the sense in which I have defined the word, is also concerned with individuals invented in imitation of those which are the subject of true history; yet with this difference, that it commonly exceeds the measure of nature, joining at pleasure

---

13 See Aristotle, *Poetics*, IX, 3-4.
14 Dryden, "Letter to Rt. Hon. Charles Montague" (probably October 1699), *The Letters of John Dryden*, ed. C. E. Ward (Durham: Duke University Press, 1942), p. 120.

things which in nature would never come to pass; just as Painting likewise does. This is the work of Imagination.[15]

> There is no suggestion here of the dynamic power of the imagination to create entirely new mental experiences, such as was to be the basis of Coleridge's theory of the imagination. For Bacon the emphasis is outward from the mind, to what the imagination can do with objects in the external world, rather than inward to the life of the imagination itself. And in this his ideas are typical of those prevailing throughout the seventeenth century, which seems to have found little to interest it in the actual mental life or feelings of the poet. It was more interested in things themselves than in the experiencing of things.

> Frye turns elsewhere to the important consideration of the autonomous unity of the literary work:

verbal structures may be classified according to whether the *final* direction of meaning is outward or inward. In descriptive or assertive writing the final direction is outward. Here the verbal structure is intended to represent things external to it, and it is valued in terms of the accuracy with which it does represent them . . . .

In all literary verbal structures the final direction of meaning is inward. In literature the standards of outward meaning are secondary, for literary works do not pretend to describe or assert, and hence are not true, not false . . . Literary meaning may best be described, perhaps, as "hypothetical", and a hypothetical or assumed relation to the external world is part of what is usually meant by the word "imaginative". . . . In literature, questions of fact or truth are subordinated to the primary aim of producing a structure of words for its own sake, and the sign-values of symbols are subordinated to their importance as a structure of interconnected motifs. Wherever we have an autonomous verbal structure of this kind we have literature. Wherever this autonomous structure is lacking, we have language, words used instrumentally to help human consciousness do or understand something else.[16]

> Dryden was indeed vitally concerned with "producing a structure of words"; but of poems like *Absalom and Achitophel* and *Religio Laici* it is obviously wrong to say that they do

---

15 Francis Bacon, "De dignitate et augmentis scientiarum libros IX" (London, 1623), *The Philosophical Works of Francis Bacon*, ed. J. Spedding and R. H. Ellis (5 vols.; London: 1861).

16 Northrop Frye, *The Anatomy of Criticism* (Princeton: Princeton University Press, 1957), p. 75.

not "pretend to describe or assert" or that they exist simply "for their own sake". Frye has merely substituted the autonomous nature of the poem for Miss Langer's insistence on its unique role as the expression of the poet's experience, as a means of giving poetry an existence independent of other forms of discourse. And unfortunately for such theories, Dryden's poetry of statement is a self-conscious structure of words, but it is also intended to state something that has relevance beyond the poem. Indeed, the very structure of words depends largely for its character as a structure on the clarity and precision with which it does just this.

Thus there is much in Frye's ideas that can be applied only with difficulty to the rhetorically or didactically conceived poetry of the seventeenth century, particularly if the intention of the poet is considered. This is especially so with his interpretation of the nature of poetic "fiction", which he relates to the autonomous structure of the poem. The Renaissance concept of poetic fiction freed poetry from the need for an exact correspondence with the things of the immediate external world, but as a means of revealing a more perfect beauty, a more fundamental or universal truth, rather than as a way of achieving internal consistency or artistic coherence for their own sakes. Concepts of artistic unity were of course not unknown in the seventeenth century: far from it, indeed, in a period dominated by the "rules" and with a great deal of interest in the concept of poetic genres. But the rhetorical tradition, with its moralistic, didactic emphasis, and its primary interest in affecting an audience, meant that this unity was seen less as an internal coherence than as a properly organized artistic imitation of nature: that is, "the final direction of meaning" was still outward for the sake of its representation of things external to itself, rather than inward for its own sake.

Yet it cannot be denied that even such a poem as *Religio Laici* retains its interest largely because it has the kind of autonomous unity described by Frye. It will not necessarily matter for our appreciation of the poem today if we should happen to regard its arguments as either mainly dead or mistaken. And, as Frye goes on to say, "it often happens that an originally descriptive piece of writing, such as the histories of Fuller and Gibbon, survives by virtue of its 'style', or interesting verbal pattern, after its value as a representation of facts has faded".[17] But if *Religio Laici* does survive "by virtue of its 'style' ", this is because the style has power to give an appearance of reality to the statement. The "verbal pattern" is not simply "interesting" in itself, but gives interest and vitality to the subject, so that, at least within the limits of our experience of reading it, the poem's original purpose as an imitation intended to teach and delight continues to be achieved. *Religio Laici* survives because, while its subject is tied to a particular background of belief that may be no longer regarded as important, its imaginative dimension is of universal appeal. But this imaginative dimension itself only has interest and meaning as an extension of the statement: it can survive only by virtue of its ability to give life to the subject.

In the light of the foregoing speculations as to the nature of the poetry of statement, it would be interesting to restudy the appreciation of *Religio Laici* provided by Mark Van Doren:

It may not be too fantastic to say that Dryden's brains were in his fingers, that he thought in meter. Alliteration in him binds words, phrases, lines, couplets, paragraphs together. Rhyme, by holding the reader's mind, as Taine says, "on the stretch", gives to the poet's statements a strange factitious potency, so that they satisfy the curiosity of the ear rather than that of the mind. Alexandrines close discussions as if forever. *Enjambment* allows the imagination leisure to thread its way through meditative passages. Series of well-chosen adjectives advance a proposition with steady strides:

Not that tradition's parts are useless here,
When general, old, distinterested and clear.

Metaphors unobtrusively employed clinch a point before the reader is aware of the advantage being taken of him:

This was the fruit the private spirit brought,
Occasioned by great zeal and little thought.
While crowds unlearn'd, with rude devotion warm,
About the sacred viands buz and swarm.

17 *Ibid.*

Exclamations draw many meanings briskly together. Queries serve for transitions. Catchwords and connectives like "then", "granting that", "True, but—", "thus far", " 'tis true", keep the game of ratiocination animated and going. Aphorisms set off arguments. Repetition and refrain speak proselyting sincerity or else confessional ecstasy. Abrupt apostrophes seem to denote overwhelming conviction suddenly arrived at. Passages of limpid and beautiful statement appear the issues of a serenely composed conscience. Angry, headlong digressions subside into mellow confessions of faith.[18]

> This is a comprehensive appreciation of the poem, and it introduces or implies most of the points raised in the previous discussions of *Religio Laici* in this study, without, however, "becoming exercised over the question" as to which of them properly belong to a consideration of the work specifically as a poem. Van Doren begins with metre as an aid to the organization of thought, moves quickly to its effectiveness in rhetorical persuasion, then on to the use of couplet rhetoric and syntactical rhythm as a means of significant patterning, and finally to a suggestion of the movement of the poem as an image of the poet's mental and spiritual life. All these things are to be found in the poem: they are all part of the imitation, part of the ornament, which, in Renaissance terms, makes it a poem. Yet, judged by some common twentieth century concepts of poetry, it is a poem only by virtue of the last named. Seen against the background of the Renaissance ideal of poetry, on the other hand, as a heightened and adorned imitation, all aspects of the poem's thought and expression become part of a richer and more satisfying poetic experience.

Critics such as Bateson and Eliot who have described Dryden's work as poetry of statement have been right, but not wholly right. His words are "precise"; they are shorn of their secondary and irrelevant associations to release the full emphasis of their primary meanings; they are "logical"; their suggestiveness, in the usually accepted poetic sense of the

18 Mark Van Doren, *John Dryden: A Study of His Poetry* (Bloomington, Indiana: Indiana University Press, 1946), pp. 170-71.

term, is often "nothing". These things are true, at least as a general rule;[19] but unfortunately they seem to lead to an appreciation of Dryden's work as statement rather than as poetry—a position stated categorically by Arnold, and also I think accepted by implication in Bonamy Dobrée's elevation of Milton above Dryden as a poet:

To discuss which of them [Milton or Dryden] is the greater poet is invidious: the answer will depend upon what you expect of poetry, though few, I think will deny the crown to Milton, who, however, did much damage to the language, while Dryden conferred upon it benefits which are speaking strictly, inestimable. In that respect his method is better. But Milton's purely personal idiom has one great advantage: his poems are much more than Dryden's independent objects, complete experiences in themselves. Dryden's, for all their lovely limpidity, as often as not demanded outside reference. Milton paid the price of his glories by being outrageously distorted and infractious: Dryden paid for his masterly statement, for his finality, by needing external support.[20]

In other words, Dryden's works are examples of "masterly statement", but they are not poems, at least not in the sense of Frye's "autonomous structures". For Dobrée the reason for this is the familiar one that whereas Milton "could only use as material ... such things as had seared his emotions", Dryden "was not interested in emotions, and he used best the material he had grasped by means of the intellect".

But what I think Dobrée is missing here is that with Dryden "masterly statement" need not be "flat": it can achieve the depth, the multidimensional existence achieved in other ways by Milton, without losing its finality, its precision and clarity, and without necessarily being transfused with emotion. Thus *Absalom and Achitophel* or *Religio Laici* may require outside reference if considered as occasional discourse, but as poetry they do achieve independence through a richness of statement that makes them "complete experiences" in themselves. Dryden's poetry of statement, in

19 The conventional statement of the exceptions to the rule might be provided from J. E. Butt's *The Augustan Age* (London: Hutchinson & Co., 1950), p. 26: "We might say that he was weak in imaginative poetry if we forget the opening lines of *Religio Laici* and the concluding verses of *To the Memory of Mr. Oldham* ... we would never forget how strong he is in the poetry of statement and declamation." But these are not really exceptions; their qualities are ultimately those of all his best poetry.
20 Bonamy Dobrée, "Milton and Dryden", *ELH*, III (1936), 99-100.

fact, shows that poetry need not necessarily be a thing of emotion—that material grasped by the intellect, that is, ideas, are just as susceptible as emotion to being given imaginative life and reality through poetry.

Indeed, the claim that Dryden's poetry "lacks suggestiveness" is true only if the reference is to a narrowly emotional kind of suggestiveness; and even then it is often less true that his words lack suggestiveness than that this quality is pushed into the background of the reader's awareness by other, more powerful effects. And paradoxically, these more powerful effects, which have their own kind of suggestiveness that transforms *Religio Laici* from a theological discourse into a poem, are in large part a function of those very qualities of precision that have been seen as substituting for suggestiveness. Poetry, in fact, cannot do without some form of suggestiveness, for it must image or imitate or reflect something beyond its mere prose content, or it is no longer poetry. Thus far, I think, any definition of poetry must go; and this would never have been denied by the seventeenth century: when combined with an apparent lack of poetic sensitivity it was what caused Francis Bacon to reject all lyric and reflective poetry as containing no "feigned history", and therefore as not being poetry at all, because to him these kinds of verse containing no imitation have no dimension beyond their direct statement and belong consequently to "philosophy and the arts of speech" rather than to poetry.[21] Poetry to the seventeenth century was an art of imitation, not of statement, and imitation is a matter of imaging, of suggesting, not of "stating". Poetry and realism are not the same thing, for in its imitation of nature poetry was expected to improve on the things of the everyday world; a Renaissance commonplace developed from the Aristotelian view of the nature of poetry that Dryden clearly restates in his *Parallel of Poetry and Painting*.

But though poetry cannot do without suggestiveness, there are other means to suggestiveness than imagery or the associative power of words. These latter, more familiar, means to suggestiveness are dependent, at least to a degree, on a weakness in the logical structure of the poetry. They often depend, as Bateson says, on their ability to "repel the logical and

21 See his *De augmentis scientiarum*, Spedding and Ellis, *op. cit.*, IV, 314-15.

progressive tendencies that are always active in speech":
tendencies which in so far as they retain their strength will
determine more or less narrowly those particular associations
that are appropriate. This opposition between poetic suggestiveness and logical progression is much emphasized by
present-day poetic theory, and it is undoubtedly to be found
in that modern poetry which seeks to achieve an immediate
and intuitive, as against a reasoned, logical, apprehension of
reality. It is less likely to appear in the poetry of an age when
imaginative writing is seen as necessarily under the control
of a strictly non-imaginative reason. In such poetry, in the
dialectically organized lyrics of Donne as well as in the
logically discursive arguments of Dryden, this logical structure is as much a part of the technique as are the metre, the
rhymes, the alliteration, the associative value of words, the
images, the "passions": all are part of poetry's delightfulness.

The problem as it was seen by the neoclassic poet was not
one of working against, or of breaking through the inherent
discursiveness or logicality of discourse. To do that would
simply be irrational, and therefore unworthy of man as a
rational being. Rather he must seek to use the resources of
poetry to enrich, to reinforce, to extend, the structural statement in order that it may present a picture that is more
lively, delightful, verisimilar, and therefore more convincing
and effective to the reader. But the basic statement remains,
and as something more essential than simply a framework on
which to hang the poetry. Indeed, one significant lesson that
is to be learned from Dryden's failure in parts of the *Aeneid*,
for example, or of *To the Memory of Mrs. Anne Killigrew*,
is that when he does fail it is usually because of an undue
emphasis on the distinctively poetic elements, such as imagery,
rather than because of the domination of his verse by what
might be called prose elements. He succeeds as a poet when
his great power of discursive statement remains in control of
the poetic ornament, so that the statement and ornament
combine to form a new whole, organically conceived and
integrated, and significant beyond the scope of either the
statement or the ornament. He fails when this control fails:
when either because of a temporary weakness of the statement, or too great a striving for poetic effect, the poetic
organism is caused to disintegrate into its component parts
of statement and ornament.

T. S. Eliot has said of Dryden's work that it is "one of the tests of a catholic appreciation of poetry". If this is true, and I am sure it is, then the limitations of much influential poetic theory of the present century may be revealed when faced with the test his poetry provides: which, of course, is not to deny that modern poetic theory and practice may also reveal the limitations of the poetry of statement. The Romantic interest in the sensibilities and emotions of the poet as the true material of poetry, and the aesthetic interest in the poem as an autonomous work of art created within the imaginative experience and sensitivity of the poet, have produced poetry of a kind to which Dryden did not and almost certainly could not have aspired; but they make no provision for an essentially rhetorical poetry, concerned to create delightful imitations of reality for the entertainment and moral edification of an audience. It is in those ideas of the nature and function of poetry of the tradition to which Dryden's work belongs—in what is now most commonly regarded as an outmoded concept of poetry as an art of imitation, an art of ornamentation—that this provision must be looked for. Indeed to go beyond this tradition is likely to be misleading. In Sidney, in the Italian critics and theorists of the *Cinquecento*, and in the general rhetorical approach to poetry (which despite the changes that were already beginning to take shape was still the main influence on Dryden as a poet, linking him with his Renaissance and classical heritage), may be found all that is needed. Or rather, all that is needed to go as far as it is possible to go towards an explanation of Dryden's art. For like all real poetry his best work is ultimately beyond explanation. One thing though is certain: any explanation must take account of his ability to use poetry to give an imaginative dimension to forceful, precise, and direct statement, and to the familiar accents of the speaking voice.

Dryden's concept of poetry, while it both imposed certain restrictions on the poet and also allowed him a degree of licence denied other writers, made no fundamental distinction between poetry and prose as forms of discourse. As a form of discourse, and not simply as poetry, the poetry of statement has an advantage that derives from its position midway between a plain, "neutral", form of expression, and a purely imaginative, affective, use of words. Having firmly established its centre of gravity, as it were, such a broadly based form of expression is in a position to move freely in either direction, without losing its own innate character of clarity combined with vitality. In this respect the poetry of statement is more closely related to the flexibility of modern prose than it is to modern poetry, and Matthew Arnold may indeed have spoken with some truth when he described Dryden as a "classic not of our poetry but of our prose".

George Young, in his *English Prosody on Inductive Lines* (1928), says of Dryden that his mastery in the heroic couplet "is due to his mastery as a writer of prose; prose of a time when the language had newly reached its present level of adaptability to the requirements of modern thought". But this, I think, is to get things in the wrong order. In reading Dryden's prose one is continually reminded of his poetry, and it is the qualities, or rather the combination of qualities, that his prose shares with his poetry that separates it from so much else in seventeenth century prose writing, whether belonging to the oratorical tradition of the Renaissance or to the newer search for a plain, straightforward style. It was, I believe, Dryden's experience as a writer of verse, particularly of dramatic verse, that enabled him to combine in prose, a natural, unselfconscious vitality with the clarity and precision demanded by the advocates of plain style. The great Preface to the *Fables*, Dryden's finest achievement in prose, stands as a monument to his achievement in the poetry of statement. He has been credited with being the father of modern prose—of prose that is neither prosaic nor poetic, prose that has now taken over so much of the territory which for him was the preserve of verse and for which his poetry of statement was so admirably suited. But to some extent at least it is his poetry of statement that is the real source of his influence on modern prose.

The tendency of twentieth century poetry to retreat into a wholly imaginative area of expression and virtually to disqualify itself from what it regards as the "non-poetic" use of words, has led to a splendid and exciting enrichment of expression within this area. But from a wider viewpoint, this tendency has meant not only an impoverishment of poetry, but also an impoverishment of the resources of verbal expression itself. Modern flexible forms of prose have to a large extent met the need left otherwise unfilled by the virtual disappearance of the poetry of statement. But prose cannot, I think, entirely take the place of the more formal structures of verse. Because these formal structures are expected and accepted, verse can use them to help build up imaginative patterns, particularly in sound and movement, of a strength which if attempted in prose would become so obtrusive as to inhibit much more strongly the reader's response to the statement as such. And, too, the unity deriving from the formal structure of the poem as a whole can give to its imaginative dimension a tangible existence as a complete thing which again would hardly be possible in a prose work except as a much more dominant element of it.

It is not, I think, going too far to say that in the poetry of statement is to be found the staple material of all verbal expression, in verse or prose, that seeks the flexibility necessary to allow it to meet the widest variety of demands. This is the essence of Dryden's achievement.

Bibliography

This bibliography lists all the works referred to in the text and notes, in addition to a *selection* of books and articles not specifically mentioned in the text but related to the study of Dryden's poetry. It is in five sections:

Dryden bibliographies

The principal collected editions of Dryden's works, arranged in chronological order

Primary sources for the study of the background of ideas and theory, covering works published for the first time prior to *ca.* 1800

Secondary sources—i.e. works published for the first time prior to *ca.* 1800—concerned directly with Dryden

Secondary sources of a more general nature but with some relation to the study of Dryden's poetry.

ABBREVIATIONS: In addition to the usual abbreviations of journal titles, the following abbreviations have been used:

HOOKER: E. N. HOOKER (ed.). *The Critical Works of John Dennis.* 2 vols. Baltimore: Johns Hopkins Press, 1939.

KER: W. P. KER (ed.). *Essays of John Dryden.* 2 vols. Oxford: Clarendon Press, 1900.

KINSLEY: J. KINSLEY (ed.). *The Poems of John Dryden.* 4 vols. Oxford: Clarendon Press, 1958.

SPINGARN: J. E. SPINGARN (ed.). *Critical Essays of the Seventeenth Century.* 3 vols. Oxford: Clarendon Press, 1909.

Dryden Bibliographies

DOBELL, PERCY J. *The Literature of the Restoration ... with particular reference to the writings of John Dryden.* London: P. J. and A. E. Dobell, 1918.

MACDONALD, H. *A Bibliography of Early Editions of Dryden and of Drydeniana.* Oxford: Clarendon Press, 1939.
The standard bibliographical work on early material connected with Dryden.

MONK, S. H. "Dryden Studies: A Survey, 1920-1945", *ELH*, XIV (1947), 46-63.

————. *John Dryden: A List of Critical Studies published from 1895 to 1948.* Minneapolis: University of Minnesota Press, 1950.

WISE, THOMAS J. *A Dryden Library. A Catalogue of Printed Books, Manuscripts, and Autograph Letters by John Dryden.* London: privately printed. 1930.

Collected Works

Works. 4 vols.; London: 1691-95.
The first collected edition of Dryden, comprised of separate editions of plays and poems.

The Comedies Tragedies and Operas. The Works. 4 vols. London: 1701.

MALONE, EDMOND (ed.). *The Critical and Miscellaneous Prose Works of John Dryden.* 3 vols. in 4. London: 1800.
The earliest genuinely critical edition of Dryden's work. Also contains a life of Dryden.

SCOTT, SIR WALTER (ed.). *The Works of John Dryden.* 18 vols. Edinburgh: 1808.
The first and still the only complete edition of Dryden. Contains an extensive life.

SCOTT, SIR WALTER and SAINTSBURY, GEORGE (eds.). *The Works of John Dryden.* 18 vols. London: 1882-92.
A revision by Saintsbury of Scott's 1808 edition.

KER, W. P. (ed.). *Essays of John Dryden.* 2 vols. Oxford: Clarendon Press, 1900.

NOYES, G. (ed.). *The Poetical Works of Dryden.* Cambridge, Mass.: Houghton Mifflin, 1909 (2nd ed. 1950).
Contains all the original poems and translations.

SUMMERS, MONTAGU (ed.). *The Dramatic Works of Dryden.* 6 vols. London: Nonesuch Press, 1930-31.

WARD, C. E. (ed.). *The Letters of John Dryden.* Durham, N.C.: Duke University Press, 1942.

HOOKER, E. N., and SWEDENBORG, H. T., *et al.* (eds.). *The Works of John Dryden.* 21 vols. Berkeley, California: University of California Press, 1954-
An eventual replacement for the Scott-Saintsbury editions. Volumes I and VIII so far available.

KINSLEY, JAMES (ed.). *The Poems of John Dryden.* 4 vols. Oxford: Clarendon Press, 1958.

KINSLEY, JAMES (ed.). *The Poems and Fables of John Dryden.* London: Oxford University Press, 1962.
The Oxford Standard Authors edition. Contains the full text of the 1958 edition with the exception of the *Aeneid.*

Primary Sources

ALEXANDER, SIR WILLIAM, Earl of Stirling. *Anacrisis: or, a censure of some poets ancient and modern.* London, 1634. Ed. SPINGARN. I, 180-89.
A defence of Aristotle's theory of poetry as imitation.

ARISTOTLE. *Poetics.*
The ultimate basis of almost all Renaissance poetic theory, though subject to continual reinterpretations influenced particularly by the *Ars Poetica* of Horace, by Plato, and by the whole classical, medieval, and Renaissance poetical and rhetorical traditions.

BACON, FRANCIS, Baron Verulam, Viscount St. Albans. "De dignitate et augmentis scientiarum libros IX". London, 1623. *The Philosophical Works of Francis Bacon,* eds. J. SPEDDING and R. H. ELLIS. 5 vols. London, 1861. IV, 275-479 (trans. of Bks. I-IV).

————. "The twoo bookes of Francis Bacon, of the proficiencie and advancement of learning, divine and human", London, 1605. *The Philosophical Works of Francis Bacon,* eds. J. SPEDDING and R. H. ELLIS. 5 vols. London, 1861. III, 253-492.

BLOUNT, SIR THOMAS POPE. *De re poetica: or, Remarks upon Poetry.* London, 1694.
An interesting compendium of neoclassic critical commonplaces, drawn largely from the French critic, Rapin.

BYSSHE, EDWARD. *Art of English Poetry*. London, 1702.
Indicates the changing emphasis, by comparison, for instance, with Puttenham's *Arte of English Poesie* (1589), in that it deals much more rigidly and extensively with metrics, and ignores the rhetorical figures of thought and sound.

CLIFFORD, MARTIN. *Notes upon Mr. Dryden's Poems in Four Letters*. London, 1687.

DANTE ALIGHIERI. *La Vita Nuova*. London: Dent, 1903.

DANTE ALIGHIERI. *De vulgari eloquentia*. London: Dent, 1904.

D(AVIES), J(OHN) (trans.). *Reflections upon Monsieur Des Cartes Discourse of a Method*. London, 1655.

DENNIS, JOHN. *The Advancement and Reformation of Modern Poetry*. London, 1701. Ed. HOOKER. I, 197-278.

————. *The Causes of the Decay and Defects of Dramatick Poetry, and of the Degeneracy of the Publick Tast*. London, 1725. Ed. HOOKER. II, 275-99.

————. *The Grounds of Criticism in Poetry*. London, 1704. Ed. HOOKER. I, 325-73.

————. *The Impartial Critic: or, some observations upon a late book entitled "A Short View of Tragedy" written by Mr. Rymer*. London, 1693. Ed. HOOKER. I, 11-14.

————. *Reflections Critical and Satyrical, upon a late rhapsody, called an Essay upon Criticism*. London, 1711. Ed. HOOKER. I, 396-419.

DRYDEN, JOHN. *A Discourse concerning the Original and Progress of Satire*. London, 1693. Ed. KER. II, 15-114.

————. *An Essay of Dramatic Poesy*. London, 1668. Ed. KER. I, 28-108.

————. *"A Parallel of Poetry and Painting"*, prefixed to his version of Du Fresnoy's *De Arte Graphica*. London, 1695. Ed. KER. II, 113-53.

————. Dedication of the *Aeneis*. London, 1697. Ed. KER. II, 154-240.

————. Dedicatory Letter prefixed to *Eleonora: a Panegyrical Poem*. London, 1692. Ed. KINSLEY. II, 582-85.

————. *"A Defence of an 'Essay of Dramatic Poesy'"*, prefixed to the second edition of *The Indian Emperour*. London, 1668. Ed. KER. I, 110-33.

————. *"Epistle Dedicatory to the Duke of York"*, prefixed to *Almanzor and Almahide: or, The Conquest of Granada*. London, 1672. Ed. SCOTT-SAINTSBURY. IV, 11-17.

————. Epistle Dedicatory to *The Rival Ladies*. London, 1664. Ed. KER. I, 1-9.

————. *"Postscript to the Reader"*, annexed to the *Aeneid*. London, 1697. Ed. KER. II, 238-51.

————. Preface to *Albion and Albanius, An Opera*. London, 1685. Ed. KER. I, 270-81.

————. Preface to *Annus Mirabilis: The Year of Wonders MDCLXVI*. London, 1667. Ed. KER. I, 10-20.

————. Preface to *Fables, Ancient and Modern*. London, 1700. Ed. KER. II, 246-74.

————. Preface to *Religio Laici; or, a Layman's Faith. A Poem*. London, 1682. Ed. KINSLEY. I, 302-11.

————. Preface to *The Hind and the Panther. A Poem, in Three Parts*. London, 1687. Ed. KINSLEY. II, 468-70.

————. Preface to the translation of *Ovid's Epistles*. London, 1680. Ed. KER. I, 230-43.

————. Preface to *Troilus and Cressida*. London, 1679. Ed. KER. I, 202-29.

————. Preface to *Tyrannick Love: or, The Royal Martyr*, ed. SCOTT-SAINTSBURY. III, 349.

————. "The Author's Apology for Heroic Poetry and Poetic Licence", prefixed to *The State of Innocence and Fall of Man, an Opera*. London, 1677. Ed. KER. I, 178-90.

FRACASTORO, GIROLAMO. *Girolamo Fracastoro Navgerius sive de poetica dialogvs* (1555). R. KELSO (trans.). *Univ. of Ill. St. in Lang. and Lit.*, IX (1924), No. 3. Pp. 49-88.
Perhaps the clearest, and most readily available, statement of the Renaissance concept of poetry as an art of ornamentation.

GASCOIGNE, GEORGE. "Certayne Notes of Instruction concerning the making of verse or ryme in English, written at the request of Master Eduardo Donati", London, 1575. *Elizabethan Critical Essays*, ed. GREGORY SMITH. 2 vols. Oxford: Clarendon Press, 1904. I, 46-57.
An early attempt to formulate principles of English poetic technique, as distinct from the application of rhetorical theory to poetry.

GEOFFREY of Vinsauf. *Nova Poetria*.

HOBBES, THOMAS. *Leviathan*. London, 1651.

HORACE. *Ars Poetica*.
Widely influential throughout the whole medieval and Renaissance periods, particularly in giving a didactic and moralistic bent to poetic theory.

JOHNSON, SAMUEL. *Lives of the English Poets*. London, 1779. Ed. G. BIRKBECK HILL. 3 vols. Oxford: Clarendon Press, 1905.

JONES, SIR WILLIAM. "On the Arts, commonly called Imitative", in "Poems consisting chiefly of translations from the Asiatic Languages", Oxford, 1772. *The Works of Sir William Jones*, ed. Lady Jones. 6 vols. London: 1799. IV, 549-61.

The first explicit challenge to the concept of poetry as an "art of imitation", on which so much Renaissance poetic theory had depended.

JONSON, BEN. *Timber: or, Discoveries: Made upon Men and Matter; As they have flow'd out of his daily Readings; or had their Refluxe in his Peculiar Notions of the Times*, London, 1640. Ed. C. H. HERFORD and E. SIMPSON. 12 vols. Oxford: 1947. VIII, 561-649.

LANGBAINE, G. *An Account of the English Dramatic Poets*. Oxford, 1691.

LIONARDI, ALESSANDRO. *Dialogi di Messer Alessandro Lionardi, della inventione poetica*. Venice, 1554.
An interesting work for the manner in which it relates "invention" to the "fable" or "imitation".

"LONGINUS". *Longinus on the Sublime*. Translated W. RHYS ROBERTS. Cambridge: Cambridge University Press, 1899.

PEACHAM, HENRY, the Elder. *The Garden of Eloquence, conteyning figures of grammar and rhetorick*. London, 1577.

PHILLIPS, EDWARD. *Theatrum Poetarum; or, a compleat Collection of the Poets; with some Observations and Reflections upon many of them, particularly those of our own Nation*. London, 1675. Ed. SPINGARN. II, 256-72.

POOLE, JOSHUA. *The English Parnassus; or, a help to English poesie*, with a Preface by J. D., London, 1657.
It has been suggested that the J. D. of the Preface may be John Dryden.

PUTTENHAM, GEORGE. *The Arte of English Poesie*. London, 1589. Ed. G. D. WILLCOCK and A. WALKER. Cambridge: Cambridge University Press, 1936.
One of the most thorough applications of the machinery of rhetoric to poetic theory. Deals with 121 "figures" originating mainly in the classical writings on oratory, and particularly in Quintilian.

SIDNEY, SIR PHILIP. *An Apologie for Poetrie*, London, ca. 1583. *Elizabethan Critical Essays*, ed. GREGORY SMITH. 3 vols. Oxford: Clarendon Press, 1909. I, 148-207.
The classic statement for English poetic theory of the Renaissance synthesis of classical and medieval ideas of the nature and function of poetry.

SMITH, JOHN. *The Mysterie of Rhetorique Unvail'd wherein above 130 of the tropes and figures are severally divided from the Greek into English together with lively definitions*. ... London, 1657.

SPRAT, THOMAS. *The History of the Royal Society of London for the improving of Natural Knowledge*. London, 1667.

TEMPLE, SIR WILLIAM. *Of Poetry*, London, 1690. Ed. SPINGARN. III, 73-109.

WARTON, JOSEPH. "An Essay on the Genius and Writings of Pope", London, 1756. *Eighteenth Century Critical Essays*, ed. SCOTT ELLEDGE. 2 vols. New York: Cornell University Press, 1961. II, 717-63.

WEBSTER, JOHN. *Academarium examen*. London, 1653.

WELSTED, LEONARD. "A dissertation concerning the perfection of the English tongue, and the state of Poetry &c.", London, 1724. *Critical Essays of the Eighteenth Century 1700-1725*, ed. W. H. DURHAM. New Haven: Yale University Press, 1915. Pp. 355-95.

WILSON, THOMAS. "The Arte of Rhetorique, for the use of all suche as are studious of eloquence ...", London, 1553. *Wilson's Arte of Rhetorique 1560*, ed. G. H. MAIR. Oxford: Clarendon Press, 1909. The last, most important, and only really complete Ciceronian rhetoric to appear in English before the arrival of the English Ramists (after whom Ciceronian rhetoric never fully recovered its original form).

YOUNG, EDWARD. "Conjectures on original composition", London, 1759. *English Critical Essays (Sixteenth, Seventeenth and Eighteenth Centuries)*, ed. E. D. JONES. Oxford: Clarendon Press, 1922. Pp. 315-64. One of the first demands for "originality" in poetry—something that had not loomed large at all in Renaissance poetic theory.

Secondary Sources—Dryden

ADEN, JOHN M. "Dryden and the Imagination: The First Phase", *PMLA*, LXXIV (1959), 28-40.

———. *The Critical Opinions of John Dryden: A Dictionary*. Nashville, Tenn.: Vanderbilt University Press, 1963.

BREDVOLD, L. "Dryden, Hobbes and the Royal Society", *MP*, XXV (1928), 417-38.

———. *The Milieu of John Dryden*. Ann Arbor: University of Michigan Press, 1934.

BROWER, R. A. "Dryden and the 'Invention' of Pope", *Restoration and Eighteenth-Century Lit.*, XXVII (1964), 211-33.

BROWN, DAVID D. "John Tillotson's Revisions of Dryden's 'Talent for English Prose' ", *RES*, XII (1961), 24-39.

DOBRÉE, BONAMY. *John Dryden*. London: The British Council, 1956.

———. "Milton and Dryden", *ELH*, III (1936), 83-100.

ELEANOR, MOTHER MARY, S.H.C.J. "Anne Killigrew and MacFlecknoe", *PQ*, XLIII (1964), 47-54.

ELIOT, T. S. "John Dryden", in *Homage to John Dryden: Three Essays on the Poetry of the Seventeenth Century*. London: L. & V. Woolf, 1924.

EMSLIE, McD. "Dryden's Couplets: Imagery Vowed to Poetry", *CritQ*, II (1960), 51-57.

FEDER, LILIAN. "John Dryden's use of Classical Rhetoric", *PMLA*, LXIX (1954), 1258-78.

FROST, WILLIAM. *Dryden and the Art of Translation*. New Haven: Yale University Press, 1955.

HOEFLING, SISTER MARY C. *A Study of the Structure of Meaning in the Sentences of the Satiric Verse "Characters" of John Dryden*. Washington: Catholic University of America Press, 1946.

HOFFMAN, ARTHUR. *John Dryden's Imagery*. Miami: University of Florida Press, 1962.

HOLLIS, CHRISTOPHER. *Dryden*. London: Duckworth, 1933.

HOPE, A. D. "Anne Killigrew, or The Art of Modulation", *Southern Review*, I (1963), 4-14.

JEFFERSON, D. W. "Aspects of Dryden's Imagery", *EC*, IV (1954), 20-41.

KIRSCH, A. C. *Dryden's Heroic Drama*. Princeton: Princeton University Press, 1965.

LEVINE, J. A. "John Dryden's Epistle to John Driden", *JEGP*, LXIII (1964), 450-474.

LEWIS, C. S. "Shelley, Dryden and Mr. Eliot", in *Rehabilitations*. Oxford: Clarendon Press, 1939.

LLOYD, C. "John Dryden and the Royal Society", *PMLA*, XLV (1930), 967-76.

McFADDEN, G. "Dryden and the Numbers of his Native Tongue", *Essays and Studies in Lang. & Lit.*, XXIII (1964), 87-109.

MASSON, D. J. "Dryden's Phonetic Rhetoric: Some Passages from his Original Poems", *Proc. Leeds Phil. & Lit. Soc., Lit. & Hist. Sect.*, XI (1964), 1-5.

MILES, JOSEPHINE. *Concordance to the Poetical Works of John Dryden*. Berkeley, California: University of California Press, 1957.

MILLER, C. H. "The Styles of 'The Hind and the Panther'", *JEGP*, LXI (1962), 511-27.

MINER, EARL. "Some Characteristics of Dryden's Use of Metaphor", *SEL*, II (1962), 309-20.

PROUDFOOT, L. *Dryden's "Aeneid" and its Seventeenth Century Predecessors*. Manchester: University of Manchester Press, 1960.

RALEIGH, SIR WALTER. "John Dryden and Political Satire", The Henry
    Sidgwick Memorial Lecture, delivered at Cambridge, November
    1913, in *Some Authors*. Oxford: Clarendon Press, 1923.

ROPER, A. H. "Dryden's 'Medall' and the Divine Analogy", *ELH*,
    XXIX (1962), 396-417.

――――. *Dryden's Poetic Kingdoms*. London: Routledge & Kegan Paul,
    1965.

SAINTSBURY, GEORGE. *John Dryden*. London: Macmillan Co., 1881.

SCHILLING, BERNARD. *John Dryden and the Conservative Myth*. New
    Haven: Yale University Press, 1961.

SMITH, D. NICHOL. *Dryden*. Cambridge: Cambridge University Press,
    1950.

TILLYARD, E. M. W. "Dryden: Ode on Anne Killigrew, 1686", in *Five
    Poems 1470-1870*. London: Chatto & Windus, 1948.

VAN DOREN, MARK. *John Dryden: A Study of His Poetry*. Blooming-
    ton, Indiana: Indiana University Press, 1946. Originally published
    as *The Poetry of John Dryden*. New York: Harcourt, Brace &
    Co., 1920.

WALLERSTEIN, RUTH. "To Madness near allied: Shaftesbury and his
    place in the design and thought of 'Absalom and Achitophel' ",
    HLQ, VI (1943), 445-71.

WARD, C. E. *The Life of John Dryden*. Chapel Hill: University of
    North Carolina Press, 1961.

Secondary Sources—General

ARNOLD, MATTHEW. "The Study of Poetry", *Essays in Criticism: Second
    Series*, ed. S. R. LITTLEWOOD. London: Macmillan Co., 1938.

ATKINS, J. W. H. *English Literary Criticism: The Medieval Phase*.
    London: Methuen & Co., 1952.

――――. *English Literary Criticism: The Renascence*. London: Methuen
    & Co., 1947.

――――. *English Literary Criticism: 17th and 18th Centuries*. London:
    Methuen & Co., 1951.

――――. *Literary Criticism in Antiquity*. 2 vols. London: Methuen &
    Co., 1952.

BALDWIN, C. S. *Ancient Rhetoric and Poetic*. New York: Macmillan
    Co., 1924.

――――. *Medieval Rhetoric and Poetic*. New York: Macmillan Co.,
    1928.

————, and CLARK, D. L. *Renaissance Literary Theory and Practice.* New York: Macmillan Co., 1939.

BALDWIN, T. W. *William Shakespeare's Small Latin & Lesse Greeke.* 2 vols. Urbana, Illinois: University of Illinois Press, 1944.

BATESON, F. W. *English Poetry and English Language: An Experiment in Literary History.* Oxford: Clarendon Press, 1934.

BETHELL, S. L. *The Cultural Revolution of the Seventeenth Century.* London: Dobson, 1951.

BOND, D. F. " 'Distrust' of Imagination in English Neo-Classicism", *PQ*, XIV (1935), 54-69.

————. "Neo-Classical Psychology of the Imagination", *ELH*, IV (1937), 245-64.

BREDVOLD, L. "The Tendency towards Platonism in Neo-Classical Aesthetics", *ELH*, I (1934), 91-119.

BROWN, W. C. *The Triumph of Form: A Study of the Later Masters of the Heroic Couplet.* Chapel Hill: University of North Carolina Press, 1948.

BUNDY, M. W. "Bacon's True Opinion of Poetry", *SP*, XXVII (1930), 244-64.

————. " 'Invention' and 'Imagination' in the Renaissance", *JEGP*, XXIX (1930), 535-45.

BUTT, J. E. *The Augustan Age.* London: Hutchinson & Co., 1950.

CHAGNARD, B. *Rhetoric and Poetry in the Renaissance.* New York: Macmillan, 1922.

CLARK, D. L. *Milton at St. Paul's School.* New York: Columbia University Press, 1948.

————. *Rhetoric and Poetry in the Renaissance.* New York: Columbia University Press, 1922.

CRAIG, HARDIN. *The Enchanted Glass.* New York: Oxford University Press, 1936.

CRANE, W. *Wit and Rhetoric in the Renaissance.* New York: Columbia University Press, 1946.

CROLL, M. W. "The Cadence of English Oratorical Prose", *SP*, XVI (1919), 1-55.

————. "Attic Prose in the Seventeenth Century", *SP*, XVIII (1921), 79-128.

CUNNINGHAM, J. V. "Logic and Lyric", *MP*, LI (1953), 33-41.

DAVIE, DONALD. *Articulate Energy.* London: Routledge & Kegan Paul, 1955.

DEANE, C. V. *Dramatic Theory and the Rhymed Heroic Play.* Oxford: Clarendon Press, 1931.

EMPSON, WILLIAM. *Seven Types of Ambiguity*. London: Chatto & Windus, 1947.

FRYE, NORTHROP. "Levels of Meaning in Literature", *KR*, XII (1950), 246-62.

————. *The Anatomy of Criticism*. Princeton: Princeton University Press, 1957.

GRIERSON, H. J. C. *Cross Currents of Literature of the XVIIth Century*. London: Chatto & Windus, 1929.

HAMILTON, K. G. *The Two Harmonies: Poetry and Prose in the Seventeenth Century*. Oxford: Clarendon Press, 1963.

HILL, MARY A. "Rhetorical Balance in Chaucer's Poetry", *PMLA*, XLII (1927), 846-47.

HOPE, A. D. "The Discursive Mode; Reflections on the Ecology of Poetry", *Quadrant*, I (1956-57), 28-33.

HOUSMAN, A. E. *The Name and Nature of Poetry*. Cambridge: Cambridge University Press, 1933.

JACK, IAN. *Augustan Satire*. Oxford: Clarendon Press, 1952.

JONES, R. F. "Science and English Prose in the Third Quarter of the Seventeenth Century", *PMLA*, XLV (1930), 977-1009.

LANGER, SUSANNE. *Feeling and Form: A Theory of Art Developed from Philosophy in a New Key*. London: Routledge & Kegan Paul, 1953.

LEWIS, C. S. *English Literature in the Sixteenth Century Excluding Drama*. Oxford: Clarendon Press, 1954.

MACK, MAYNARD. "Wit and Poetry and Pope: some observations on his Imagery", *Pope and His Contemporaries: Essays Presented to George Sherburn*, ed. J. L. CLIFFORD and L. A. LANDER. Oxford: Clarendon Press, 1949.

MACLEAN, NORMAN. "From Action to Image: Theories of the Lyric in the Eighteenth Century", *Critics and Criticism*, ed. R. S. CRANE. Chicago: University of Chicago Press, 1952, pp. 408-60.

NICOLL, ALLARDICE. *A History of English Drama 1660-1900*. 6 vols. Cambridge: Cambridge University Press, 1952.

READ, HERBERT. *Collected Essays in Literary Criticism*. London: Faber & Faber, 1938.

SCHELLING, FELIX E. "Ben Jonson and the Classical School", *PMLA*, XIII (1898), 221-49.

SHARP, R. L. *From Donne to Dryden*. Chapel Hill: University of North Carolina Press, 1940.

SMITH, A. J. "The Metaphysic of Love", *RES*, IX (1958), 362-75.

SPINGARN, J. E. *Literary Criticism in the Renaissance*. New York: Columbia University Press, 1899.

STOCKDALE, PERCIVAL. *Lectures on the Truly Eminent English Poets*. 2 vols. London, 1807.

SUTHERLAND, JAMES. *Preface to Eighteenth Century Poetry*. Oxford: Clarendon Press, 1948.

THORPE, C. DeW. *The Aesthetic Theory of Thomas Hobbes*. Ann Arbor: University of Michigan Press, 1940.

TILLYARD, E. M. W. *Poetry Direct and Oblique*. London: Chatto & Windus, 1934.

TUVE, ROSAMUND. *Elizabethan and Metaphysical Imagery*. Chicago: University of Chicago Press, 1947.

WALLERSTEIN, RUTH. *Studies in Seventeenth Century Poetic*. Wisconsin: University of Wisconsin Press, 1950.

————. "The Development of the Rhetoric and Metre of the Heroic Couplet, Especially 1625-1645", *PMLA*, L (1935), 166-210.

WASSERMAN, EARL R. "The Return of the Enjambed Couplet", *ELH*, VII (1940), 239-52.

WEINBERG, BERNARD. *A History of Literary Criticism in the Italian Renaissance*. 2 vols. Chicago: University of Chicago Press, 1961.

WILLEY, BASIL. *The Eighteenth Century Background*. London: Chatto & Windus, 1940.

————. *The Seventeenth Century Background*. London: Chatto & Windus, 1934.

WILLIAMSON, G. E. "Strong Lines", *English Studies*, XVIII (1936), 152-59.

————. *The Proper Wit of Poetry*. London: Faber & Faber, 1961.

————. *The Senecan Amble: A Study of Prose Form from Bacon to Collier*. London: Faber & Faber, 1951.

————. "The Rhetorical Pattern of Neo-Classical Wit", *MP*, XXXIII (1935), 55-81.

Index of Names

Aristotle, 135, 167
Arnold, Matthew, 4, 5, 172, 176

Bacon, Sir Francis, 21, 167-68, 173
Bateson, R. W., 62, 159, 171, 173-74
Boccaccio, 140, 141, 146
Bredvold, L., 33
Brown, W. C., 27n
Busby, Dr., 10
Butler, Samuel, 109
Butt, J. E., 172n

Chaucer, Geoffrey, 43, 114, 124-25, 138-41, 143-44, 146, 154
Cleveland, J., 97
Clifford, Martin, 96
Coleridge, Samuel Taylor, 3, 168
Cowley, Abraham, 4, 114
Croce, B., 162
Croll, M., 26, 134

Dante, 86, 163n
Davie, Donald, 30, 31, 43
D(avies), J(ohn), 96
Dennis, John, 1, 9, 22, 53n
Dobrée, Bonamy, vi, 172
Donne, John, viii, 4, 46, 61, 72, 102, 107, 137, 150, 174
Dryden, John,
    Plays
    Secret Love, 101n
    The Conquest of Granada, 65-66
    The Spanish Fryar, 9
    The State of Innocence, 56, 94
    Poems
    Absalom and Achitophel, vii, 10-19, 22, 36, 38-45, 56-57, 59-60, 65, 68-70, 73-75, 77-78, 81-82, 85-87, 101, 104, 108-13, 115-17, 130-33,
135-36, 145, 158, 160, 163-64, 166, 168, 172
    Absalom and Achitophel, Part II, 38, 54, 63-65, 75-76, 123
    Aeneid, 14, 88, 108, 135, 140, 144-46, 148, 153-54, 163
    Alexander's Feast, 49, 82
    Annus Mirabilis, 12, 84-85, 98, 99, 101n, 108, 111, 116, 118, 132-33, 150
    Astrea Redux, 96
    Cymon and Iphigenia, 147
    Eleonora, 137-39, 154, 163
    Heroique Stanza's, 84, 118-19
    MacFlecknoe, vii, 11, 15-16, 37-38, 48, 54-57, 74, 76, 80-81, 86-87, 104, 112-14, 158
    Ovid's "Metamorphoses", 55n
    Palamon and Arcite, 124, 139-40, 143-44
    Religio Laici, vii, 12, 18, 22-36, 39, 45, 58-61, 64, 75, 91-92, 97-101, 105-9, 111, 115, 117, 121-22, 133, 135, 141n, 145, 149-54, 157-60, 163-66, 168, 170-73
    Sixth Satyr of Juvenal, 142-43
    Song for St. Cecilia's Day, 82-89
    The Cock and the Fox, 55
    The Hind and the Panther, vii, 22, 35, 54, 70, 100, 106, 117, 158, 160
    The Medall, vii, 55-57, 74, 78-79, 81, 88, 103-11, 114, 160
    Theodore and Honoria, 140, 141
    Threnodia Augustalis, 102-3, 112
    To the Memory of Mr. Oldham, vii, 6, 18, 76-77, 131-34, 155-56, 172n
    To the Memory of Mrs. Anne Killigrew, vii, 18, 118-22, 130, 135-37, 140, 149-50, 155, 174

Dryden, John, *continued*
Upon the Death of Lord Hastings,
   97-98, 111, 130
Prologues and Epilogues 68
Prologue to "The Assignation", 68
Prologue to "Love Triumphant", 71
Prose
Apology for Heroic Poetry, 93
Dedication to the "Aeneis", 70-139
*Dedicatory Letter prefixed to
   "Eleonora"*, 137
*Defence of an "Essay of Dramatic
   Poesy"*, 21, 23, 95, 130, 160-61
Discourse on Satire, 8, 39, 41, 53,
   161
*Epistle Dedicatory to "The Conquest
   of Granada"*, 161
*Epistle Dedicatory to "The Rival
   Ladies"*, 50, 67, 95
Essay of Dramatic Poesy, 24, 50, 67
*Letter to Rt. Hon. Charles Mon-
   tague*, 167
Parallel of Poetry and Painting, 129,
   173
Postscript to the "Aeneid", 153-54
Preface to "Albion and Albanius",
   83
Preface to "Annus Mirabilis", 33,
   52, 99, 129
Preface to the "Fables", 129, 176
Preface to "Ovid's Epistles", 138
Preface to "Religio Laici", 8, 23, 151
Preface to "Sylvae", 145
*Preface to "The Hind and the
   Panther"*, 34
Preface to "Troilus and Cressida",
   52
Preface to "Tyrannick Love", 161

Eliot, T. S., 6, 7, 9, 36, 114-15, 117,
   147, 157, 171, 175
Empson, W., viii, 45, 51, 83, 103
Euripides, 90

Feder, L., 161n
Fletcher, J., 4
Fracastoro, G., 125, 127, 145
Frost, Robert, 26
Frost, W., vi, 138
Frye, Northrop, 50, 165-70, 172
Fuller, T., 169

Gay, John, 89
Geoffrey of Vinsauf, 125
Gibbon, Edward, 40, 169
Goldsmith, Oliver, 43
Graves, Robert, 63
Gray, Thomas, 25, 84-85

Hamilton, K. G., v, vi, ix, 5n, 53n,
   93n, 96n, 147n, 159n
Heraud, J. A., 3
Hill, M., 139

Hobbes, Thomas, 58
Hoefling, Sister M., vi
Hoffman, A., vi
Hollis, C., 25
Hooker, E. N., 101n
Hope, A. D., x, 25-26
Hopkins, Gerard Manley, 51, 134
Horace, 8
Housman, A. E., 124-25, 128, 130-31,
   143, 146

Jack, Ian, vi
Jefferson, D. W., 116
Johnson, Dr. Samuel, 2, 4, 24-25, 29-30,
   31, 51-52, 58, 89, 97, 103, 116, 135,
   136, 144, 150
Jonson, Ben, 21
Juvenal, 142

Keats, John, 3, 134, 164

Landor, Walter Savage, 149
Lewis, C. S., 125-26
Lionardi, Alessandro, 147, 154
"Longinus", 90, 93-95, 122, 126, 152

Mack, Maynard, 45-46, 48-49, 108
Malone, Edmond, 1, 3
Miles, Josephine, 14n
Milton, John, 3-4, 33, 60, 61, 94, 115-16,
   146, 172

Needham, Marchmont, 117
Nicoll, Allardice, 68n

Pater, Walter, 4-5
Patten, J., ix
Pope, Alexander, 2-4, 31, 36, 46, 49,
   52, 54, 55n, 73, 89, 101n, 112n, 130,
   157
Proudfoot, L. D., vi, 145-46, 154

Quintilian, 161

Raleigh, Sir Walter, 4
Ratcliffe, Alexander, 97
Read, Herbert, 51n
Reid, H. T., 3
Roberts, W. R., 126
Roper, A., vi
Rossetti, D. G., 4

Saintsbury, G., 149-50
Sampson, G., 33n
Sandys, George, 14, 146
Schilling, B., vi
Scott, Sir Walter, 3
Shakespeare, William, 3-4, 52, 65-66,
   103-5, 124
Sharp, R. L., 6-8
Shelley, P. B., 3, 151, 164
Sidney, Sir Philip, 21, 165n, 174
Spencer, Edmund, 3

Stockdale, P., 24
Sutherland, J., 67
Swedenborg, H. T., Jr., 101n
Swinburne, A. C., 88
Sylvester, Joshua, 14, 146

Tate, Nahum, 65
Tennyson, Lord Alfred, 88, 151
Theocritus, 155
Thomas, Dylan, 96n
Turner, G. E., 4
Tuve, Rosamund, viii
Tuveson, E., 101n

Van Doren, Mark, vi, 6-7, 17, 24-25,
    42, 45, 84, 94-95, 101n, 122, 126,
    128, 131, 137, 140, 142, 170-71

Vaughan, H., 151
Vico, G., 162
Virgil, 99, 138-39, 144-45, 148, 154

Waller, Edmund, 4, 12
Wallerstein, Ruth, 27n, 97
Warton, Joseph, 2, 69
Welsted, Leonard, 22, 162n
Wilkins, J., 54
Williamson, G. E., 27n, 42n, 47n, 130n
Wilson, Thomas, 34, 126
Wimsatt, W. K., Jr., 45, 47-49
Wordsworth, William, 3, 70, 132, 164
Wright, Dr. Louis, x

Yeats, W. B., 117
Young, George, 176